"*Damage Control*, Second Edition, is a timely update on the law of just cause dismissal. It provides me with an easy-to-use resource tool when I need to know the answer immediately."

Sue DiPoce
Vice President Human Resources
DCCI Inc.

"The authors have provided us with an extremely useful review of the current trends on the law of just cause. Since the *McKinley* case was decided in 2001, this has become an increasingly difficult area of the law and to have *Damage Control*, Second Edition at my fingertips is reassuring."

Trish Hewitt
Vice President Human Resources
Harlequin Enterprises Ltd.

"*Damage Control*, Second Edition, is well written, concise and provides a current review of the most recent cases involving just cause. I highly recommend this to any Human Resources professional who has to deal with this area of the law."

Claire Renaud
Manager Human Resources
Canadian Chamber of Commerce

"The authors have done an excellent job on providing the reader with the most up-to-date review of the law of just cause. My job demands that I make the right decisions and *Damage Control*, Second Edition, will definitely be a useful resource tool for me and my human resources team."

Mike Annable
Vice President Human Resources
Linamar Corporation

DAMAGE CONTROL

An Employer's Guide to Just Cause Termination

Second Edition

Malcolm J. MacKillop
B.A., LL.B.

James G. Knight
B.A., LL.B.

Kerry D. Williams
B.A., LL.B.

CANADA LAW BOOK INC.
240 Edward Street, Aurora, Ontario, L4G 3S9
www.canadalawbook.ca

Library and Archives Canada Cataloguing in Publication

MacKillop, Malcolm
    Damage control : an employer's guide to just cause termination — Malcolm J. MacKillop, James G. Knight, Kerry D. Williams. — 2nd ed.

Includes bibliographical references and index.
ISBN 0-88804-426-7

    1. Employees—Dismissal of—Law and legislation—Canada.
I. Knight, Jamie   II. Williams, Kerry D.   III. Title.

KE3262.M23 2005   344.7101'2596   C2005-900953-5
KF3471.M23 2005

To Judy and Evan

Malcolm J. MacKillop

To Betty, Geoff, Jenny and Alison, for all of their love and support

James G. Knight

To John Craighead, mentor and friend

Kerry D. Williams

✧ FOREWORD ✧

In the fall of 1997, Malcolm MacKillop published the first edition of this book, *Damage Control: An Employer's Guide to Just Cause Termination*. It was the first (but not the last) text dedicated solely to the topic of "just cause" in Canadian employment law. Malcolm, Jamie Knight and Kerry Williams have most capably updated the original edition in many essential ways. This text is now very current, as a result of their painstaking revisions. I noted an increased reference to arbitral jurisprudence, revisions of various statutory references, cross referencing, and most importantly, a thorough updating of the case references.

Notably, over the past five years, our Supreme Court of Canada has rendered three significant decisions in *Dowling, Wallace* and *McKinley*. The impact of these three judgments has dramatically affected employment law and, in particular, the area of "just cause". *Dowling* single-handedly eliminated any thought of a doctrine of "near cause"; *Wallace* has had a monumental impact on how damages are formulated in cases involving inappropriate employer conduct at the time of dismissal; and *McKinley* has entrenched a "contextual approach" into the court's consideration of just cause. This second edition has also included a new feature in its Appendix A. For the first time there is found a useful summary of significant Supreme Court of Canada and appellate level decisions concerning just cause. This will be of great assistance to the employer or practitioner looking for a quick answer. Additionally, Messrs. MacKillop, Knight and Williams have updated the Bibliography to provide a complete and current listing of other available resources.

Knowing Malcolm MacKillop as I have since 1989, I am certain that in this revised text he set out to continue to offer practical and useful guidance to fellow lawyers, human resource professionals, and employers. He and Messrs. Knight and Williams have succeeded admirably. Malcolm is a leader in the Fraser Milner Casgrain Employment & Labour Group and a pre-eminent Canadian employment law practitioner. Not only has he acted as lead counsel in litigation at all levels of courts, published widely, appeared on radio, television and video, taught at several universities, is regularly called upon to chair leading symposia, but he has been recognized by Lexpert as one of the leading 500 lawyers in Canada. The reader will not go wrong in seeking guidance from this clearly written and user-friendly text. Congratulations on a job well done!

January, 2005   The Honourable Mr. Justice Randall Scott Echlin
Superior Court of Justice (Ontario)
Toronto, Ontario

✧ PREFACE ✧

It has been over seven years since the first edition of *Damage Control* was published. Many things have changed for me personally over those seven years. The law of wrongful dismissal has seen significant changes as well.

On a more personal note, my close friend and mentor, Randy Echlin, left 25 years of practising employment law behind to become a Superior Court Judge. Subsequent to Randy's departure from the firm, I also left to join a close friend and colleague, James Knight, at Fraser Milner Casgrain. Jamie, along with his other partners, brought together a highly successful and experienced coterie of employment and labour lawyers and built them into one of Canada's largest and most recognized employment knowledgeable groups in Canada. My role as the newest member of the FMC group was to expand upon the employment litigation practice.

The idea for a second edition of *Damage Control* originated during a conversation between Jamie and myself. Jamie, who is a well-respected author of several employment and labour law texts, is committed to providing the human resources community with useful, current legal literature. So it was without hesitation that Jamie supported the concept of a second edition and the project began to unfold.

Regrettably for me, Jamie chose to pursue his career with a labour boutique firm. Nevertheless, we decided to continue this endeavour together. Before Jamie left our firm, he made certain that this writing project had the support of our firm and that the necessary resources were made available. I am truly thankful for the tremendous support Jamie provided both before and during this project.

Some of Jamie's efforts were expended in enlisting the help of a young associate. He suggested Kerry Williams, now a co-author of this edition of *Damage Control*. Kerry is one of the most dedicated and hard-working associates whom I have come across. Without his focus and commitment this book would never have been completed. Both Jamie and I owe Kerry our lasting gratitude for "keeping his eye on the ball" during this entire project.

I would also like to acknowledge the valuable contribution made by our FMC law students, Meighan Ferris, Cristiano Papile, Wesley Novotny, Christina Hall, Scott Yelle, Douglas Stewart, William Willis and Megan Stewart who provided research and writing during this project.

Since 1997, the concept of "just cause" has undergone significant change largely because of the legal reasoning pronounced in the leading Supreme Court of Canada decision of *McKinley v. B.C. Tel.* In that case, the Supreme Court adopted a "contextual approach" to whether "dishonesty" was cause for dismissal. This was a substantial departure from the historical thinking that if dishonesty were proven, then cause existed. The importance of the *McKinley* judgment cannot be overstated. Since *McKinley* was decided in 2001, judges have expanded the application of the "contextual approach" to all types of misconduct beyond just dishonesty. Because of this development, large portions of *Damage Control* had to be rewritten to reflect the effect of the *McKinley* decision on the various grounds for dismissal.

Many thanks to those who have expressed to me over the years how helpful they found the first edition of *Damage Control* to be. Hopefully this second edition of *Damage Control* will also prove to be a reliable resource tool.

Toronto, Ontario   Malcolm J. MacKillop
January, 2005

✧ TABLE OF CONTENTS ✧

PART II
✧ GROUNDS FOR TERMINATION ✧

PART III
✧ THE TERMINATION ✧

✦ TABLE OF CASES ✦

✧ INTRODUCTION ✧

1 ✧ PURPOSE OF BOOK

As one might gather from its title, this book is about "just cause" terminations. The book's primary purpose is twofold: (1) to provide an explanation and overview of the just cause concept; and (2) to give the reader an appreciation of what must be demonstrated to establish cause in a particular case. In the area of employment and dismissal law, the phrase "just cause" is used to describe those fact situations where there are grounds or reasons recognized in law to justify the termination of an individual's employment. If a court is satisfied that such grounds or reasons exist, employers can successfully defend legal actions brought against them by former employees who claim they deserve monetary compensation for being "wrongfully dismissed", that is, fired without cause.

The existence of just cause means that an employee can be dismissed immediately and without notice where his or her conduct is inconsistent with expressed and implied employment duties. If just cause is present, the employer is not obligated to provide the employee being fired with reasonable notice of termination or with pay in lieu of notice.

To facilitate the dual purpose of explaining just cause and describing how it is proven, this book discusses a number of concepts important to the area of employment and dismissal law. Also included are practical points that should be kept in mind when firing an employee, methods to follow when conducting a termination interview and advice about defending wrongful dismissal claims where the employer is relying on just cause.

2 ✧ TARGET AUDIENCE AND FOCUS OF BOOK

Although legal practitioners may find it useful as well, this book is primarily aimed at human resource professionals and all other individuals who manage employees. In most cases, these people must make decisions or offer opinions as to whether or not an employee should be let go. If employees are dismissed improperly or "wrongfully", the consequences employers can expect to suffer are expensive and time consuming. For those assessing these situations, it is therefore crucial to know beforehand when an employee's immediate dismissal can be legally justified. Such knowledge should be based on a good appreciation and understanding of the circumstances and grounds which constitute just cause for termination. It is this appreciation and understanding that *Damage Control: An Employer's Guide to Just Cause Termination* attempts to foster in its readers.

The focus of this text is on just cause terminations and, as such, it does not provide analysis on other subtleties in the area of employment and dismissal law. Rather, the book discusses the many grounds which can (and cannot) constitute just cause, thereby warranting an employee's immediate or summary termination. Moreover, the elements that need to be established to prove just cause are set out together with the factors and circumstances which can strengthen a particular case for cause. In this way, the various conditions that must be satisfied before a finding of just cause can be made are provided to the reader in a functional manner. Finally, the book will provide practical advice and tips on how to dismiss employees properly and, if necessary, deal with an employee's refusal to acknowledge that cause for termination did in fact exist.

3 ✧ A WORD OF WARNING

It is not possible to provide the reader with the "right answer" to every employment problem which may give rise to a termination on the basis of just cause. Ultimately, whether the employer has just cause to support a summary dismissal will depend on the particular facts applicable to the situation at hand. Simply put, facts are crucial in every case and caution should be exercised in approaching any situation where termination for cause is being contemplated. Although this book is intended to provide a general overview of the many different reasons that may constitute cause for dismissal, it cannot and should not be relied upon to the exclusion of a thorough consideration of the facts and sound legal advice from a lawyer specializing in employment law.

PART I

✧ GENERAL CONCEPTS ✧

1 ✧ THE COMMON LAW

The common law, known also as judge-made law, refers to the body of recorded decisions and corresponding reasons rendered by judges of the courts, which are subsequently relied upon and used as authority by legal counsel and judges when cases are argued and decided. In contrast, when one speaks of statute law, reference is being made to legislation created by the various levels of government.

Over time, the common law has identified and defined the duties, rights and obligations of employers and employees in employment relationships. For instance, employees have a duty to serve their employers faithfully and loyally and employers are obligated to give employees sufficient notice that their employment is being terminated.[1] Absent just cause,[2] an employer who fails to provide the required common law notice will have to pay damages to the dismissed employee.

This book focuses on the employer's common law right to terminate an employment contract or relationship for just cause. Like other common law duties, rights and obligations, the types of misconduct that constitute just cause for dismissal have been described and delineated over time by the decisions and corresponding reasons of judges in court cases and by arbitrators and adjudicators in similar cases arising under statutory law or in a trade union context. The existence of just cause cancels an employer's common law obligation to provide an employee with reasonable notice of termination. In many cases, such behaviour also cancels the employer's obligation either to continue employment or to provide statutory notice as required by the various legislative enactments that govern employment relationships.[3]

---

[1] See discussion under Heading 3, "Common Law Reasonable Notice", of this Part.
[2] See discussion under Heading 7, "Just Cause — The Contextual Approach", of this Part.
[3] See discussion under Heading 4, "Statutory Notice, Termination Payments and Severance Payments", of this Part.

2 ✧ EMPLOYMENT CONTRACTS

Employment contracts are agreements that govern the relationship between an employer and employee and incorporate the respective rights and obligations of each party. The terms of an employment contract come from a combination of the following sources: written documents; oral agreements; rights, duties and obligations implied by law; sometimes informally applied workplace policies and procedures; and the conduct of the individual employer and employee.

Certain terms are incorporated into all employment contracts as a result of the common law while other provisions are incorporated as a result of employment standards legislation. Employment law primarily falls under provincial jurisdiction, so there is legislation in each province; the *Canada Labour Code*[4] and other federal legislation governs the minority of relationships that fall under federal jurisdiction. Attention must be paid to the precise wording of any applicable legislation because some statutes stipulate that their provisions apply only to particular relationships and jurisdictions. For the most part, the terms of an employment contract cannot violate the legislation that applies to it. For instance, a contractual term that deals with terminating an individual's employment will not be valid if it is inconsistent with the minimum statutory requirements that govern the employment relationship in question. In contrast, obligations and terms implied by the common law can be altered or displaced entirely by specifically expressing so in the employment contract.[5]

3 ✧ COMMON LAW REASONABLE NOTICE

The concept of common law reasonable notice is very important to the area of employment and dismissal law. It refers to the fact that employees who are dismissed without cause are entitled to receive notice that their employment is to be terminated or to receive a sum of money instead of notice. This principle stems from a long history of judicial pronouncements and applies to all employees unless they are hired for a definite period of time or unless the terms of their contracts limit or modify the amount of notice they would otherwise be entitled to receive. Subject to these exceptions, the employer must abide by the common law reasonable notice rule if a termination cannot be justified by employee misconduct that amounts to just cause for dismissal or, more rarely, due to a frustration of contract.[6] The failure to provide reasonable notice will permit a terminated employee to successfully sue an

---

[4] R.S.C. 1985, c. L-2.
[5] *Machtinger v. HOJ Industries Ltd.* (1992), 91 D.L.R. (4th) 491 (S.C.C.), at pp. 508-9.
[6] See discussion under Heading 7, "Just Cause — The Contextual Approach", of this Part.

employer for wrongful dismissal and, as a consequence, be awarded monetary damages by the court to be paid by the employer.

The period of common law notice that employers provide must be reasonable. What amounts to reasonable notice has been examined and explained in a great number of cases decided in the area of employment and dismissal law. The classic definition of reasonable notice still widely applied today throughout Canada was first set out as follows in the case of *Bardal v. Globe & Mail Ltd.*:[7]

> There could be no catalogue laid down as to what is reasonable notice in particular classes of cases. The reasonableness of the notice must be decided with reference to each particular case, having regard to the character of the employment, the length of service of the servant, the age of the servant and the availability of similar employment, having regard to the experience, training and qualifications of the servant.

As one can gather from the preceding quote, a precise equation for calculating common law reasonable notice does not exist. Therefore, to determine what amount of notice is most appropriate for a given case, employers must consider the judicial decisions rendered in similar dismissal situations, together with the factors identified in *Bardal*:

- the character of an employee's employment;
- the length of service with the employer;
- the employee's age;
- the availability of similar employment having regard to the employee's experience, training and qualifications.

A rule of thumb that an employer may wish to follow requires a base period of notice to be calculated at one month for every year of an employee's service. The remaining *Bardal* factors must then be considered in order to determine whether the notice period should be adjusted upwards or downwards. It is generally the case that older employees and those who have served their employers for a long time are entitled to greater notice periods. It is important to understand that this rule of thumb is not a matter of law, but simply a matter of useful practice, and it is only a starting point for evaluation of the claim. In at least one province, namely Ontario, the Court of Appeal has held that 12 months is the maximum amount of common law notice that administrative employees are entitled to, notwithstanding the factors of age and length of service.[8] It is not clear that this is still good law and the authors would urge judicial reconsideration of any such position as it is inconsistent with the prevailing trends. Indeed, the notion of a 12-month cap

---

[7] (1960), 24 D.L.R. (2d) 140 (Ont. H.C.J.), at p. 145.
[8] *Cronk v. Canadian General Insurance Co.* (1994), 6 C.C.E.L. (2d) 15 (Ont. Ct. (Gen. Div.)), vard 128 D.L.R. (4th) 147 (C.A.).

for non-managerial or clerical employees has been put in doubt by a more recent decision from the Ontario Court (General Division).[9] In that decision, the court expressed the view that no such cap or ceiling on the period of reasonable notice exists based on the character of an individual's employment. Instead, the prudent employer should examine and apply all of the factors initially identified in the *Bardal* decision when determining the amount of notice to provide. It is also a good idea to consider any other factors that may affect the employee's ability to secure comparable alternative employment.[10] Such factors include an employee's health, communication skills, citizenship and ability to relocate to another community or city. Even so, it will be a relatively rare case involving a non-managerial, non-professional, or administration employee where the period of reasonable notice is set higher than 12 months.

In a similar non-binding way, it is common for practitioners in this area to assume that there is a cap of 24 months for managerial and professional employees. This cap should not be accepted as anything more than a rough guide for settlement discussions. There have been cases, albeit not very many, where this cap has been exceeded, and it is unlikely that there would be any current court that would uphold such a cap as a legal barrier to higher awards.

In most employment terminations, rather than having employees work through the period of notice they are owed, employers provide them with a sum of money equivalent to the salary and employment benefits they otherwise would have earned during this time. The sum can be paid all at once or spread over a number of pay periods. The goal is to treat the employee as if he or she were still actively employed during the notice period, at least with respect to salary and benefits. It is also possible to give working notice of a termination of employment. However, this can create a problematic work environment, where disruptive behaviour by the terminated employee will not likely be found to be just cause, due to the employer's role in having brought about the situation.[11]

Reasonable notice is supplied for the purpose of providing a dismissed employee with time to look for and attain comparable employment. By dismissing employees with notice or pay instead of notice, they can seek out other employment options while having some financial security. In some cases an offer of employment, even if not accepted by the employee, can be deemed to mitigate the situation, freeing the employer from having to pay damages.[12] However, the goal is not to guarantee that comparable employment is found during the specified notice period. The actual time required to

---

[9] *McKay v. Eaton Yale Ltd.* (1996), 31 O.R. (3d) 216 (Gen. Div.).
[10] *Beatty v. Canadian Mill Services Assn.*, [2003] B.C.J. No. 1617 (QL) (S.C.).
[11] *Elg v. Stirling Doors*, [2002] O.T.C. 539 (S.C.J.).
[12] *Mothersele v. Gulf Canada Resources Ltd.* (2003), 24 C.C.E.L. (3d) 139 (Alta. Q.B.).

find a new position may not be equal to the amount of notice ultimately found to be reasonable.[13]

4 ✧ STATUTORY NOTICE, TERMINATION PAYMENTS AND SEVERANCE PAYMENTS

(a) Statutory Notice and Termination Payments

Each province and territory has employment standards legislation which affects an employer's right to dismiss employees who do not work in a unionized setting.[14] At the federal level, the *Canada Labour Code*[15] governs the employment of individuals in federally controlled agencies, departments and workplaces. Employers should note that the dismissal of an employee in the federal jurisdiction may attract different consequences than a dismissal in the non-federal domain.

The statutes of each jurisdiction set out the minimum notice requirements that an employer must provide to all employees who are dismissed. The employer either could require employees to work out the notice specified in the legislation or make a termination payment equivalent to the amount of salary and benefits the employee would have earned while working during the legislated notice period. Statutory notice is different from common law reasonable notice discussed earlier. The notice set out by statute is the minimum amount of notice that employers must provide to employees they dismiss. In contrast, the required common law notice will vary depending on the particular circumstances of the dismissal. Inevitably, such common law notice will at least be equal to and will usually be greater than statutory notice.[16] In practice, by providing employees with the proper amount of common law notice, an employer simultaneously satisfies the applicable statutory notice requirement. In this way, common law notice exists "instead of" and not "as well as" statutory notice. If the employee is only given notice or termination pay equivalent to the minimum set by statute, it would in most circumstances be deemed insufficient and the employer potentially could be sued and ordered to pay wrongful dismissal damages. The amount of damages is generally equivalent to what the employee would have earned by working during the common law notice period to which he or she was entitled. In such cases, the courts and legal counsel have agreed that any statutory

---

[13] *Ansari v. British Columbia Hydro and Power Authority* (1986), 13 C.C.E.L. 238 (B.C. S.C.), affd 55 B.C.L.R. (2d) xxxiii (C.A.).
[14] Labour relations laws govern employers whose workplaces are unionized.
[15] R.S.C. 1985, c. L-2. See discussion under Heading 6, "The Canada Labour Code", of this Part.
[16] Unless otherwise stated, use of the terms "notice" and "reasonable notice" elsewhere in this book refers to the notice period implied and required by the common law.

termination pay received by the employee must be deducted when calculating the award of damages for wrongful dismissal.[17] That is, the award of damages cannot be "stacked" on top of termination pay already received.

A number of exemptions to the statutory notice requirements are found in employment standards legislation. Most of these statutes recognize that some acts or examples of misconduct disentitle an employee to notice or termination pay.[18] However, the kind of misbehaviour that cancels an employer's obligation to provide legislated notice or termination pay differs among jurisdictions. For instance, an Ontario employer need not provide statutory termination pay or notice where the employee has been guilty of "wilful misconduct, disobedience or wilful neglect of duty that is not trivial and has not been condoned by the employer".[19] The legislation governing the jurisdiction of the particular employer must be examined to determine exactly which exemptions are available to an employer.

Behaviour that constitutes just cause for termination as defined and implied by the common law[20] will occasionally fall within one of the legislated exceptions to statutory notice. In these circumstances, an employee could be dismissed without common law reasonable notice and the employer would be exempted from providing statutory notice or termination pay. Generally speaking, however, the exemptions of employment standards legislation are only triggered by serious employee misconduct and are narrower in scope than the grounds for just cause for termination. Therefore, where just cause for termination exists and the employer is not required to provide common law reasonable notice, an employee still may be entitled to receive minimum statutory notice or termination pay.

(b) Statutory Severance Payments

In addition to the provisions that deal with statutory notice and termination payments, Ontario and federal legislation contain severance pay provisions. These jurisdictions require certain employers to provide certain dismissed employees with defined payments of severance in specific recog-

---

[17] See, *e.g.*, *Brown v. Black Clawson-Kennedy Ltd.* (1989), 29 C.C.E.L. 92 (Ont. Dist. Ct.).

[18] The only jurisdictions whose statutes do not presently recognize disentitlement on this basis are British Columbia, Prince Edward Island and Saskatchewan.

[19] *Termination and Severance of Employment*, O. Reg. 288/01, s. 9(1), para. 6 (under the *Employment Standards Act, 2000*, S.O. 2000, c. 41).

[20] See discussion under Heading 7, "Just Cause — The Contextual Approach", of this Part.

nition of an employee's length of service.[21] Unlike statutory termination payments which need not be made if proper termination notice is provided, statutory severance payments are mandatory. However, only Ontario and federal employers must be concerned with this additional obligation. Also, although the law was previously unsettled in this area, recent Ontario decisions have ruled that the amount of statutory severance paid to an employee must be deducted from any awards of wrongful dismissal damages that are subsequently ordered by a court.[22] Even so, care should be taken either to structure the payments or to draft a settlement document or release that clearly identifies that the employer has satisfied the statutory obligation to provide severance pay or has provided the employee with a greater benefit.

5 ✧ WRONGFUL DISMISSAL VERSUS CONSTRUCTIVE DISMISSAL

Wrongful dismissal and constructive dismissal are separate but related concepts. As mentioned earlier, wrongful dismissal refers to the situation where an employee is not provided with adequate notice of termination and the employer is unable to establish a case for just cause. In these circumstances, the employee is said to have been wrongfully dismissed and is entitled to damages on this basis.

On the other hand, constructive dismissal occurs in situations where although an employee is not fired outright the effect of the employer's conduct is to create the circumstances that justify a resignation by the affected employee.[23] That is, while the individual's employment is not explicitly terminated, the terms and conditions of his or her employment are unilaterally changed by the employer in a way that is both negative and material. In such circumstances, the employee can treat the employer's actions as a termination of employment and a wrongful dismissal action can be commenced just as if the employee had been expressly fired. The danger for an employee, and it is a very serious risk, is that the employer could oppose the employee's allegation of a constructive dismissal and defend any claim on the basis that the employee quit. Not every unilateral change will found a claim for constructive dismissal. If, in the end, the employee were unsuccessful, he or she would receive nothing and would have to pay the legal costs of the employer.

---

[21] In Ontario, employers must provide employees who have at least five years of service with statutory severance pay if more than 50 employees are terminated within a six-month period due to the closing of a plant or an operation. Federal employees with at least 12 consecutive months of service are entitled to statutory severance pay.

[22] See, *e.g.*, *Stevens v. Globe and Mail* (1996), 135 D.L.R. (4th) 240 (Ont. C.A.).

[23] *Palumbo v. Research Capital Corp*, 2003 C.L.L.C. ¶210-023 (Ont. S.C.J.), appeal allowed in part [2004] O.J. No. 3633 (QL) (C.A.).

6 ✧ THE CANADA LABOUR CODE

The *Canada Labour Code* governs employers in the federal jurisdiction.[24] These are employers of individuals in fields such as banking, transportation and shipping. Like the employment standards legislation for non-federal jurisdictions, the Code imposes an obligation on federal employers to provide a minimum amount of notice or pay when terminating an employee. Specifically, the employer must give an employee who has completed three consecutive months of employment at least two weeks notice of termination or its equivalent in pay. The Code also requires the employer to provide employees with severance pay if they have completed at least 12 consecutive months of employment.[25] An employee entitled to severance pay must be given an amount that is equivalent to wages for a total of five days or two days of wages for each completed year of service, whichever is greater. Although the employer's obligation to provide both severance pay and a minimum amount of notice or pay in lieu of notice is mandatory, the obligation does not exist where there is just cause for an employee's termination. This exemption is specifically provided for by the Code, although the type of employee misconduct that will constitute just cause for the Code's purposes is not defined.

When terminating an employee, the federal jurisdiction employer must provide common law reasonable notice in addition to the minimum notice required by the Code, unless just cause for the termination exists. However, the principle against "stacking" would also apply, which allows the employer credit for payment of statutory termination and severance pay as against what is owed as reasonable notice. Employees in the federal domain who do not receive reasonable notice and feel they have been wrongfully dismissed can pursue two options. An action for wrongful dismissal can be commenced in the courts or the employee can use the process outlined in the Code which provides for the appointment of an adjudicator. Both options can be initiated but once a decision is made by either the court or the adjudicator, the other loses authority over the matter.

The procedures and remedies set out in the Code provide protection against and compensation for wrongful dismissal, that is, termination without reasonable notice. They are available to any non-unionized and non-manage-

---

[24] For further information see J. Knight and P. Leiper, *Canada Labour Code Quick Reference Guide* (Toronto: Thomson Carswell, 2004).

[25] Only employers in the federal jurisdiction and non-federal employers in Ontario are required to provide employees with severance pay. In this regard, severance pay is distinct from termination pay and is given in recognition of an employee's time with the employer. This is different from termination pay which is aimed at compensating employees for the loss of employment and providing some financial security while they look for another job.

rial employee who has completed at least 12 months of continuous employment with a federal jurisdiction employer.[26] Under the Code, if such an employee believes that he or she has been dismissed unjustly, a written complaint can be made to an "inspector" within 90 days of the dismissal. Should the inspector be unable to effect a settlement between the employee and employer, the Minister of Labour will appoint an adjudicator to hear the complaint where it appears to have some merit. However, a complaint will not be heard if the employee was laid off because of lack of work or because the job became redundant.[27]

As in the case of a wrongful dismissal action brought before the court, the termination of an employee in the federal jurisdiction will be justified if just cause for the termination exists. The employer who defends a dismissal before an adjudicator must rely on decisions that have been rendered by other adjudicators in similar circumstances. In this respect, employers should note that the jurisprudence has created a more stringent test with regard to just cause for the purpose of the Code as compared to the test established by the case law. In other words, a finding of just cause for termination is generally more difficult to obtain from an adjudicator than a court.

A termination will be found to be unwarranted where an adjudicator concludes that there was no just cause for termination. If this conclusion is reached, the adjudicator has the power to order the employer to reinstate the employee with or without compensation for earnings lost since the dismissal. The remedy of reinstatement is unique and is unavailable to an employee who chooses to initiate legal proceedings in a court rather than file a complaint pursuant to the Code. Further, the role of a court differs from that of an adjudicator in that the adjudicator is expected to formulate a remedy that is appropriate for each particular unjust termination. This has resulted in unique and individually tailored remedies such as ordering an employer to provide the employee with a reference letter, reinstating an employee but ordering probation for a specified amount of time and converting a discharge into a suspension without pay. The point being made here is that a federal jurisdiction employer may be directed to do much more than simply pay monetary damages for wrongful dismissal if just cause for an employee's termination is not established. The employer may be ordered to provide a more onerous remedy than that which a court would typically require. Even so, the ultimate burden for the employer of reinstating the employee is relatively rare.

---

[26] A managerial employee in this context refers to someone with the authority to make policy decisions that affect the employer's business. Employers should note that short or temporary lay-offs do not interrupt a period of employment where it is very likely that the employee will be recalled to work.

[27] *Canada Labour Code*, s. 242(3.1) (en. 1985, c. 9 (1st Supp.), s. 16).

To minimize the possibility of an order of reinstatement, the employer should provide the adjudicator with any available evidence that the employee would be unlikely to perform in a satisfactory manner and do an effective job if reinstated or that, prior to the employee's dismissal, the interpersonal relations of the workplace were impaired. These are factors that the adjudicator will consider when determining whether or not an employer must reinstate an employee. In addition, reinstatement is less likely to be required where the employee has served the employer for only a short period of time, where there is a problem with the employee's attitude, or where there continues to be a personality conflict even though the employee cannot be blamed for it or is not primarily at fault.

7 ✧ JUST CAUSE — THE CONTEXTUAL APPROACH

The concept of just cause is an exception to the fundamental rule that an employer must provide an employee with reasonable notice of termination or, alternatively, a sum of money equivalent to the salary and employment benefits that the employee would otherwise have earned during the required notice period. Just cause refers to the fact that if certain grounds exist, an employer will have legal justification for dismissing the employee summarily (*i.e.*, without notice or pay in lieu of notice).

The grounds that constitute just cause for termination primarily refer to the behaviour or conduct of the dismissed employee. However, not all occurrences of employee misconduct will warrant a finding of just cause. For an employee's misconduct to amount to just cause for termination, the behaviour must be of such a character as to violate the essential conditions of the employment contract or breach the trust inherent in the employment relationship. A contextual approach is now employed to determine whether an employee's conduct has voided the employment relationship such that there is just cause for termination.

Pursuant to the decision of the Supreme Court of Canada in *McKinley v. B.C. Tel.*[28] not every dishonest act or misconduct amounts to cause for dismissal; rather, the context of the act must be taken into consideration when assessing whether or not there are grounds to dismiss an employee for cause. The Supreme Court recognized the importance of protecting employee rights based on the principle that employment is a fundamental aspect of people's lives that should not be treated lightly. In *McKinley*, the issue of misconduct arose when Martin McKinley, after 16 years of service, took a leave of absence from work due to health problems. Mr. McKinley expressed an interest in returning to work in a less stressful position; however, B.C. Tel did not

---

[28] (2001), 200 D.L.R. (4th) 385 (S.C.C.).

offer him alternative employment. Eventually, B.C. Tel terminated Mr. McKinley who rejected the accompanying offer of severance and commenced a wrongful dismissal action.

At first, B.C. Tel argued it had offered Mr. McKinley a reasonable compensation package and had used its best efforts to locate an alternative position for him. Three days into trial, however, B.C. Tel discovered a letter from Mr. McKinley's physician and changed its defence to allege that Mr. McKinley had lied about his medical condition and the available treatments. In the letter Mr. McKinley's physician had recommended that he take a certain medication upon returning to work. Based on this letter, B.C. Tel claimed that McKinley had deliberately withheld the fact that he could safely return to work if he took the medication.

The main issue before the court was whether the dishonesty was of a degree that undermined the employment relationship. Reviewing the judicial history, the court noted two distinct lines of jurisprudence. The first held that the circumstances of the dishonesty must be considered in order to determine whether just cause for termination existed. The second provided that any degree whatsoever of employee dishonesty constituted just cause for termination.

Preference was given to the contextual approach wherein the specific form of employee dishonesty must be considered in the circumstances of the case, and only more serious instances of employee dishonesty will be held to constitute cause for termination. Accordingly, grounds for just cause exist where the employee's misconduct amounts to a breakdown in the employment relationship. The court outlined a two-step approach. First, does the evidence establish the employee's dishonest conduct on the balance of probabilities and, if so, does the nature and degree of the dishonesty warrant summary dismissal? Second, an evaluation must be conducted of the surrounding circumstances of the misconduct, its level of seriousness and the extent to which it has detrimentally affected the employment relationship. Only once all such factors have been assessed can the court determine whether the misconduct violated the essential conditions of the employment contract, or breached the trust inherent in the employment relationship.[29]

Even prior to *McKinley*, many lower courts across the country had already started to adopt a contextual approach in cases of alleged wrongful dismissal. This trend has strengthened since the *McKinley* decision. In *Thompson v. Lex Tec Inc.*,[30] the court considered the case of an employee who arrived an hour late for work on one occasion. When his supervisor aggressively pursued him for an explanation for his lateness, the employee

---

[29] For further examples of the application of the contextual approach see Heading 4, "Dishonesty", of Part II, "Grounds for Termination".

[30] (2001), 149 O.A.C. 106 (C.A.).

responded with profane language and shoved his supervisor in the chest before leaving the workplace. The trial judge adopted a contextual approach to find there was no just cause for dismissal. The employee had been to a doctor's appointment and was not habitually late for work. Interestingly, the appeal was heard after the release of the *McKinley* decision. In upholding the trial court decision, the Ontario Court of Appeal noted that factors to consider when applying a contextual analysis include: the individual's employment history with his or her current employer, his or her relationship with their immediate supervisor, the supervisor's role in the relevant events, the nature and degree of the misconduct, and the effect of the misconduct on the employer's business.

While the court in *Thompson* subtly expanded the scope of the contextual approach to include just cause dismissal, the court in *Bonneville v. Unisource Canada Inc.*,[31] adopted a much bolder approach. Although the factors to be considered were similar in both cases, in the latter decision, Barclay J. held that *McKinley* was "meant to apply to all situations where the defence of misconduct is raised by the employer".[32] *Bonneville* involved an employee who shot a rifle at a set of metal lockers near a customer pickup door during work hours. Applying the contextual approach, the court held the employer should have resorted to less serious forms of discipline and therefore just cause was not established. One significant mitigating circumstance in this case was the employee's unblemished 24-year employment record with the company. As this case demonstrates, with a contextual approach, it is often more difficult to dismiss a long-term employee for cause.

In *Henry v. Foxco Ltd.*,[33] the New Brunswick Court of Appeal adopted a more balanced, contextual approach to just cause dismissal. In *Foxco*, the employee worked at a garage doing auto body work. He was asked to remove decals from two vans and did not complete the task as quickly as required by his employer. A confrontation ensued with the employee repeatedly telling his employer to "go ahead and fire me". Following the exchange, the employer obliged the employee and dismissed him.

In determining whether there was just cause for dismissal, the court unanimously agreed that the contextual approach should be applied in cases of employee misconduct. Turnbull J.A. affirmed: "I would not limit [the application of *McKinley*] to 'dishonest conduct'".[34] Robertson J.A. agreed by criticizing the conventional approaches of assessing cause for dismissal, preferring instead the contextual approach for all cases of employee misconduct.

---

[31] (2002), 18 C.C.E.L. (3d) 174 (Sask. Q.B.).
[32] *Supra*, at para. 35.
[33] (2004), 31 C.C.E.L. (3d) 72 (N.B.C.A.).
[34] *Supra*, at para. 32.

For the most part, the terms of an employment relationship are determined by the parties themselves. In fact, the parties may go so far as to specify types of conduct that would justify summary dismissal. However, it is not possible to identify every ground that conceivably could amount to just cause. The courts have come to recognize that certain types of behaviour warrant immediate termination of an individual's employment and have, over time, defined categories of grounds that constitute just cause. Notwithstanding the evolving nature of these categories, the following statement relating to just cause still holds true:

> If an employee has been guilty of serious misconduct, habitual neglect of duty, incompetence, or conduct incompatible with his duties, or prejudicial to the employer's business, or if he has been guilty of wilful disobedience to the employer's orders in a matter of substance, the law recognizes the employer's right summarily to dismiss the delinquent employee.[35]

Accordingly, it is generally true that only serious misconduct or a fundamental breach of a term or condition of an employment contract will qualify as just cause for termination. Whether an employee's behaviour is severe enough to justify summary dismissal is a question of fact that a court of law must determine on a case-by-case basis. In some instances, an employer's subjective opinion of the employee's behaviour might be a factor for consideration. For the most part, however, the court will evaluate the conduct impartially and make an objective decision as to whether it was grave enough to meet the just cause requirement.

8 ✧ BAD FAITH DISCHARGE

If a court finds that just cause for termination did not exist and that the employee was dismissed without any or adequate notice or pay in lieu of notice, the employee is said to have been wrongfully dismissed. Where this occurs, the court will order the employer to pay the employee a monetary award of damages as compensation for the failure to provide notice of termination. Except in very rare cases, a court is not permitted to order specific performance of the employment contract because common law principles provide that an employer cannot be forced to re-employ a dismissed employee. Employers should also note that courts will consider awarding punitive or aggravated damages in cases where the manner of termination caused an employee to suffer mental distress, or was otherwise deserving of censure in the opinion of the court. This kind of result is more likely if the

---

[35] From the dissenting reasons of Schroeder J.A. in *Port Arthur Shipbuilding Co. v. Arthurs* (1967), 62 D.L.R. (2d) 342 at p. 348 (Ont. C.A.), revd 70 D.L.R. (2d) 693 (S.C.C.).

employer has alleged just cause but has been unsuccessful in convincing the court. The more typical trend in the last several years, especially in the face of an unsuccessful allegation of just cause, is for the courts to award damages for the employer's failure to act fairly and in good faith toward a dismissed employee, a trend more commonly referred to as a "bad faith discharge" or "*Wallace* damages". The quantity of damages is usually framed as an extension of the reasonable notice period. Bad faith discharge damages are often awarded instead of, and possibly in addition to, aggravated damages if there is evidence of distressful *and* humiliating treatment of an employee by an employer during the course of a dismissal. The authority in dealing with this issue is the Supreme Court decision in *Wallace v. United Grain Growers Ltd.*[36]

(a) Wallace Damages

In *Wallace*, an employee was hired by the competitor of his former employer of 25 years. In the course of being hired, the employee sought and received assurances from his new employer concerning tenure, fair treatment and remuneration. Until his summary dismissal 14 years later, the employee was the employer's top salesperson. The employer originally alleged cause for dismissal, only to withdraw the allegation on the eve of the trial. As a result of the manner in which he was dismissed, the employee had difficulty finding replacement work. He also required psychiatric treatment for the psychological and emotional distress caused by the dismissal and false allegations made against him.

The court found that several circumstances in *Wallace* warranted extension of the notice period, including the fact that the employer had induced the employee away from secure employment, the employer had made assurances concerning both job security and fair treatment and, although other employees had salary arrangements, the employer had offered the employee a commission-based pay arrangement. Most importantly, the court found that the employer's "callous and insensitive treatment" in dismissing the employee should be compensated for by an increase in the notice period awarded. The court refused to go so far as to import a tort of "bad faith discharge". Even so, the court recognized that bad faith behaviour on the part of an employer in the course of dismissing an employee is worthy of censure, and that such censure should be expressed as an extension of the period for which damages for reasonable notice are awarded.

Examples of bad faith behaviour cited by the court included: *Trask v. Terra Nova Motors Ltd.*,[37] where an employer falsely accused a departed

---

[36] (1997), 152 D.L.R. (4th) 1 (S.C.C.).
[37] (1995), 9 C.C.E.L. (2d) 157 (Nfld. C.A.).

employee of theft and communicated this accusation to potential employers of the dismissed employee; *Jivrag v. Calgary (City)*,[38] where similar false accusations were combined with a refusal to provide a reference letter; *Corbin v. Standard Life Assurance Co.*,[39] where an employer fired an employee on disability leave because of suffering depression as soon as the employee returned to work; and *MacDonald v. Royal Canadian Legion*,[40] where an employee, after a three-month layoff, learned of his dismissal by seeing his former position advertised in a newspaper at a lower rate of pay. While citing these examples as conduct that may merit extended notice damages, the court noted that such damages are not automatic, and that "the trial judge must examine the nature of the bad faith conduct and its impact in the circumstances".[41]

More recently, the courts have awarded *Wallace* damages ranging from between two to four months and up to eight to 12 months extension of the notice period.[42] While most courts have awarded *Wallace* damages as a separate head of damages, many have included an unspecified extension of the notice period as *Wallace* damages.[43] In *Singh v. British Columbia Hydro and Power Authority*,[44] the plaintiff, who had started with the company as a janitor and attained the position of Mail Room Supervisor after 18 years of service, was terminated as part of a company-wide restructuring. The court found that the company had recently sent out several internal communications assuring employees of their job security before terminating the plaintiff. Promises of job security, along with the fact that the plaintiff was terminated

---

[38] (1986), 13 C.C.E.L. 120 (Alta. Q.B.), vard 18 C.C.E.L. xxx (C.A.).

[39] (1995), 15 C.C.E.L. (2d) 71 (N.B.C.A.).

[40] (1995), 12 C.C.E.L. (2d) 211 (N.S.S.C.).

[41] *Wallace v. United Grain Growers Ltd., supra*, footnote 36, at p. 35.

[42] See, for example, *Musgrave v. Levesque Securities Inc.* (2000), 50 C.C.E.L. (2d) 59 (N.S.S.C.), wherein the notice period was extended from 8 to 16 months based on a finding that the employer's conduct bordered on slander and defamation. The employer was dishonest in communicating to the employee and clients why he was being dismissed, and made it virtually impossible for the employee to continue in the same industry. See also *Wal-Mart Canada Inc. v. Day* (2000), 4 C.C.E.L. (3d) 226 (N.S.C.A.), where the notice period was extended from 17 to 29 months because the employer had alleged cause in terms of dishonesty that a jury found were unsubstantiated; and *George v. Imagineering Ltd.* (2001), 14 C.C.E.L. (3d) 102 (Ont. S.C.J.), affd 23 C.C.E.L. (3d) 31 (C.A.), where the notice period was extended from 25 to 30 months.

[43] See *Silvester v. Lloyd's Register North America Inc.* (2003), 24 C.C.E.L. (3d) 18 (N.S.S.C.), appeal allowed in part 30 C.C.E.L. (3d) 200 (C.A.); *Barakett v. Levesque Beaubien Geoffrion Inc.* (2001), 8 C.C.E.L. (3d) 96 (N.S.S.C.), affd 12 C.C.E.L. (3d) 24 (C.A.), leave to appeal to S.C.C. refused [2002] 3 S.C.R. ix; and *Delaquis v. College de Saint-Boniface* (2000), 144 Man. R. (2d) 266 (Q.B.).

[44] (2001), 12 C.C.E.L. (3d) 214 (B.C.C.A.), leave to appeal to S.C.C. refused [2002] S.C.R. ix.

upon his return to work from a two-month leave of absence during which he was treated for depression, were considered aggravating *Wallace* factors by the court. As such, the notice period was increased from 20.5 to 27 months.

In *Marshall v. Watson Wyatt & Co.*,[45] the plaintiff, a communications consultant who accepted a company's offer over a competing job offer, was employed for one year before she was terminated. A jury found that the employer had acted dishonestly and in bad faith when dismissing her and awarded an additional three months notice. The Court of Appeal upheld the jury's award based on evidence that the employer alleged cause right up until the start of trial, refused to pay the plaintiff approximately $80,000 in commissions owed and delayed several months in providing her with her employment record required to obtain employment insurance benefits. The courts have subsequently elaborated on the employer's obligation of good faith and applied it to various types of employer behaviour. For example, courts have considered how this obligation relates to an employer's actions during a termination interview, when drafting a termination letter and when structuring a settlement offer. The case law dealing with this issue continues to evolve, as some trial judges demonstrate an increased willingness to place more emphasis on the obligation of fair dealing. However, *Wallace* damages are generally not awarded without some degree of bad faith or malice on the part of the employer during the course of an employee's dismissal.

Failure of an employer to deal appropriately with an employee's disability during the course of a dismissal can give rise to an entitlement to *Wallace* damages. One case that underscores this point is *Zorn-Smith v. Bank of Montreal*.[46] Ms. Zorn-Smith, who suffered from stress-related breakdowns throughout her career with the Bank of Montreal, was terminated after she refused the bank's demand that she either return to her old position without accommodation or take a new position at a significant salary cut. Justice Aitken of the Superior Court of Justice held that Ms. Zorn-Smith had been wrongfully dismissed. In awarding *Wallace* damages to compensate Ms. Zorn-Smith for the bank's bad faith conduct, Justice Aitken took note not only of the manner in which the plaintiff had been terminated, but also of the fact that the bank had wrongfully discontinued her benefits, failed to contact her family physician for more medical information (as had been requested) and failed to provide specific information about the process for appealing benefit discontinuation. Although it is arguable that Justice Aitken exceeded the scope of *Wallace* damages, until her decision is overruled or successfully appealed it is important for employers and human resources professionals to

---

[45] (2002), 209 D.L.R. (4th) 411 (Ont. C.A.).
[46] (2003), 31 C.C.E.L. (3d) 267 (Ont. S.C.J.).

remember her findings when terminating disabled employees, or those who claim to be disabled.[47]

(b) Contracting out of Wallace Damages

The issue of whether it is possible to contract out of *Wallace* damages has received some attention from the courts. In *Barnard v. Testori Americas Corp.*,[48] Simon Barnard executed an employment contract that limited his right to recovery to eight weeks' salary in lieu of notice of termination. Mr. Barnard was subsequently terminated without cause and he sued for wrongful dismissal. Mr. Barnard sought an extension of the notice period on account of his employer's bad faith conduct upon termination. The trial judge awarded him compensation well in excess of the amount set out in the employment agreement. Testori appealed the trial judge's decision on the basis that *Wallace* damages are not available when the employment contract specifically sets out entitlement upon termination. The Prince Edward Island Court of Appeal agreed with Testori and held that *Wallace* damages did not apply in a situation where an employment agreement contained an express provision with respect to the employee's entitlement upon termination without notice. The Court of Appeal reasoned that since the termination provision in the employment agreement waived the implied term of reasonable notice, there was no implied reasonable notice period to be extended for bad faith consideration and noted that *Wallace*, unlike the case at hand, involved a situation where the contract did not contain any express provisions regarding termination.

Conversely, in the British Columbia case of *Duprey v. Seanix Technology (Canada) Inc.*,[49] a different conclusion emerged, with the court suggesting that a well-drafted termination clause may not protect an employer from its bad faith conduct. In this case, Joseph Duprey was hired by Seanix Technology (Canada) Inc. as Director of Retail Sales to help increase Seanix's retail computer sales. The parties signed an employment agreement that fixed the length of notice required upon dismissal. Mr. Duprey was abruptly terminated from his employment after three months of employment. During Mr. Duprey's brief period of employment, he managed to broker an 82 million dollar deal. Mr. Duprey alleged that Seanix terminated his contract in order to avoid its obligation to pay him commission on the deal, while Seanix alleged that it terminated him based on his poor performance. The trial judge found that Mr. Duprey's employment was terminated because Seanix did not want to pay his commission. With respect to Mr. Duprey's notice

---

[47] See also *Montague v. Bank of Nova Scotia* (2004), 30 C.C.E.L. (3d) 71 (Ont. C.A.).
[48] (2001), 11 C.C.E.L. (3d) 42 (P.E.I.C.A.), revg 194 Nfld. & P.E.I.R. 119 (S.C.).
[49] (2002), 20 C.C.E.L. (3d) 136 (B.C.S.C.).

period, the court held that since he had signed a valid employment agreement limiting his termination entitlement to the minimum statutory requirement, Mr. Duprey had waived his entitlement to reasonable notice. However, the fact that Mr. Duprey had executed an employment contract which limited his entitlement to notice did not prevent the court from awarding a further payment of one month's notice to compensate for Seanix's bad faith conduct.

Given the conflicting decisions on this issue, it is difficult to determine whether an employer will be protected from bad faith damages by an employment agreement limiting the notice period or pay in lieu of notice to which an employee is entitled. In any event, to avoid liability for *Wallace* damages, prudent employers should ensure that employees are treated in a fair and equitable manner, not only at and around the time of dismissal, but also following the dismissal.

(c) Mitigation of Wallace Damages

Is it possible to avoid the kind of complications, confrontations and harsh words that can lead a court to award *Wallace* damages? In a word, yes. Although it is very difficult to predict exactly what a court may view as bad faith conduct, there are several concrete steps that employers can take to ensure a smooth and relatively painless dismissal. To minimize confusion and miscommunication during a termination, it is important to provide the employee with a termination letter setting out the reasons for and terms of his or her dismissal. If the option of resigning rather than dismissal is offered, allow the employee a reasonable amount of time to contemplate the offer and to seek independent legal advice. In *Geluch v. Rosedale Golf Assn.*,[50] Justice Himel reprimanded Mr. Geluch's former employer for offering him the option of resigning but then giving him only a few minutes to make a decision. Mr. Geluch was ultimately awarded two months in *Wallace* damages, in addition to 15 months of reasonable notice.

It is also advisable to provide outplacement counselling, particularly with professional or managerial employees. Discharged employees are far less likely to turn litigious if they feel that the employer is making a sincere effort to help them find a new job. Courts will also be less inclined to punish an employer who has tried to help an employee's transition into a new job. The timing, location and manner of dismissal should all be designed to minimize humiliation, confusion and hurt feelings. Courts have found that terminations communicated by voice mail[51] or by posting the employee's position

---

[50] (2004), 32 C.C.E.L. (3d) 177 (Ont. S.C.J.).
[51] *Carter v. Packall Packaging Inc.*, [2004] O.J. No. 334 (QL) (S.C.J.).

in a newspaper at a lower rate of pay[52] will warrant *Wallace* damages because of their callous and humiliating nature.

Where there is reason to believe that the termination meeting will be especially difficult, it may be advisable to have a counsellor present. Do not make false allegations of cause. Do not communicate false or exaggerated allegations of cause to others within the relevant business community. Courts will take such statements very seriously because of the damaging impact they can have on an employee's re-employment prospects. In fact, even if there is good reason to believe that the termination was justified by the employee's actions, it is still advisable not to communicate that opinion. After termination, provide the employee with all documentation he or she may need to claim employment insurance benefits.[53] It is never advisable to withhold such documentation, regardless of any outstanding issues the employer may have with the employee.

When faced with a claim of disability, employers should take the obligation to act in good faith during dismissal even more seriously.[54] Ensure that the employee has any forms, publications or instructions that might be needed in order to apply for disability benefits or to appeal a decision rejecting his or her claim for such benefits. Inform the employee exactly what kind of medical information will be required for the determination of entitlement to benefits and allow time for the employee to consult with specialists or other health care practitioners. Keep in mind that the courts will perceive the employee as being particularly vulnerable at this time. An employee struggling with physical or emotional issues will require extra help in dealing with employment matters and courts expect the employer to provide that help, even during the course of a termination. Finally, take any and all complaints about a poisoned work environment very seriously. Investigate complaints and keep detailed records of any offered or implemented solutions. Allowing a workplace to become harmful or overly stressful to employees can result in an extended period of notice upon termination.

The implications of the *Wallace* decision cannot be underestimated. Its impact continues to resonate as courts struggle to apply the concept of bad faith to terminations. Employers who ignore their obligations to discharge employees in good faith face an increased risk of wrongful dismissal litigation and longer notice periods. Taking steps to ensure a relatively peaceful and successful termination at the outset can substantially reduce an employer's ultimate exposure to litigation costs.

---

[52] *MacDonald v. Royal Canadian Legion* (1995), 12 C.C.E.L. (2d) 211 (N.S.S.C.).
[53] *Singh v. British Columbia Hydro and Power Authority, supra*, footnote 44.
[54] *Marshall v. WatsonWyatt & Co., supra*, footnote 45.

9 ✧ NEAR CAUSE

The concept of near cause once applied to cases where an employee's misconduct was not quite grave enough to support a finding of just cause for termination but was serious enough to warrant some reduction in the amount of termination notice to which the employee would otherwise be entitled. Near cause served as a compromise to the strict approach of classifying an employee's behaviour as either completely justifying dismissal or not justifying it at all. This compromise probably evolved in response to the rigid standards that have been used to determine whether or not an act or particular behaviour constitutes just cause and therefore warranted dismissal. Near cause probably has no further application in Canadian courts and it is unlikely to be revived as a "consolation prize" for employers in the future.

The Supreme Court of Canada made its views about near cause clear when it considered a Nova Scotia case that had been friendly to the concept.[55] A stationary engineer who had been employed by the city of Halifax for 25 years was dismissed based on allegations that he had failed to disclose his interest in a contracting company that bid on city contracts. The trial judge, however, found no factual basis for the allegations. The employer then contended that additional facts that had come to light after the employee's dismissal constituted just cause. The employer argued that the employee fraudulently preferred a particular contractor and discouraged other bidders, costing the city "thousands of dollars". Based on the employee's 25 years of service, the trial judge found grounds for a serious reprimand, but not summary dismissal. In assessing the amount of notice to be awarded, the trial judge adopted the principle of "moderated damages" to reduce the amount of notice. He also made reference to the doctrine of near cause, but did not adopt it. The Court of Appeal ruled that there was authority for applying the near cause principle and, therefore, the trial judge was correct in reducing the employee's notice. However, in a short unanimous decision, the Supreme Court rejected all arguments relating to near cause and remitted the case to the Nova Scotia Supreme Court to determine the appropriate amount of notice.[56]

Even when the doctrine of near cause had some application, employers had to know that they would likely have to pay an employee damages for wrongful dismissal if the incident or behaviour that prompted termination was not sufficiently severe to constitute just cause. On the other hand, even now that the doctrine has been discredited and while it may be legally incorrect to do so, if the employee appears undeserving of sympathy, the courts

---

[55] *Dowling v. Halifax (City)* (1995), 15 C.C.E.L. (2d) 299 (N.S.S.C.), affd 136 D.L.R. (4th) 352 (C.A.), revd 158 D.L.R. (4th) 163 (S.C.C.).

[56] For a recent application of the Supreme Court of Canada decision see *Liebman v. Trafalgar Industries of Canada Ltd.*, [2004] O.J. No. 582 (QL) (S.C.J.).

may be influenced to do indirectly what they can no longer do directly. All courts recognize that the assessment of damages is not a science and that reasonable notice generally falls within a range of possibilities or notice scale. Simply put, a court might be more inclined to award damages at the lower end of the reasonable notice scale where it finds some culpability on the part of the employee. Putting aside the question of where an employee will end up on the notice scale, the disappearance of the near cause doctrine can leave an employer in a tough spot. If you allege cause and do not succeed, not only will you lose the case but, with the emergence of *Wallace* damages, you may face a counter-attack of bad faith discharge. As a result, the disappearance of the near cause doctrine, combined with the prominence of *Wallace*, could have a chilling effect on the willingness of employers to allege cause.

10 ✧ AFTER ACQUIRED CAUSE

After acquired cause is a concept that allows an employer to justify an employee's dismissal with behaviour that did not come to the employer's attention until the individual's employment had already been terminated. That is, an employee's conduct can act to establish just cause for termination despite the fact that the employer was unaware of it at the time the employee was fired. In one case, it came to the employer's attention that a dismissed employee was dishonest in claiming for moving expenses that had been paid for by his former employer.[57] The court held that this misconduct constituted after-acquired cause. However, the conduct can be relied upon only if it took place prior to the dismissal. Misbehaviour or other conduct that occurs after an employee is terminated cannot serve to constitute just cause. Notwithstanding this principle, serious misconduct that is engaged in after an employee receives adequate notice of termination may warrant immediate dismissal if it takes place prior to the date on which the individual's employment legally terminates in accordance with the end of the reasonable notice period. In one case for example, an employee was given notice that his employment would end in a few months.[58] The employee continued to work following receipt of the notice but during this period engaged in wilful misconduct that constituted just cause for termination. The court concluded that the employer was justified in terminating the employee immediately, even though the misconduct took place after the employee had been told that his employment was ending. However, in another case the employer, through the use of working notice, was deemed to have created a predictable environment

---

[57] *O'Donnell v. Bourgault Industries Ltd.* (1999), 182 Sask. R. 117 (Q.B.), affd 223 Sask. R. 132 (C.A.).

[58] *Aasgaard v. Harlequin Enterprises Ltd.* (1993), 48 C.C.E.L. 192 (Ont. Ct. (Gen. Div.)), affd 70 A.C.W.S. (3d) 80 (C.A.).

of hostility and anger that ultimately led to the employee's immediate termination. As a result of the employer's role in creating the hostile environment, it was not permitted to rely on just cause to end the employee's employment, but rather was required to pay the notice period determined by the court.[59] This kind of reasoning arguably applies even in situations where the employee is still within the period of reasonable notice, although no longer actively at work.

In most cases, courts will differ in the weight they give to misconduct that employers say was discovered after the employee was dismissed. Misbehaviour will generally not be afforded weight if it is insignificant or if the nature of the conduct is such that the employer is very likely to have known about it, or should have known prior to notice of dismissal. On occasion, an employer might deliberately avoid inquiry into whether just cause for termination existed before the employee was actually fired. In circumstances where the employer intentionally avoids dealing with an employee's misconduct when it occurs in the course of employment, the court will likely conclude that it was excused and cannot be used to justify termination retroactively.[60] Similarly, there may be times when a court will find that an employer ought to have known about an employee's behaviour if the workplace was being managed properly. Courts are less inclined to conclude that misconduct constitutes after acquired cause where the failure to discover it before an employee's termination was the result of poor management practices.

While there are cases where little weight is given to misconduct discovered after an employee's dismissal, an employer may still benefit from carrying out a post-dismissal investigation for the purpose of possibly uncovering other acts of misconduct. An employee who has engaged in one misdeed may have engaged in others, proving true the adage that "where there's smoke, there's fire". After-acquired knowledge of misconduct may also be useful in strengthening existing arguments for cause in wrongful dismissal cases commenced by fired employees. Consequently, the value of after-acquired knowledge in respect of an employee's misbehaviour should not be underestimated.

11 ✧ ONUS OF PROOF

Where an employer claims that a termination was for cause, it is the employer's responsibility to prove the existence of grounds constituting just cause for termination. That is, the employer bears the burden of proving the

---

[59] *Elg v. Stirling Doors*, [2002] O.T.C. 539 (S.C.J.).
[60] See *Olson v. Ritchie Bros. Construction Ltd.* (unreported, May 5, 1994, Alta. Q.B.). See also discussion under Heading 13, "Condonation", of this Part.

facts necessary to establish just cause once an individual has shown that he or she was employed and subsequently dismissed by the employer.

As canvassed below,[61] the existence of just cause must be determined objectively rather than according to the subjective beliefs or impressions of the employer who has summarily dismissed an employee. Although an employer may honestly believe that there is cause for an employee's dismissal, reasonable notice of termination or pay in lieu of notice must still be provided if just cause, objectively defined, cannot in fact be established.

12 ✧ STANDARD OF PROOF

Employers must meet a certain threshold of proof when they attempt to demonstrate the existence of just cause for termination. Just cause must be proven on a balance of probabilities. That is, it must be more likely than not that just cause for an employee's dismissal existed. Some courts have suggested that more compelling evidence is required to establish cause where the employer alleges that an employee is guilty of criminal or dishonest conduct. For instance, allegations of theft, misappropriation of company property, breach of trust, etc., may require that a higher standard of proof be met. This higher standard will fall somewhere along the scale between proof on a balance of probabilities and proof beyond a reasonable doubt. The latter is a more difficult standard to achieve, well beyond "likely true" and approaching certainty. Even at its highest, however, the standard of proof necessary to establish just cause is less stringent than that required in a criminal case where the guilt of an accused must be proved beyond a reasonable doubt.

Whether just cause exists will depend on the particular facts in each case of dismissal and on whether an objective third party would consider the employee's conduct to be sufficiently serious to warrant summary dismissal. The contextual approach is applied, requiring employers to meet the following two-step test to justify dismissal for cause: first, the evidence must establish misconduct on the balance of probabilities, and second, the nature and degree of the employee's dishonesty must warrant summary dismissal.[62] However, the contextual approach is not applied as stringently where the employee has engaged in a serious form of misconduct such as fraud, misappropriation, or theft. In such cases, a single incidence of such misconduct is usually sufficient to justify summary dismissal. Where an employee commits a serious form of misconduct, the employer must demonstrate that the employee intended to and actually did engage in the deceitful conduct in order to dismiss the employee for cause. On the other hand, the courts must

---

[61] See the discussion under Heading 12, "Standard of Proof", of this Part.
[62] *McKinley v. B.C. Tel* (2001), 200 D.L.R. (4th) 385 (S.C.C.).

still apply the contextual approach to determine whether the dismissal was appropriate in the circumstances. While the courts continue to do so in all situations of serious misconduct, the finding of theft or fraud, especially by an employee who holds a position of trust, is usually sufficient to justify dismissal for cause.[63]

The honest good faith beliefs of the employer as to the character and conduct of the dismissed employee are of little relevance, except perhaps as background information or in defence of a claim of bad faith discharge. To demonstrate just cause, an employer must satisfy the court that, in fact, the employee engaged in real misconduct or exhibited true incompetence. It should be noted that just cause is somewhat easier to establish where an employee's behaviour causes harm to the employer. The kind of harm that an employer might suffer includes injury to his or her reputation, property damage and production or profit losses.

Finally, employers should always consider whether or not a written employment contract with the employee defines conduct that would constitute just cause. It is almost always the case that the terms of such an agreement will prevail so long as the contract is otherwise enforceable. A contractual term that defines what behaviour qualifies as just cause may make it easier for an employer to meet the standard of proof required to establish just cause for termination. However, if just cause is being defined in an employment contract, it should be broadly defined and avoid all-inclusive language. For example, the termination provision should start with a "boilerplate" statement such as: "The parties agree that the employee may be terminated for just cause for any omissions or commissions that constitute just cause at law and, without limiting the generality of the foregoing, for the following specific acts . . ." This approach provides employers with both the basic protection pursuant to common law principles of just cause and the more specific terms of an employment contract that may provide more latitude to the employer.

13 ✧ CONDONATION

Condonation is a concept related to situations where employers overlook behaviour that would otherwise constitute just cause for dismissal. Employers who become aware of employee misconduct serious enough to justify termination will be found to have excused it if they continue to employ the employee for a considerable period of time after discovering the misconduct.

---

[63] See the discussion under Heading 4, "Dishonesty", of Part II, "Grounds for Termination".

Where an employee alleges that his or her conduct was condoned by an employer, the burden of proving such condonation rests on the employee. An essential element that must be established is intention on the part of the employer to excuse the behaviour. For such intention to be established, the employee must demonstrate that the employer had real and actual knowledge of the conduct constituting just cause. Simply being aware of rumours that pertain to the behaviour of an employee will generally not qualify as real and actual knowledge of the employee's transgressions.[64]

Misconduct can be condoned by both action and inaction on the part of an employer. For instance, the employer might learn of an employee's misbehaviour and do nothing, continuing to retain the individual for a considerable period of time, or offering to renew an empoloyee's contract.[65] Similarly, behaviour may be excused where the employer knows about it and goes on to give the employee good performance reviews.[66] Another way in which an employer might be seen to condone an employee's misconduct is by reprimanding the employee but subsequently doing nothing else.[67] A court might also conclude that conduct was condoned where an employee is laid off for a substantial period of time before the employer alleges that just cause for the termination existed. Finally, an employer likely will be seen as excusing an employee's poor performance where the performance was accepted for a long period of time. If an employer wants to rely on such performance to constitute just cause for termination, it must first provide its employee with ample warning that the performance will not be tolerated any longer. Notwithstanding the comments made thus far, it should be noted that subsequent instances of similar misconduct can serve to nullify an employer's earlier condonation, in certain circumstances. A court has held that although conduct prior to the condonation cannot be completely ignored, it is up to the trial court judge to determine what weight it should carry in a subsequent action.[68] In another case, it was held that although prior excused conduct cannot be relied upon as cause for dismissal, it may be taken into account as being indicative of the employee's general attitude towards his responsibilities and provides a contextual background to the events surrounding a dismissal.[69]

There is some uncertainty as to whether providing termination pay constitutes condonation of conduct. Where an employer dismisses an employee and provides some sort of a severance or termination package, it can be

---

[64] *O'Malley v. Pacific Customs Brokers (Airport) Ltd.* (1984), 10 C.C.E.L. 98 (B.C.S.C.).
[65] *Chambers v. Omni Insurance Brokers* (2002), 17 C.C.E.L. (3d) 179 (Ont. C.A.).
[66] See, *e.g.*, *Connor v. Canada Life Assurance Co.* (1991), 108 N.S.R. (2d) 361, supplementary reasons 108 N.S.R. (2d) at p. 369 (S.C.T.D.).
[67] See *Fournier v. Robichaud* (1987), 80 N.B.R. (2d) 329 (Q.B.).
[68] *Chambers v. Omni Insurance Brokers, supra*, footnote 65.
[69] *Henson v. Champion Feed Services Ltd.*, [2003] A.J. No. 1454 (QL) (Prov. Ct.).

argued that the employer forfeits the right to claim that just cause for dismissal existed. However, it is often the case that despite the existence of just cause, an employer will provide a fired employee with a payment as a gesture of good will and to make the termination less difficult. In these circumstances, the employer should make it abundantly clear that termination is for cause and that the payment is being made gratuitously. If the employee subsequently brings an action for wrongful dismissal, the employer can argue that there was just cause to dismiss the employee and that the pay-out provided was given strictly to assist the employee in his or her search for future employment.

In this respect, an employer would be prudent to issue a dismissal letter stating that termination was for cause and that the employer is willing to provide an offer of settlement involving a termination payment in good faith, without prejudice and without admission of liability. Employees should be required to sign back acceptance of such an offer. If any payment is made without sign-back, the employer should issue a separate letter to that effect. Employers also should be careful not to say or do anything at the time of dismissal that could later be viewed as inconsistent with a claim of just cause for termination. Accordingly, a letter of reference should not be provided where cause for an employee's dismissal is being asserted. Instead, employers should only supply a confirmation of employment letter that describes the nature of the employer's business and specifies the dates and duration of the employee's employment and the position(s) the employee held during that time.

14 ✧ DOCUMENTATION

The importance of documentation relates to the practice of recording all occurrences of misconduct by employees that independently or cumulatively could constitute just cause for termination. Such occurrences should be recorded by an employer in an individual file maintained for each employee. As part of the record of corrective action, the employer should specifically record warnings an employee is given about his or her behaviour. Proper documentation will assist the employer in proving that just cause for an employee's termination did in fact exist and that, where it was required, the employer provided adequate warning to the employee about the consequences of continued misconduct.

Prudent documentation consists of giving employees a copy of what is actually recorded in their employment files. However, employers should do more and ensure that each employee sufficiently understands the significance of what is being documented. Failure to do so could result in employees successfully arguing that they did not appreciate the nature of the details recorded in their employment files and were not advised as to the consequences of their behaviour, especially the potential for just cause dismissal.

It is the employer who has the ultimate responsibility of proving that a warning as to the consequences of certain behaviour was given and understood by the dismissed employee. In this respect, employers should ask employees to sign an acknowledgement stating that they understand and agree with the warning/discipline received or at least acknowledge its receipt.

If a warning is made in writing, a copy of it should be placed in the employee's file. Where warnings are not in writing, they should be made in a clear and unmistakable manner. The fact that a warning was given and when it was made should also be recorded in an employee's file, as should the particulars of the warning and the name and position of the person who issued it.

An employer should avoid providing only verbal warnings and placing written notes concerning the employee's conduct in his or her file without communicating the concern directly to the employee. A court will not give significant weight to any documentation in an employee's file that was never provided to the employee. In the result, even if an oral warning is provided to an employee, if a record is created for the file, as it should be, a prudent employer will provide a copy of that record to the employee. In this way, many employers have adopted the concept of a "written verbal" warning as the first stage of the disciplinary process.

15 ✧ PROGRESSIVE AND CORRECTIVE DISCIPLINE

From the preceding sections, especially "Just Cause", "Near Cause", "Condonation" and "Documentation", it is apparent that employers are well served by using a system of discipline that is both corrective and progressive. In the context of unionized workplaces, progressive discipline is well known and refers to a method of disciplining employees on a cumulative basis for successive transgressions or incidents of incompetence. The notion of corrective action is that employers should be motivated by a good faith intention to improve the behaviour and performance of their employees, rather than build a record to justify dismissal. Naturally, by doing the former, you should achieve the latter. An effective system of progressive and corrective discipline should not be unique to unionized workplaces. The authors recommend that employers use the same kind of system in non-union workplaces or for employees who are not represented by a trade union, including supervisory employees.

In essence, progressive and corrective discipline requires that increasingly severe disciplinary consequences be imposed on employees in a graduated manner. Dismissal should be reserved as the ultimate disciplinary response. For instance, in dealing with an employee's misconduct, an employer might first issue a number of verbal and written warnings and then proceed to suspend the employee (with or without pay) a few times (for progressively longer periods) before finally terminating employment. For those employers who choose to follow a system of progressive and corrective discipline, just cause for an employee's termination will generally not be established unless increasingly more serious penalties have been imposed. As will be discussed at the end of this section, particularly egregious misconduct could still result in an immediate dismissal.

Progressive and corrective discipline has also been characterized in terms of the "culminating incident" principle. This principle suggests that a certain act may justify an employee's dismissal if he or she received a number of prior warnings and suspensions even if the act itself would not have justified dismissal. The act or incident serving to warrant termination constitutes the culminating incident and is often described as "the straw that broke the camel's back". It permits an employer to justify the firing of an employee by relying on his or her disciplinary record, notwithstanding the relatively minor nature of the final incident itself. However, no matter how trivial the culminating incident is, it must still be deserving of some discipline in order to qualify as just cause for termination.

Employers who follow a corrective action plan should have an easier time justifying an employee's summary dismissal. For instance, using progressive and corrective discipline may satisfy an employer's duty to provide employees with warnings prior to termination about the consequences of their misconduct or incompetence. Also, progressive and corrective discipline can be viewed as a method by which to ensure that an employer is not seen as having condoned or excused the misbehaviour of an employee.

Depending on the facts and circumstances of a given situation, warnings may or may not be required. For instance, where certain conduct or incidents are annoying but trivial, a warning is likely required before just cause for a dismissal can be established. However, where there have been several occurrences of serious misbehaviour or incompetence, the collective nature of the incidents may make it unnecessary to have warned an employee that termination might be imposed. This could be the case notwithstanding the fact that each incident is not severe enough by itself to justify dismissal.[70] In exceptional circumstances, a single transgression might justify summary dismissal if it is extremely prejudicial to the employer.[71] The test is whether the alleged misconduct was such as to interfere with and prejudice the safe and proper conduct of the employer's business. Put another way, even where a policy of discipline exists, it need not be followed where an employee's behaviour amounts to a fundamental breach or violation of the terms that govern the

---

[70] *Fonceca v. McDonnell Douglas Canada Ltd.* (1983), 1 C.C.E.L. 51 (Ont. H.C.J.).
[71] *Stilwell v. Audio Pictures Ltd.*, [1955] O.W.N. 793 (C.A.).

employment relationship with the employer.[72] Examples of misconduct that do not require warnings of termination include theft, a physical altercation with the employer and sabotage of the employer's property or business.

16 ✧ MITIGATION

The concept of mitigation refers to the fact that, despite entitlement to reasonable notice or pay in lieu of notice, an employee is required to take all reasonable steps to minimize losses suffered as a result of not being given such notice or pay. A court will conclude that an employee was wrongfully dismissed where it finds that the employee was terminated without just cause and without adequate notice or pay. In such a case, the court generally orders the employer to pay the employee a monetary sum. Even so, a court will refuse to order full compensation where the employer is able to demonstrate that the employee did not do enough to minimize loss of salary, benefits, etc. The onus is on the employer to establish this fact and unless clear and convincing evidence exists the employee will be presumed to have made reasonable and sufficient mitigation efforts.

The most common way in which a dismissed employee can mitigate the losses suffered is to earn employment income and to replace, if possible, the employment benefits lost as a result of the termination. In some cases, an employee may be obligated to purchase health care benefits under an individual insurance policy. The employee is not required, however, to take any employment. Rather, the obligation to mitigate is limited to accepting a job comparable to the position from which the employee was terminated or one consistent with the employee's skills, qualifications and experience. Alternatively, an employee could commence self-employment or, where it is an option, could accept another position with the same employer, at least until alternative employment is found. Notwithstanding the duty to mitigate, a court will not expect an employee to continue working for the same employer if that would be unreasonable. For example, where working conditions are likely to be substantially different or where the employment relationship is acrimonious or disagreeable, it is patently unreasonable to expect an employee to accept continuing employment in mitigation of damages.[73] Further, where a predictably hostile work environment results from the employer's use of working notice, the employer cannot then rely on this as a basis for just cause termination.[74]

---

[72] *Mant v. Buckerfield's Ltd.* (1991), 36 C.C.E.L. 193 (B.C.S.C.).
[73] *Mifsud v. MacMillan Bathurst Inc.* (1989), 63 D.L.R. (4th) 714 (Ont. C.A.), leave to appeal to S.C.C. refused 68 D.L.R. (4th) vii.
[74] *Elg v. Stirling Doors*, [2002] O.T.C. 539 (S.C.J.).

If an employee is re-employed with a new employer for essentially the same salary and benefits, the claim for reasonable notice cannot be made since the employee will not have suffered any losses from his or her dismissal. As noted above, this may also apply if the terminating employer provides the employee with alternative employment on comparable terms. On the other hand, where the employee obtains a new position that pays less in terms of salary and benefits, the terminating employer is responsible to pay the difference for the required period of notice. In either situation, however, the employee is still entitled to receive termination and severance pay (where applicable) pursuant to employment standards legislation as statutory payments are not subject to the doctrine of mitigation. In other words, and unless the employee remains in employment in a different position with the same employer, a dismissed employee would continue to have statutory entitlements even if he or she found comparable employment immediately after dismissal and suffered no loss.

PART II

✦ GROUNDS FOR TERMINATION ✦

1 ✦ PROBATIONARY STATUS

Probationary status alone will not justify dismissal without notice. However, it is generally easier to establish just cause for termination with respect to probationary employees than with respect to permanent employees. An individual who is a probationary employee is hired subject to successful completion of a probation period. During this time, the employee's suitability for permanent employment is assessed, as well as the employee's ability to meet the requirements of the job in question. Where the employee is ultimately found to be unsuited for permanent employment and/or unable to meet the job requirements, he or she can be summarily dismissed within the probation period. In this regard, the employer must be sure to terminate the employee within the probation period initially established, unless the period has been extended prior to its expiry.

A question that often arises is whether or not the employee has probationary status at the time of dismissal. The fact that an employer has a policy of hiring employees subject to completion of a testing or trial period is not enough to support a finding of probationary employment. At the very least, an employee should be advised of the probationary aspect of his or her hiring and ideally terminology to this effect should appear in the employment contract.[1] For example, if a prospective employee is given an employment manual setting out the terms of probation, a court will likely conclude that the probationary nature of the hiring was sufficiently disclosed.[2]

Employers who act in good faith are given a significant amount of latitude when it comes to firing probationary employees. The standard of proof or degree of misconduct required to establish just cause for a probationary employee's termination is less than that needed to dismiss a permanent employee. Furthermore, the type of unsuitability that will justify termination of a probationary employee is broad in scope and can include a consideration of the following factors: the employee's compatibility; the employee's character; and the employee's ability to meet present and future demands of the

---

[1] See *Miller v. Goldfan Holdings Ltd.* (1992), 44 C.C.E.L. 224 (Ont. Ct. (Gen. Div.)).
[2] See *Kirby v. Motor Coach Industries Ltd.* (1980), 1 C.C.E.L. 260 (Man. Co. Ct.), revd on other grounds 10 Man. R. (2d) 36 (C.A.).

job in question. A court will not question an employer's decision to fire a probationary employee if he or she is fired on the basis of one or more of these factors and the employer's judgment and discretion are exercised in a *bona fide* manner (*i.e.*, in good faith).

In contrast, a court will conclude that a termination without notice was wrongful if it finds there was no legal justification to dismiss the probationary employee and the employer acted on the basis of an improper motive or for reasons other than the employee's unsuitability.[3] This is why employers are required to show that they acted fairly and with reasonable diligence in determining whether a probationary employee was suitable for the job. In addition, the employee must be given a reasonable opportunity to demonstrate his or her ability to meet the standards set by an employer at the time of hiring. If both conditions are satisfied, summary dismissal within a probation period will be justified. These conditions were satisfied in a case involving a human resources manager hired by a meat-packing company subject to a six-month probation period.[4] During this time, the company decided that the manager was unsuitable for permanent employment. The company found that the manager was aggressive and abrasive towards staff members, was not inclined to listen to other persons' points of view and had a tendency to act unilaterally without consulting the company's supervisors. The court confirmed that when a probationary employee is dismissed an employer must show that the individual is ill-suited for permanent employment in the position for which he or she was hired. The court concluded that the company had acted fairly and with reasonable diligence in determining that the manager was not suited for the human resources position. Moreover, it was found that the manager had been given a reasonable opportunity to demonstrate whether he could meet the standards the company had set at the time of his hiring. While these standards might relate to the testing of an employee's skills, the court noted that they could also deal with an employee's ability to work in harmony with others, the employee's potential usefulness in the future and any other factors that an employer deems essential to the proper performance of the position.

The dismissal of a probationary employee is justified where the cumulative effect of several problems causes the employer to lose confidence in the employee's judgment. The case for termination will be even stronger if the employee occupies a managerial position of trust with significant responsibilities. These were the circumstances where the board of directors of a credit union dismissed an employee hired for the position of general manager subject to a six-month term of probation.[5] A number of concerns relating to the

---

[3] *Kirby v. Motor Coach Industries Ltd., supra.*
[4] *Ritchie v. Intercontinental Packers Ltd.* (1982), 2 C.C.E.L. 147 (Sask. Q.B.).
[5] *Rocky Credit Union Ltd. v. Higginson* (1995), 10 C.C.E.L. (2d) 1 (Alta. C.A.).

manager's conduct arose during this period. In particular, the manager submitted a claim for his relocation expenses that included several items not covered by his employment contract. Further, the manager permitted his loan with the credit union to fall overdue, did not address problems associated with his mortgage and often failed to follow the board of directors' instructions and directives. The concerns relating to the manager's conduct were assessed by the members of the board prior to expiry of the manager's probation period. The board members decided that confidence in the manager had been lost and that he could not be entrusted with the significant responsibilities associated with his position. As a result, the manager's employment was summarily terminated. The court concluded that the termination was justified given the manager's conduct in a position of trust, his responsibilities as general manager and the board's need to have absolute confidence and faith in his judgment, advice and reliability. In essence, just cause for the manager's dismissal was established by the totality of the evidence, the cumulative effect of the board's concerns and the nature of the manager's position. The court agreed that the standard of proof required to establish just cause for a probationary employee's termination is less than that needed for dismissing a regular employee. In the particular circumstances, however, the difference between the two standards of proof was not important. Regardless of whether or not the manager was a probationary employee, the court concluded that the facts of the case clearly amounted to just cause for termination.

Finally, a probationary employee may be summarily dismissed without reasons being given where there are serious concerns about the employee's compatibility with others in the workplace. Termination on this basis is very likely to be justified where the job in question requires the employee to work as part of a team in the employer's organization. In one case, for instance, a newly hired corporate secretary was unable to demonstrate her ability to work harmoniously in a small organization where teamwork was essential to its operations.[6] While there were no problems with her work performance, concerns arose in the secretary's probation period as to whether her personality, management style and business approach were compatible with the employer's organization. These concerns were based on a number of factors that included complaints from co-workers and the organization's solicitor who all found it very difficult to work with the secretary. Her abrasive and condescending approach toward people eventually caused a junior employee to resign. The concerns relating to the secretary were investigated and confirmed by the employer. The employer ultimately decided that she was not compatible with the organization's "team approach" and terminated her employment within the probation period. The court accepted that an

---

[6] *Jadot v. Concert Industries Ltd.* (1995), 10 C.C.E.L. (2d) 13 (B.C.S.C.), affd 33 C.C.E.L. (2d) 29 (C.A.).

employer is entitled to use a probation period to consider not only the technical skills of a potential permanent employee but also to assess the applicant's character and to determine whether he or she was likely to work harmoniously in the employer's organization. In this case, the secretary was required to adapt to a small, casual environment. While the requirement was made clear to the secretary at the time of hiring, she was unable to demonstrate her ability in this respect. The court concluded that the employer acted in good faith when the secretary's suitability for permanent employment was assessed and when the determination was made that she could not work harmoniously in the organization. Further, the court said that the employer was not required to notify the secretary of his concerns or give her an opportunity to respond to them because reasonable steps had been taken to ensure that the decision about her suitability was made in good faith. The employer had discharged its onus of showing that the secretary was dismissed for *bona fide* reasons of unsuitability and her dismissal was therefore justified.

It should be noted that everything said so far about probationary employees applies to private sector employers and employees. Where an individual is the holder of a public office, a police officer for example, additional considerations apply. In particular, a duty of procedural fairness is imposed on employers who want to fire this type of probationary employee and certain statutes govern the manner in which they can be dismissed. An employer's failure to comply with the applicable legislation may result in reinstatement of the dismissed employee.

It should also be noted that all jurisdictions have employment standards legislation that sets out minimum notice requirements that employers must provide to all employees who are dismissed.[7] In most instances, employees are not entitled to receive statutory notice until they have worked a minimum period of time. These periods are specified in the legislation that applies to each jurisdiction. For example, an Ontario employer is not required to provide statutory notice unless an employee has been in its employ for at least three months. However, the employer may still have to provide individuals employed for fewer than three months with common law reasonable notice where just cause for termination does not exist. Furthermore, while employers may be able to justify a probationary employee's termination on the basis of unsuitability, the employee will usually be entitled to statutory notice where he or she has worked the minimum amount of time prescribed in the relevant legislation. This means that an employer cannot use a term of probation to contract out of statutorily imposed notice periods.

---

[7] See discussion under Heading 4, "Statutory Notice, Termination Payments and Severance Payments", of Part I, "General Concepts".

Employers sometimes want to put a regular or permanent employee on probation when they see problems in an employee's work performance. Caution must be exercised in these circumstances because imposing a probation period without the employee's consent will sometimes be treated as constructive dismissal. Even where there is consent, a permanent employee is entitled to the full period of probation to demonstrate his or her abilities. An employer cannot dismiss a permanent employee prior to expiry of the probation term. Furthermore, the degree of misconduct or unsuitability required to dismiss a permanent employee on probation is more onerous than that needed for the termination of a "traditional" probationary employee. In these circumstances, it is preferable to avoid using probationary terminology altogether. The employee should be placed on a performance review plan instead. The plan should outline the employee's shortcomings and the specific job requirements and provide the employee with a reasonable period in which to improve.

Overview

A probationary employee can be dismissed without notice on the basis of unsuitability. In this respect, a less onerous standard of proof is required to establish just cause for a probationary employee's termination than that required for dismissing a regular employee. However, the employer must be able to justify the manner in which the decision to terminate the employee was reached and the basis of the decision as well. Sufficient cause for the termination of a probationary employee exists where employers can show that they acted fairly in determining the probationary employee's suitability for permanent employment and gave the employee a reasonable opportunity to demonstrate his or her abilities. Any of the following circumstances will strengthen the case for employers:

1. The probationary employee was not fired on the basis of an improper motive or for reasons other than unsuitability.
2. Co-workers and others in the workplace had problems when dealing with the employee.
3. The employee's personality was incompatible with the workplace environment of the employer's organization.
4. The cumulative effect of problems and concerns caused the employer to lose confidence in the employee.
5. The employee held a managerial position of trust with significant responsibilities.
6. During the probation period the employee was unable to meet the requirements of the job.
7. The termination occurred within the probation period.

2 ✧ MISREPRESENTATION PRIOR TO HIRING

At some point in the employment relationship, an employer may discover that during the hiring process an employee intentionally misrepresented his or her background, skills or qualifications. Employees who mislead prospective employers in this manner often do so to ensure that they obtain the desired position. Generally speaking, dishonesty or misrepresentation by an employee in an interview, on a job application or in employment negotiations is just cause for dismissal where certain factors exist.

To establish a case for cause based on misrepresentation by the employee prior to being hired, the employer must demonstrate that the misrepresentation was material; that is, it must pertain to a qualification or skill required for the job in question. Alternatively, the misrepresentation must relate to matters that would have resulted in the employee not being hired had they been accurately presented. In one case, an employee misled a company during job negotiations with respect to several material items by misrepresenting his qualifications and falsely claiming to hold a secure and senior position of employment.[8] The employee also lied about the remuneration he was receiving at the time. The court agreed that the company would never have hired the employee on the agreed upon terms had it known the truth. It was held by the court that the employee was justifiably fired without notice due to the misrepresentations made. The same conclusion was reached in a case where an employee's résumé showed that he was employed when he applied for a sales supervisor position.[9] The reality was that he had been unemployed for seven months following a nervous breakdown and a period of hospitalization. The employee's résumé was inaccurate in another respect as well. It falsely stated that he had taken a university business course relevant to the position he was seeking. The employer was able to satisfy the court that the employee would likely not have been interviewed nor offered the position of sales supervisor if he had been truthful about his employment status and education. Just cause for his termination was therefore established.

Related to the requirement of materiality is the need for a misrepresentation to have prejudiced an employer or at least have had the potential to do so. In this respect, errors that are minor, inadvertent or inconsequential are not apt to constitute just cause for termination. For instance, accidentally providing an incorrect date with respect to past employment will not usually be sufficient grounds for a summary dismissal where nothing turns on the date's accuracy. In contrast, a dismissal might be justified if the misrepresentation reveals that the employee cannot be trusted. This was one of the concerns a utility company had about continuing to employ someone who had lied about

---

[8] *Schafer v. Pan Matrix Informatics Ltd.* (1987), 80 A.R. 378 (Q.B.).
[9] *Cornell v. Rogers Cablesystems Inc.* (1987), 17 C.C.E.L. 232 (Ont. Dist. Ct.).

his education before commencing employment.[10] When the company discovered that the employee did not have a Bachelor of Commerce degree in marketing, its concerns were twofold. First, it felt the employee would be unable to perform the marketing duties he had been hired to perform. In this respect, the court accepted that the employee would not have been hired if the company had known he lacked the relevant degree. Secondly, the company was concerned about retaining someone as a sales supervisor who would lie about his credentials. This was something everyone in the organization would eventually know about and the company was worried that it would send out the wrong message. Notwithstanding the company's concerns, its president was willing to offer the employee a lower position with reduced remuneration. This offer was made mainly out of sympathy for the employee because he and his wife were expecting a child. It was also made because the employee seemed remorseful about his conduct and appeared to have the potential to be an asset in areas other than marketing. However, as the offer was not accepted by the employee, he was terminated for having deceived the employer about his education. While the employee tried to maintain that the misrepresentation was inadvertent, he could not explain why he had said nothing when his arrival was announced in the company newsletter and referred to the fact that he had a business degree. Accordingly, the court concluded that the employee had intentionally misstated his education and that the company had just cause for terminating him on this basis.

Another element required to establish just cause in this area involves the need for the misrepresentation to have been expressly or blatantly made by the employee during the hiring process. For example, if a prospective employee makes no positive statement as to the income and benefits attached to his former or present employment, a case for cause based on a misrepresentation in respect of remuneration cannot be supported. These were the circumstances in one case where a court concluded that a transport company did not have just cause for terminating its manager on the basis of misrepresented facts.[11] The court said that statements made by the employee prior to commencing employment were not misrepresentations about his former income level and benefits. Rather, they were "innuendos" that made the employer think the employee may have been earning more than he was being offered. Because the employee never made any specific statements about his income level and benefits, the company was precluded from successfully arguing that just cause on the basis of misrepresentation existed. Furthermore, although the employee had said he could generate substantial profits as manager of the employer's company, the court concluded this was "mere puffery" about his future potential and did not constitute a misrepresentation as to his present or

---

[10] *Werle v. SaskEnergy Inc.* (1992), 103 Sask. R. 241 (Q.B.).
[11] *Earle v. Grant Transport* (1995), 15 C.C.E.L. (2d) 313 (Ont. Ct. (Gen. Div.)).

past achievements. Consequently, such a declaration was insufficient to support a dismissal for just cause.

Normally, an employee is not required to disclose past misconduct unless specifically asked by a prospective employer or unless the position being sought is a fiduciary one.[12] In one case, for example, a lawyer made arrangements with an organization to accept a position in its legal department that would require him to deal extensively with governmental agencies.[13] At the time of hiring, the lawyer did not tell his prospective employer that he was the subject of a police investigation for a criminal offence. Prior to commencing employment in his new position, the lawyer was actually arrested and charged. The organization decided to cancel his employment even though the lawyer was ultimately acquitted of the charge laid against him. Notwithstanding the acquittal, the court said the lawyer owed a duty to his prospective employer to disclose the possibility of being criminally charged. This duty existed because, in addition to its professional nature, the relationship between lawyers and their employers is of a fiduciary nature. Accordingly, the court took the view that employees such as lawyers are required to tell potential employers about any wrongdoing of which they may be suspect. In the circumstances of this case the court concluded that by not disclosing the possibility of a criminal charge being laid against him, the lawyer had failed to meet the standard of good faith required for negotiating the contemplated fiduciary relationship.

The final point to be made in respect of a dismissal based on employee misrepresentations relates to timing. The employer who wants to rely on the making of a misrepresentation as grounds for termination should dismiss the employee immediately or soon after the misrepresentation is discovered. A case for cause will be more difficult to support where an employee is given the chance to perform the job for which he or she was hired despite the employer's knowledge of the misrepresentation. In such circumstances, the employer might be seen as condoning the misrepresentation. However, a case for cause will not necessarily fail if the employee is offered a different and/or substantially lower position from the one currently being held.[14]

Overview

Just cause for termination can be established where an employee is found to have purposely made one or more misrepresentations during the hiring process. A case for cause on this basis exists where the following factors and circumstances exist:

---

[12] See discussion under Heading 17, "Breaching Fiduciary Duties", of this Part.
[13] *Courtright v. Canadian Pacific Ltd.* (1983), 5 D.L.R. (4th) 488 (Ont. H.C.J.), affd 18 D.L.R. (4th) 639*n* (C.A.).
[14] *Werle v. SaskEnergy Inc.*, *supra*, footnote 10.

1. The misrepresentation was material in that it pertained to a qualification or skill required by the job in question or related to matters that accurately presented would have prevented the employee from being hired.
2. The misrepresentation prejudiced or potentially prejudiced the employer. This includes circumstances where a misrepresentation revealed that the employee could not be trusted.
3. The misrepresentation was not trivial or inconsequential.
4. The misrepresentation was expressly or blatantly made by the employee or could reasonably be inferred from his or her conduct.
5. The employee was a fiduciary and prior to hiring failed to disclose wrongdoings of which he or she was then suspected.
6. The employee was dismissed soon after the employer learned of the misrepresentation.

3 ✧ PERFORMANCE PROBLEMS

A common reason for wanting to dismiss an employee relates to the employee's performance in carrying out the duties and responsibilities of the job. Problems associated with the way in which an employee's work is discharged or with the work product of the employee can give rise to just cause for termination. However, mere dissatisfaction is generally not sufficient to justify an employee's dismissal.[15] Rather, the employer must be able to demonstrate that there are real problems with the employee's performance that were not ameliorated despite the issuance of clear instructions and warnings. All factors that may explain the problems must be examined, especially if they are caused by the employer. The specific nature of the problem will often determine whether a case for just cause can be established. Three categories of performance problems that have been identified are: those associated with incompetence; those that relate to carelessness; and those that can be seen as neglect of duties.

(a) Incompetence

An employee's incompetence may amount to just cause for termination of employment. In this context, incompetence refers to circumstances where individuals lack the necessary skills or are unqualified or unable to perform the tasks or functions required for the positions they hold. An employer who claims that a worker was fired on this basis must prove that the employee's performance fell below an objective standard of competence. The nature of such a standard will necessarily depend on the type of work the employee was

---

[15] *Kenzie v. Standard Motors (77) Ltd.* (1985), 40 Sask. R. 228 (Q.B.).

hired to perform. It will also depend on any representations that the employer and employee respectively make about the job's requirements and the employee's ability to satisfy them. In any event, an implied term of all employment contracts is that the employee being hired has the ability to perform the job competently.[16] However, if the employee is performing in a satisfactory manner, incompetence will not be established even where the employer is able to show that someone else could do a better job.[17]

Unless gross incompetence is being alleged, the employer must warn an employee about the consequences of continued poor performance. This will be the case where an employee is performing below the objective standard of competence demanded by the employer's organization. The employee must be told that his performance is not "up to speed" and that failure to improve could result in loss of employment. Adequate warning by the employer consists of the following elements, all of which must take place before the termination:

(a) telling the employee that his or her performance is below standard and identifying precisely what problems exist in relation to how the duties of the job are being discharged;

(b) providing the employee with a clear description of the job's requirements and the level(s) of competence demanded;

(c) informing the employee that failure to improve in the areas identified could lead to the termination of employment; and

(d) assisting in the employee's attempts to meet the required level(s) of competence and giving the employee a reasonable opportunity to demonstrate improvement in job performance.

To provide proper assistance, the employer should meet with the employee periodically and discuss how things are going. The employer might also consider establishing a review period and perhaps setting a reasonable target date for improvement. Both should be based on the employee's length of service, position and responsibilities. In general, longer review periods and target dates further into the future are warranted for long-serving employees in more senior positions. Any deadlines that are set for improving performance must be respected. In this regard, a poorly performing employee cannot be dismissed during a period of review before the deadline for improvement expires.[18]

---

[16] *Halsbury's Laws of England*, 4th ed., vol. 16, p. 437, para. 644, as cited in *Matheson v. Matheson International Trucks Ltd.* (1984), 4 C.C.E.L. 271 (Ont. H.C.J.), at p. 275.

[17] *Russell v. Molson Breweries (Ontario) Ltd.* (1995), 9 C.C.E.L. (2d) 277 (Ont. Ct. (Gen. Div.)).

[18] *Renwick v. MacMillan Bloedel Ltd.* (1995), 9 C.C.E.L. (2d) 255 (B.C.S.C.).

Poor performance is also rarely a basis for summary dismissal.[19] An isolated incident of substandard performance will generally not constitute cause for dismissal unless the incident demonstrates severe or gross incompetence on the part of the employee or has very serious consequences. In some cases, courts seem to be suggesting that even several incidents of poor performance will not justify termination unless they amount to gross incompetence. More recent case law, however, suggests that several occurrences of deficient performance can cumulatively amount to just cause for termination where a company can show that an objective standard of competence was not being met and the employee was given adequate warning in respect of poor performance.[20]

In practice, termination for cause on the ground of incompetence may be difficult to prove. Part of the difficulty lies in defining the objective standard of competence required for a specific position and work environment. Where a contract of employment does not specifically define competence, employers will often define it in terms of performance results. What an employer should do is provide employees with a clear understanding of the actual performance levels that must be met. Failure to do this will likely lead to a court concluding that termination based on incompetence was not legally justified.[21] On the other hand, an allegation of incompetence can sometimes be used to settle a wrongful dismissal lawsuit where the employer has taken great pains to document every incident of poor performance. Although extensive documentation in this regard might alone be insufficient to convince a judge that dismissal was justified, its existence could persuade opposing counsel that it would be better to reach a settlement than to proceed to court where there is no certainty of success.

An objective standard of competence can often be validated through the use of testing materials in the workplace. In one case, the court said the employer had a right to demand particular standards of competence that could be measured by having employees write a competency test.[22] An employee who was dismissed without notice failed the test on two occasions. Her position required her to perform efficiently and accurately and the court concluded that failure to obtain a passing score on the test was evidence of the employee's incompetence and inability to perform the required duties of her job. Further evidence of her incompetence was demonstrated by complaints made by those for whom she worked. Moreover, it was found that she had received adequate warning in respect of the consequences of her substandard

---

[19] *Milsom v. Corporate Computers Inc.* (2003), 27 C.C.E.L. (3d) 26 (Alta. Q.B.).

[20] *Matheson v. Matheson International Trucks Ltd.*, *supra*, footnote 16; *Chiang v. Intrawest Corp.*, [2002] B.C.J. No. 1492 (QL) (S.C.).

[21] *Horvath v. SAAN Stores Ltd.*, [2003] B.C.J. No. 2786 (QL) (S.C.).

[22] *Sloane v. Toronto Stock Exchange* (1988), 24 C.C.E.L. 52 (Ont. H.C.J.), revd on other grounds 5 O.R. (3d) 412 (C.A.).

performance. The employee had been told that unless her performance improved, her job would be in jeopardy. She was also given an opportunity to correct her deficiencies and the employer provided guidance and additional training in order to assist her. Despite the warning, the employee's performance did not improve. On the facts of this particular case, the court concluded that incompetence amounting to just cause for termination existed.

A termination is warranted where performance does not improve after an employee is made aware of the standards that must be met and receives adequate warning in respect of the failure to meet them. Should improvement occur, however, the employer cannot fire the employee at a later date on the basis of earlier instances of low performance unless the employee is specifically told that improvement must be maintained and that further problems of poor performance (*i.e.*, "backsliding") could possibly result in termination.[23] In such circumstances, the employer may want to consider using a monitoring system to review an employee's performance after initial improvement.

Employers should note that in certain circumstances an employee's failure to meet performance standards may not constitute just cause for termination. For instance, if the employee shows that his or her lacklustre performance was caused by the employer's failure to provide proper training, termination for incompetence will not be justified.[24] Similarly, just cause will likely not be established where an employer does not give an employee adequate instructions, support, supervision or materials, or where the employer fails otherwise to maintain suitable working conditions. Just cause will also not exist where failure to meet stated performance standards is the result of an employer's unreasonable demands. If the demands of a job are not reasonable, it will be difficult for the employer to prove that an employee failed to meet an objective standard of competence. For example, where quotas are not based on fixed criteria or are unrealistic and arbitrary, an employee cannot be penalized for failing to meet them.[25] Nor can just cause be made out where the employer hires someone known to be inexperienced and incapable of carrying out the work required for a particular position. That is, a company cannot use the ground of incompetence to justify a termination if it knew that the individual lacked the skills necessary for the job in question.[26] The employer might also be seen as condoning deficiencies in an employee's performance by failing to carry out performance appraisals on a regular basis.[27]

In contrast to the examples noted above, just cause will likely be made out where an employee lied about possessing the skills and qualifications

---

[23] *Matheson v. Matheson International Trucks Ltd.*, *supra*, footnote 16.
[24] *Smith v. Deblin's Warehouse Ltd.*, [2002] O.T.C. 231 (S.C.J.).
[25] *Stevens v. Electrolux Canada* (1985), 6 C.C.E.L. 254 (N.B.Q.B).
[26] *McIlveen v. British Columbia* (1988), 24 C.C.E.L. 197 (B.C.S.C.).
[27] *Tremblett v. Aardvark Pest Control Ltd.* (1987), 16 C.C.E.L. 306 (Ont. Dist. Ct.).

needed to meet the job's obligations.[28] In many cases, termination for incompetence can also be established if there is evidence that the employer suffered financial difficulties as a result of the employee's poor performance and failure to improve after being warned accordingly.[29]

With respect to termination on the basis of incompetence, it should be noted that, in general, it may not be advantageous for the employer to build a case for incompetence where the employee has only been with the company for a short period of time. In most circumstances, proving the existence of incompetence that amounts to just cause is both expensive and time consuming for senior management. Proper warning in respect of poor performance must be given to the employee,[30] a review period and review plan typically have to be established, the employer must meet regularly with the employee to assess progress during the review period and, most importantly, there must be clear documentation highlighting the employee's continued deficiencies with respect to performance during the review period. Unless the employee is "worth saving" (the employer believes the employee has the potential to meet the job's requirements), termination with pay in lieu of notice is probably a better route to follow. However, where a company decides to attempt to correct the performance problems, the employer must show a genuine interest in assisting the employee. Where a performance review plan is established, there must be *bona fide* or good faith intentions on the part of the employer. There must be a real commitment to help the employee. Establishing a plan so a case for cause will be easier to prove at a later date or terminating an employee prior to expiry of the review plan will be viewed with disapproval by the courts. In such circumstances, a court will likely side with an employee allegedly fired for incompetence if the court feels the employer was not really interested in improving the employee's performance or that the employee was not given a fair chance to perform for the full review period. Such an inference will reasonably stem from the employer's failure to provide guidance as to how performance could be improved.[31]

(b) Carelessness

Carelessness is another example of behaviour that can amount to just cause for termination. Like incompetence, it is a performance problem that relates to the work carried out by an employee. In this context, carelessness refers to an employee not exercising proper care or paying enough attention in the performance of his or her job duties. Employee conduct that is careless

---

[28] *Bridgewater v. Leon's Manufacturing Co.* (1984), 6 C.C.E.L. 55 (Sask. Q.B.). See also discussion under Heading 2, "Misrepresentation Prior to Hiring", in this Part.

[29] *Bridgewater, supra.*

[30] *Milsom v. Corporate Computers Inc.* (2003), 27 C.C.E.L. (3d) 26 (Alta. Q.B.).

[31] *Matheson v. Matheson International Trucks Ltd.* (1984), 4 C.C.E.L. 271 (Ont. H.C.J.).

consists of actions or omissions that are preventable by common foresight and that cause the employer some form of prejudice. The distinction between carelessness and incompetence is that in the case of carelessness we are not talking about an employee's inability to meet or perform at an objective standard of competence. Rather, we are dealing with cases where an employee chooses to carry out his or her duties recklessly or without following traditional behavioural norms and practices. A termination could therefore be warranted where an individual is sufficiently careless despite having the ability to perform competently.

The employer's business might suffer as a direct result of an employee's carelessness. In cases where the particular act of carelessness also involves an injury or a serious risk of injury to the employee, a co-worker or the public, it is likely that cause will be found to exist. For instance, a seven-year-old mentally challenged child was left on a school bus for the day when the substitute bus driver did not notice that the child had fallen asleep in the seat behind him. The court concluded that the driver had failed to conduct even a cursory check of the bus and did not appreciate the seriousness of the incident. These factors, the court felt, were sufficient to undermine the school board's confidence in the driver's ability to protect the safety of children and the board was therefore justified in dismissing the driver with cause.[32]

Generally speaking, however, unless an act of carelessness causes very serious consequences or damages, a court will usually require the employer to provide warnings about the consequences of continued carelessness or to use increasingly severe disciplinary penalties before ultimately dismissing an employee. In other words, an isolated incident of carelessness will rarely justify termination without notice. In one case, a mechanic accidentally poured antifreeze into the hydraulic system instead of the radiator of a customer's vehicle.[33] The court found no evidence of incompetency and concluded that the mechanic's conduct in making one isolated mistake was not enough to justify dismissal without notice.

Normally, a case for cause will succeed where several instances of negligent or careless conduct occur. However, the timing of the carelessness may be a factor that courts will take into account when determining if just cause has been established. In one case, for instance, while an employee had made several careless errors, her dismissal was held to be unwarranted because of when the errors occurred.[34] Since they arose during a very busy and hectic period, the court concluded that the employee's carelessness did not amount to conduct that constituted just cause for termination.

---

[32] *Patenaude v. Rosetown School Division No. 43* (2002), 220 Sask. R. 255 (Q.B.).

[33] *Lavallee v. Prairie Equipment Ltd.* (1988), 20 C.C.E.L. 182 (Man. Q.B.).

[34] *Goby v. Gordon Ironsides and Fares Co.* (1910), 15 W.L.R. 258 (Sask. Pol. Ct.).

A case for cause is also likely to fail if an employee's careless conduct relates to an area in which the employer has traditionally been unconcerned or reckless. This will especially be true where the conduct is an isolated incident of carelessness and the employee was not warned that it would result in dismissal. In one case, an employee was fired for not taking due care of the employer's company gasoline credit card while it was in his possession.[35] Although the card was ultimately used for unauthorized purchases, the employer did not accuse the employee of theft. The court concluded that the termination was not justified on the basis of the employee's carelessness because he had never been warned in this regard. He had never been told that his failure to take proper care of the credit card would result in the loss of employment. Further, the court did not find any evidence of other careless conduct or poor performance on the part of the employee prior to his dismissal. For these reasons, the court took the view that suspension would have been a more appropriate disciplinary action for the employer to take. An additional reason for concluding that cause was not established by the employee's carelessness was based on the way in which the company dealt with its credit cards generally. In particular, the evidence showed that the employer's supervision over the cards was fairly slack, that the cards were often used without authorization and that the employer could and should have enforced stricter controls over the cards. From this case the following lesson can be learned: a company wishing to build a case for cause based on carelessness should ensure that its policies are not lax or remiss in the areas touched by the careless conduct. If a court sees that an employer is reckless with regard to these matters, carelessness by the employee is less likely to be characterized as misconduct justifying dismissal.

(c) Neglect of Duty

Neglecting the duties of one's job is another reason why an employer might choose to dismiss an employee. Terminations for this reason are similar to those based on incompetence or careless conduct because they relate to problems with an employee's performance. Neglect of duty refers specifically to situations where an employee does not perform some or all of his or her duties or, alternatively, engages in a pattern of performing them reluctantly or ineffectively. In circumstances of neglect, the employee's substandard performance is not caused by lack of ability as is the case with incompetence but, like other performance problems, the neglect of duties can amount to just cause for termination because the conduct may be incompatible with the employee's obligations and prejudicial to the employer's business. Alternatively, if an employee's neglect of duty is sufficiently serious,

---

[35] *Codner v. Joint Construction Ltd.* (1989), 27 C.C.E.L. 144 (Nfld. S.C.).

just cause for summary dismissal will be found. In one case, a Superintendent of Public Works and Utilities failed to submit the required number of drinking water samples to the provincial lab over an 18-month period and submitted false reports to the town council. His explanations that he was too busy to submit the water samples to the provincial lab and that he had inadvertently filed misleading reports were deemed unsatisfactory by the town council. The court agreed, stating that it was reasonable for the council to lose confidence in the superintendent based on his behaviour, and therefore cause for dismissal was found.[36] However, a dismissal on this basis is only justified if the employee acted wilfully and was warned that continued neglect would lead to the termination of employment. In one case, for example, a hospital's administrator was fired for his neglect in ensuring that proper accounting and control procedures were maintained by the accounting department.[37] Although the court agreed that the administrator had neglected this aspect of his job, it concluded that just cause for termination did not exist. Cause was not made out because the employee had not specifically been warned that his job was in jeopardy due to his neglect nor had the employee been given a reasonable opportunity to perform more effectively. In another case, the reason given for a district manager's dismissal was that he looked for ways to avoid performing his duties.[38] After considering the evidence, the court concluded that just cause for the manager's termination had not been established. Even if the employer had legitimate grounds for complaint, dismissal without notice was not warranted since the employee was never warned that his job was in jeopardy and would be lost if he failed to "shape up".

A case for cause based on neglect will similarly fail where the employee's neglect of duties is not wilful. For example, termination is not justified if the employee performs ineffectively or not at all because of a stress-related illness brought on by the job,[39] an emotional upset in the employee's personal life,[40] or where it is the employer's actions that contribute to an employee's neglect of his or her duty.[41]

An employer wanting to fire an employee for neglect of duty must be certain that the employee acted wilfully and was warned about the consequences of his or her behaviour. In one case, an employee who worked as a "monitor" for a company that provided night patrols had the tendency of continually questioning his supervisors. He was given a letter of warning stating that this behaviour would no longer be tolerated. Over a year later, during an

---

[36] *Lane v. Unity (Town)* (2002), 228 Sask. R. 306 (Q.B.).

[37] *Manning v. Surrey Memorial Hospital Society* (1975), 54 D.L.R. (3d) 312 (B.C.S.C.).

[38] *Kozak v. Aliments Krispy Kernels Inc.* (1988), 22 C.C.E.L. 1 (Ont. Dist. Ct.).

[39] *Casey v. General Inc.* (1988), 24 C.C.E.L. 142 (Nfld. S.C.).

[40] *Robinson v. Canadian Acceptance Corp. Ltd.* (1973), 43 D.L.R. (3d) 301 (N.S.S.C.), affd 47 D.L.R. (3d) 417 (C.A.).

[41] *Belzberg v. Pollock* (2003), 23 C.C.E.L. (3d) 22 (B.C.C.A.).

incident that took place while he was on duty, the employee failed to notify headquarters when he was aware that he should have done so. The court held that based on the written warning that the employer had provided the employee and the subsequent incident that led to his dismissal, just cause could be found.[42]

The employer must also ensure that performance requirements imposed on the employee are reasonable. The requirements cannot be illegal, dishonest or likely to threaten the health and safety of the employee or other individuals. Generally speaking, the employer will not be able to build a case for cause on the basis of neglect unless all these conditions have been met and can be proven.

Furthermore, several instances of neglect are typically required to establish just cause for termination, although an isolated incident may amount to cause in some circumstances if it is sufficiently serious. In a case that illustrates this point, a certain neglectful incident was found to be severe enough to justify an insurance company's decision to fire a sales representative.[43] The company was able to show that the employee had neglected to secure pertinent information from a customer when completing an application for insurance on her behalf. His failure in this respect was wilful because, rather than asking the questions he had been told to ask, he chose to ask only those he personally thought were relevant. As a result of the employee's conduct, certain information was not disclosed to the company and the customer was given a policy of automobile insurance. In particular, the company was unaware of the fact that the customer's husband had a poor driving record and a suspended licence. The husband was subsequently in an accident while driving the vehicle insured under the policy and the company was required to pay out a substantial amount of money for claims made against it. Had it not been for the employee's neglect, the company would have known about the husband's driving record, the insurance policy would not have been issued and the company would not have suffered losses from the accident. For these reasons, the court said this was a case where one incident of neglect was serious enough to constitute just cause for termination.

As demonstrated in the case just discussed, courts will often consider the prejudice suffered by an employer's business when deciding whether just cause on the basis of neglect has been established. A case for cause is more apt to succeed where an organization loses business and the confidence of its customers as a result of an employee's neglect and incompetence.[44] By way of contrast, a factor that can mitigate against a finding of just cause is the

---

[42] *Nickson v. Industrial Security Ltd.*, [2001] N.B.R. (2d) (Supp.) No. 86 (QL) (Q.B.).
[43] *Ferguson v. Allstate Insurance Co. of Canada* (1991), 35 C.C.E.L. 257 (Ont. Ct. (Gen. Div.)).
[44] *Kellas v. CIP Inc.* (1990), 32 C.C.E.L. 196 (B.C.S.C.).

length of an employee's service as compared to the amount of time the employee was derelict in his or her duties. In one case, for instance, the court noted that a five-month period of neglectful and substandard performance prior to the employee's dismissal was relatively short in comparison to his ten years of employment with the employer.[45]

Overview

Performance problems can support a case for just cause termination in the appropriate circumstances. Practically speaking, proving the case may be onerous on account of the difficulties that lie in defining an objective standard of job performance. In addition, the employer may be required to warn an employee about the consequences of his or her conduct before the employee can be dismissed without notice. However, performance problems associated with incompetence, carelessness or an employee's neglect of duties may be relied upon to justify summary termination and the case for just cause will be strengthened where the following factors or circumstances exist:

1. The employee's performance was below an objective standard of competence.
2. The employee was warned about the problems with his or her performance (unless the employer is alleging that there has been gross incompetence or a serious incident of carelessness or neglect).
3. The employee was given a real chance to improve.
4. The warning provided by the employer was adequate in that the performance problems were identified, the performance required was specifically described, the consequences of not improving were explained and the employer assisted the employee's attempts to improve.
5. The employer provided a clear definition of what is required from the employee in terms of performance and output.
6. A review period and plan for improvement were imposed in good faith but the employee's performance did not improve.
7. A deadline that was set for improvement passed without amelioration in the employee's performance.
8. There were several incidents of incompetence, carelessness or neglect.
9. The employee failed to meet tests of competence used by the employer to measure skills and abilities.
10. The employer provided the employee with suitable working conditions, clear instructions, proper training and adequate supervision and guidance.
11. The employer's performance demands were reasonable.

---

[45] *Robinson v. Canadian Acceptance Corp. Ltd.*, *supra*, footnote 40.

12. There was a misrepresentation of the employee's skills and abilities prior to hiring.
13. The employer carried out routine performance appraisals and had not condoned the employee's deficiencies.
14. The employer suffered harm or prejudice as a result of the employee's incompetence, carelessness or neglect.
15. The employee's incompetence, carelessness or neglect may or did cause injury to the employee, to co-workers and/or to the general public.
16. The employer warned that an improvement in performance must be maintained and that failure to do so would result in the termination of employment.
17. The employer documented all instances of the employee's poor performance, in addition to the employee's performance during review periods.
18. The performance problems did not relate to an area in which the employer's policies and attitudes have traditionally been indifferent, lax or reckless.
19. The employee did not serve the employer for a substantial period of time.
20. The employee's poor performance was not caused by an illness or disability.

4 ✧ DISHONESTY

It is an implied term of employment contracts that an employer may summarily dismiss an employee for just cause. In assessing whether the alleged misconduct is sufficiently serious to warrant dismissal with cause, the nature of the misconduct must be considered, having regard for the circumstances of the case. The circumstances in which an employer is justified in summarily dismissing an employee due to the latter's dishonesty is to be determined based on a "contextual" approach, which requires an examination of the particular facts of each case, and consideration of the nature and seriousness of the employee's dishonesty to assess whether it is compatible with maintaining the employment relationship.

In the seminal case of *McKinley v. B.C. Tel*,[46] the issue of employee misconduct arose when Martin McKinley took a leave of absence from work due to health problems following 16 years of service. Upon his return, Mr. McKinley expressed an interest in working in a less stressful position; however, he was not offered an alternative position. Eventually, B.C. Tel terminated Mr. McKinley, who rejected the accompanying offer of severance and commenced a wrongful dismissal action.

At first, B.C. Tel resisted Mr. McKinley's action by claiming that it had offered him a reasonable compensation package and had used its best efforts

---

[46] (2001), 200 D.L.R. (4th) 385 (S.C.C.).

to locate an alternative position for him. Then, three days into the trial, B.C. Tel discovered a letter from Mr. McKinley's physician and changed its defence to allege that Mr. McKinley had lied about his medical condition as well as the treatments that were available to him. The letter referred to an earlier recommendation made by the physician that Mr. McKinley take a certain medication upon returning to work. Accordingly, B.C. Tel argued that Mr. McKinley deliberately withheld the fact that his physician had indicated he could safely return to work provided he took his medication.

The main issue in the case was whether Mr. McKinley's dishonesty was serious enough to undermine the employment relationship. Following a review of the case law, the Supreme Court of Canada rejected the line of decisions that held that any form of employee dishonesty constituted grounds for just cause dismissal. Rather, the Supreme Court confirmed that only some forms of dishonesty constitute cause for dismissal. Accordingly, to determine whether cause exists, the specific form and context of the employee's dishonesty must be considered to see whether it has given rise to a breakdown in the employment relationship.[47] In the result, Mr. McKinley received general damages for wrongful dismissal, as the court found that his dishonesty was not sufficiently serious to lead to a breakdown in the employment relationship.

In a case that followed the principle set out in *McKinley,* an employee was dismissed for cause when, angered by comments he received regarding his attitude and work, he sent out a memo critical of management and threatened to erase important computer files.[48] The memo was delivered on a Friday. Executives of Gulf Canada Resources discussed the memo on Monday and were concerned that the employee, Christopher Mothersele, would sabotage his computer and delete his files. He was terminated Tuesday afternoon. The court held that Mothersele's threat must be evaluated in the context of his employment record. Mr. Mothersele was a valued employee with a clean employment record who had not made prior threats and who had not previously harmed computers or software, although he had been critical of his employer's failure to store data properly.

The court held that an employer faced with this type of memo, who fears that valuable files could be at risk, should have taken immediate steps to back up and protect the vulnerable data. However, knowing that there was a possibility that Mr. Mothersele did not mean to carry out his threat, knowing his technical skills, the pride that he took in his work product and his personality, it was unreasonable for the employer to immediately dismiss him for cause. Rather, the employer should have communicated the perceived seri-

---

[47] For more details on the contextual approach see the discussion under Heading 7, "Just Cause — The Contextual Approach", of Part I, "General Concepts".

[48] *Mothersele v. Gulf Canada Resources Ltd.* (2003), 24 C.C.E.L. (3d) 139 (Alta. Q.B.).

ousness of the threat to Mr. Mothersele and assessed his state of mind. Had the employer done so, they would have realized that he was not seriously contemplating carrying out his threat. In the circumstances, the court held that a more appropriate sanction would have been to issue a stern warning with possible financial penalties.

Another case where the employee's dishonesty did not warrant dismissal for cause, concerned a middle level manager who was employed with the Hudson's Bay Company for seven years.[49] While making purchases for himself at Zeller's (a subsidiary of Hudson's Bay Company), Mr. Kidd put two items, a soap dish and vitamins, valued at $29, in his pocket and failed to pay for them. He was stopped by security, but did not identify himself as a Hudson's Bay employee as he was aware of his employer's Code of Conduct and was concerned about the repercussions of being accused of theft. On his return to the office, Mr. Kidd admitted his error and was apologetic. Mr. Kidd said he had no intention of stealing and that he had been distracted and upset upon receiving a message that a friend had died in the September 11 terrorist attacks. Nevertheless, his employment was terminated. The court held that while Mr. Kidd's failure to disclose that he was a Hudson's Bay employee was less than forthright, and in a sense dishonest, he had no intention of stealing and dismissal was a disproportionate response. Accordingly, the court held that Mr. Kidd's conduct "did not violate an essential condition of the employment relationship nor breach the faith inherent in the work relationship".[50]

Following the decision in *McKinley*, courts now consider whether the employee's dishonesty is serious enough to lead to a break down in the employment relationship before finding that a dismissal for cause is justified. One case where dishonesty warranted just cause dismissal involved an employee who was terminated for falsely inflating expense reports.[51] Mr. Cosman was employed as a group sales representative for a period of approximately 22 months. After beginning work with Viacom Entertainment Canada Inc., Mr. Cosman joined a club in order to foster sales leads. The club membership cost him $300. Mr. Cosman claimed that when he approached the Group Sales Manger to approve the expense he was told that it would not be allowed. However, according to Mr. Cosman, the Group Sales Manager suggested that he inflate his automobile mileage claims to recapture the amount of the membership. At trial, the Group Sales Manager denied any such conversation. The trial judge held that Mr. Cosman's conduct amounted to dishonesty and that his misconduct was sufficiently serious to undermine the employment relationship. The trial judge noted that Mr. Cosman's con-

---

[49] *Kidd v. Hudson's Bay Co.* (2003), 25 C.C.E.L. (3d) 102 (Ont. S.C.J.).
[50] *Supra*, at para. 26.
[51] *Cosman v. Viacom Entertainment Canada Inc.*, [2002] O.T.C. 313 (S.C.J.).

duct amounted to criminal activity that destroyed the level of trust that Viacom fairly demanded of him, stating that "his criminality poisoned the continuation of the relationship".[52]

In all employment relationships, there is an implied duty on the part of the employee to be faithful and honest. If this duty is breached by engaging in dishonest conduct, there will be just cause to dismiss the employee summarily. Dismissal is justified because failure to be honest causes an employer to lose trust and confidence in an employee and the foundation of the employment relationship is undermined. Accordingly, where a company can demonstrate dishonesty on the part of one of its employees, a court will apply the contextual approach to determine whether the employee's misconduct amounted to a breakdown in the employment relationship warranting just cause dismissal.

The contextual approach requires courts to assess all the factors surrounding the employee's dismissal including the nature and degree of the misconduct, the employment relationship and the workplace environment. Only after these factors have been assessed can the court then determine whether the misconduct violated the essential conditions of the employment contract or breached the trust inherent in the employment relationship. Yet, the contextual approach is not applied as stringently where an employee has engaged in a serious form of misconduct such as fraud, misappropriation or theft. In such cases, a single instance of serious misconduct is usually sufficient to justify dismissal for cause. However, where an employee commits a serious form of misconduct, the employer must still demonstrate that the employee intended to and did engage in the deceitful conduct to dismiss the employee for cause.[53]

With respect to the allegation of dishonesty, the employer must prove that the conduct was in fact dishonest before a contextual approach is applied. In this respect, courts consider several factors when determining whether an employee's conduct amounts to dishonesty. Although certain acts seem dishonest, an employee's transgressions cannot be viewed in isolation. Rather, they must be considered in the context within which they occur and the employee's subsequent behaviour must also be taken into account. In one case, for instance, a unit manager who worked for the Insurance Corporation of British Columbia was fired for lying to one of his superiors.[54] The manager initially denied that he had used the corporation's computer system to access another employee's poor driving record. He also denied that he wrote a letter to the president that described this employee's record and the reckless manner in which she drove a car leased by the corporation. However, the manager

---

[52] *Supra*, at para. 14.
[53] *McKinley v. B.C. Tel, supra*, footnote 46.
[54] *Petit v. Insurance Corp. of British Columbia* (1995), 13 C.C.E.L. (2d) 62 (B.C.S.C.).

immediately sought to retract his lies and to tell his superior the truth. Before deciding whether just cause for termination existed, the court said the manager's conduct had to be examined in its entirety. With respect to his use of the corporation's system, the manager did not think his conduct was unethical as he only wanted to advise the corporation of another employee's reckless driving habits. Although the manager lied to his superior about his actions, these lies were not maintained. The court ultimately concluded that the manager's conduct in its entirety was better characterized as a mistake in judgment rather than dishonesty. Because he attempted to correct this mistake immediately, the manager's employment contract was not fundamentally breached by his actions and termination was not justified.

Some employees are required to meet a higher standard of honesty than others. This means that actions by one employee may amount to just cause for termination while the same actions by another employee do not. One factor that can be used to help distinguish between seemingly similar misconduct is the nature of the position occupied by the employee. In one case, for example, an employee was dismissed when his employer learned that he had been convicted of filing false insurance claims.[55] The employer was an Ontario university that had hired the employee as a part-time lecturer to teach a course on the ethics of business. The court concluded that the lecturer's conduct in filing false claims was immoral, dishonest and deceitful and just cause for termination had been established. This conclusion rested partly on the fact that the school's reputation would likely be damaged by having on staff a faculty member convicted of fraud. Also, it was found to be inherently unacceptable for a person who practised fraudulent activity within the business community to instruct students in business ethics. In a similar case, an auditor at a hospital was terminated for cause for attempting to avoid paying GST on the purchase of a new vehicle.[56] The court held that if this had become public knowledge, the effectiveness of the hospital's audit department could be called into question. Clearly, the findings that cause existed in these cases were in large part due to the position held by the employee.

In other cases, courts have said that dishonest conduct is more likely to constitute cause for termination where the employee in question holds a position of trust. Such positions include loans or credit officers, fraud investigators, supervisors, senior officers and similar "key" positions. For example, courts have generally recognized that a higher level of trust and honesty is required from the employees of banks and financial institutions as compared to other employees.[57]

---

[55] *Pliniussen v. University of Western Ontario* (1983), 2 C.C.E.L. 1 (Ont. Co. Ct.).

[56] *Hyland v. Royal Alexandra Hospital* (2000), 5 C.C.E.L. (3d) 63 (Alta. Q.B.), affd 26 C.C.E.L. (3d) 186 (C.A.).

[57] See *Ennis v. Canadian Imperial Bank of Commerce* (1986), 13 C.C.E.L. 25 (B.C.S.C.); *Ivanore and Canadian Imperial Bank of Commerce (Re)* (1983), 3 C.C.E.L. 26 (Can. L.R.B.).

Just cause is easier to establish where an organization has been prejudiced or has suffered a loss as a result of the employee's dishonest conduct. In one case, termination was ruled justified where a company lost a substantial amount of money because its training manager authorized employees to claim overtime hours that had not in fact been worked.[58] Whether or not an employee personally benefits from his dishonest behaviour generally does not seem to be relevant to the issue of just cause. Where, for example, an employee falsifies information on a customer's loan application, the conduct will amount to just cause despite the fact that the employee derived no personal financial benefit.[59]

Dishonest behaviour warranting dismissal does not necessarily have to occur within the confines of an employee's position. In some circumstances, dishonesty by an employee in personal affairs may be used to establish just cause for termination.[60] In one case, a branch manager obtained a loan from his employer on the condition that he use the proceeds to purchase a car and pay off his credit card accounts.[61] He failed to do the latter and lied to his supervisor when asked. The manager was fired because of the employer's loss of confidence and trust based on the manager's continued assertion that his credit card balances had been paid off.

In general, an employer who wishes to terminate an employee for what is perceived to be dishonest conduct must establish misconduct on the balance of probabilities and show that the nature and degree of dishonesty warrants summary dismissal. This requires a multi-factor analysis. If the behaviour is obviously deceitful on its face and a reasonable person would conclude that it was inherently dishonest the conduct would likely support a claim of just cause for termination without notice.[62] However, "if an employer alleges dishonesty, and this is not borne out by the evidence, the employer by not meeting the standard to provide just cause then takes the chance of an increased notice period being assessed against the employer".[63]

At the present time, courts seem to be more demanding of employees with respect to honesty in that they recognize the need for trust in the employer-employee relationship. Where the employee has engaged in a serious form of dishonesty such as fraud, misappropriation or theft, the single act is usually sufficient to justify summary dismissal, especially if the employee holds a position of trust. The employer must demonstrate that the employee intended to and did engage in the misconduct in order to justify dismissal for

---

[58] *Myles v. Saint John Shipbuilding Ltd.* (1996), 17 C.C.E.L. (2d) 45 (N.B.Q.B.).

[59] *Ivanore and Canadian Imperial Bank of Commerce (Re), supra,* footnote 57.

[60] See also discussion under Heading 25, "Off-work Criminal or Improper Conduct", of this Part.

[61] *Marshall v. Pacific Coast Savings Credit Union* (1995), 10 C.C.E.L. (2d) 38 (B.C.S.C.).

[62] See *Kreager v. Davidson* (1992), 44 C.C.E.L. 261 (B.C.C.A.).

[63] *Lambe v. Irving Oil Ltd.* (2002), 219 Nfld. & P.E.I.R. 183 (Nfld. S.C.), at para. 133.

cause. At the same time, the courts will continue to apply the contextual approach to determine whether dismissal is appropriate in the circumstances of less serious instances of misconduct. Accordingly, the purpose of applying the contextual approach is to ensure that summary dismissal is a sanction that is proportionate to the employee's misconduct.

In terms of proving dishonesty, an employer is generally required to provide clear and convincing evidence of the misconduct and may be expected to meet a higher standard of proof than normally required. Illustrating exactly how an employee's conduct affected the employer's trust or caused the employer to suffer some detriment, financial or otherwise, is very important.

Overview

While an employee can be terminated without cause upon providing the proper notice or severance, where an employer wants to rely on cause for dismissal, it must keep in mind that the employment relationship will not lightly be severed by the courts. In cases where dishonesty is alleged, the context will be closely scrutinized. A court must consider the employee's behaviour in the context of all other factors surrounding the employee's dismissal, including the nature and degree of the misconduct, the employment relationship and the workplace environment. Only after all factors have been assessed can the court determine whether the employee's misconduct violated the essential terms of the employment contract or breached the trust inherent in the employment relationship. Employers must keep this in mind when alleging dishonesty as cause for termination and should also note that the case for cause will be stronger where the following factors or circumstances exist:

1. The employer or a superior was lied to and the employee made no subsequent attempts to tell the truth.
2. The employee did not disclose a transgression and lied when his or her conduct in this regard was being investigated.
3. The employee was in a senior position or one that required a high degree of trust and integrity.
4. The nature of the alleged dishonesty is inconsistent with the character of the job duties.
5. The employee's conduct resulted in harm or prejudice to the employer's operations.
6. The employer lost trust and confidence in the employee as a result of the misconduct.
7. The alleged transgressions are inherently dishonest or deceitful.
8. There is clear and convincing evidence that the employee engaged in dishonest conduct.

5 ✧ FRAUD

In this discussion, fraud refers to an employee's deceitful conduct. Fraudulent behaviour is generally worse than simple dishonesty and as such can amount to just cause for termination without notice. Employers must demonstrate that their businesses were prejudiced by the employee's conduct or that the fraudulent behaviour revealed a character inconsistent with the employee's continued employment.[64]

If the actions of an employee cause no detriment to the employer's business, a case for cause will likely be unsupportable unless the employee acted in a secretive manner. This is especially true where an employer receives some benefit from the conduct being scrutinized. In one case, the director of a Red Cross Society blood transfusion centre was dismissed for alleged misappropriation and mismanagement of funds.[65] The director had opened a personal bank account wherein she deposited donations and earnings from the various research projects in which she participated. Although the money was used exclusively for research purposes, maintaining a separate account in this manner was a breach of society policies and directives. However, the court concluded that the director's conduct did not amount to just cause for termination because there was no evidence that she intended to misappropriate, defraud or deprive her employer of property for her personal and financial benefit. Rather, she had kept a strict accounting of all money received and disbursed and her activities were carried on in a public manner. Furthermore, rather than harming the society's interests, the director's conduct benefited the society.

Depending on the nature of an individual's occupation, an act of fraud that does not occur in the course of employment can still amount to just cause for dismissal in certain circumstances. Where the fraudulent conduct conflicts with the employee's position and responsibilities, a dismissal for just cause can be more easily established.[66] In one case, for instance, a superintendent of schools defrauded the government when he sought to obtain provincial assistance for his son that the son was not legally entitled to receive.[67] The court found the fraudulent conduct constituted just cause for the superintendent's termination because it was in direct conflict with his position and employment duties. In particular, the superintendent held a position of trust that commanded integrity and trust from his teaching staff, his students, the school

---

[64] See also discussion under Heading 23, "Character Revelation", of this Part.

[65] *Rock v. Canadian Red Cross Society* (1994), 5 C.C.E.L. (2d) 231, supplementary reasons 7 C.C.E.L. (2d) 146 (Ont. Ct. (Gen. Div.)).

[66] See discussion under Heading 25, "Off-work Criminal or Improper Conduct", in this Part.

[67] *Cherniwchan v. Two Hills No. 21 (County)* (1982), 38 A.R. 125 (Q.B.).

board and the community. Further, one of the superintendent's duties was to seek school funding and grants from the government he had defrauded.

In contrast, seemingly fraudulent conduct is less apt to constitute just cause for dismissal where an employee does not occupy a high position of trust and integrity and where the employee does not intend to defraud the employer. For example, a salesperson was dismissed when the company he worked for discovered that he had falsified expense receipts for the purpose of deceiving Revenue Canada.[68] However, the employee was not defrauding the company since he had in fact paid for all the items being declared as expenses. The employee falsified the receipts because he did not have written documentation to support all the reimbursements he was entitled to receive from the employer. Without the proper documentation, the reimbursements received by the employee had to be included in his taxable income. Since the employer had not been defrauded by the employee's actions, the court concluded that a case for cause could not be maintained. Notwithstanding its decision, the court noted that the nature of an employee's position should be considered when determining whether just cause exists and that termination would likely have been warranted had the employee been the treasurer of the company rather than a salesperson.

An employer has usually been prejudiced where an employee's deceit is found to constitute cause for dismissal, but this is not always the case. Courts often find that, although the employer was not prejudiced by the employee's behaviour, the behaviour revealed a character inconsistent with his or her continued employment and therefore constituted just cause for termination.[69] In one case, an employee's deceitful conduct was found to warrant dismissal not just on the basis of its fraudulent nature but also because the employee was capable of such deceit.[70] The employee had fraudulently misdated a document for his own personal benefit and was prepared to lie about it under oath.

In some instances of alleged fraud, courts will consider an employee's intent, especially where the conduct appears to be reasonable. In one case, an employee kept a television set that was sent by a supplier as a promotional gift when the employee ordered a shipment of goods on behalf of the company for whom he worked.[71] The company had no policies in respect of such gifts so the employee treated the television as his own personal property. The court did not find that the employee's conduct amounted to fraud or that the employee had intended to be deceitful. As a consequence, the court con-

---

[68] *Homer v. Rocca* (1987), 87 N.B.R. (2d) 282 (Q.B.), affd 20 C.C.E.L. 287 (C.A.).
[69] See discussion under Heading 23, "Character Revelation", of this Part.
[70] *Lake Ontario Portland Cement Co. v. Groner* (1961), 28 D.L.R. (2d) 589 (S.C.C.).
[71] *Kreager v. Davidson* (1992), 44 C.C.E.L. 261 (B.C.C.A.).

cluded that the employee had been wrongfully dismissed and was entitled to damages.

The intentions of an employee are not always relevant. Even where they are honest in nature, just cause for termination can be established if an employee's misconduct reasonably results in an employer's loss of trust and confidence. In one case, an employee who held the position of company president was dismissed after forging a director's signature on the company's financial statements.[72] The employee maintained that he forged the signature because the director was out of town and the statements had to be executed before his return. While the court recognized that the employee's intentions may not have been deceitful, it concluded that termination was warranted on the grounds that his conduct revealed a character that caused his employer to lose trust in him. Furthermore, since the employee was company president, he occupied a position that required a high standard of honesty and integrity, a standard that was inconsistent with the act of forgery.

When an employer must prove a case for cause on the basis of fraudulent behaviour, the general rule relating to just cause dismissals applies, that is, just cause must be established by the employer on a balance of probabilities. However, some cases have suggested that a somewhat stricter test of proof within this standard must be met when allegations of fraud are being made.[73] While the standard continues to be proof on a balance of probabilities, the prudent employer will ensure that convincing and clear facts exist when serious employee misconduct is alleged.

Overview

Fraudulent behaviour by an employee can amount to grounds for just cause termination. A case for cause on this basis is strengthened when some or all of the following factors and circumstances exist:

1. The employer was prejudiced by the act or acts of fraud.
2. The employer received no benefit from the employee's misconduct.
3. The employee occupied a position associated with a high degree of trust and integrity.
4. A character inconsistent with the employee's continued employment was revealed by the fraudulent behaviour.
5. The conduct conflicted with the duties and responsibilities of the position.
6. The employer's trust and confidence was reasonably lost as a result of the employee's misconduct.
7. The employee acted in a secretive manner.

---

[72] *Jewitt v. Prism Resources Ltd.* (1980), 110 D.L.R. (3d) 713 (B.C.S.C.), affd 127 D.L.R. (3d) 190 (C.A.).
[73] *Homer v. Rocca, supra,* footnote 68.

8. The misbehaviour was not reasonable in the circumstances.
9. The employee's intentions were deceitful.

6 ✧ THEFT

Like fraudulent conduct, theft against an employer can be categorized as dishonest behaviour when establishing grounds for just cause termination. Absent strong mitigating circumstances, a single incident of theft can justify an individual's dismissal without notice. This is so because an implied term of every employment contract is that the employee will not steal from the employer. Also, an act of theft demonstrates a trait that is incompatible with the duty of loyalty and honesty owed to employers.

The characteristics of honesty and trustworthiness are particularly important where employees hold responsible or senior positions that command a high level of integrity and trust. In one case, for example, a manager was entrusted with the custody of inventory worth hundreds of thousands of dollars.[74] His dismissal was justified because he had stolen from the company. The court's reasoning was that honesty and trustworthiness are paramount requirements for a manager's position and that the manager's conduct illustrated his inability to satisfy these requirements. Similarly, a court found just cause when a self-supervising employee committed theft, breaching the employer's confidence.[75]

A strong case for cause can also be made out where the employee benefits personally from an act of theft or where the employer's interests are prejudiced as a result. However, just cause for termination can still be established even in the absence of a loss to the employer's business. In one case, for instance, an employee diverted waste oil from his employer's operations to a neighbour without authorization.[76] The court found this conduct to be an act of theft that justified termination. The fact that the employer may not have suffered a financial loss from the incident was immaterial. Instead, the fact that the employee was capable of such conduct by itself was enough to establish just cause for his dismissal.

As in all cases for cause, when theft is alleged as the reason for termination, the burden of proving the employee's misconduct is on the employer. That is, the employer must prove on a balance of probabilities that the employee did in fact engage in an act or acts of theft. Whether or not this burden of proof is met will depend on the particular circumstances. In one case, the court concluded that the employer had proven theft on a balance of prob-

---

[74] *Melanson v. Tandy Electronics* (1987), 82 N.B.R. (2d) 161 (Q.B.).
[75] *Mutton v. AOT Canada Ltd.*, [2002] O.T.C. 161 (S.C.J.).
[76] *Beyea v. Irving Oil Ltd.* (1985), 8 C.C.E.L. 128 (N.B.Q.B.), affd 14 C.C.E.L. 67 (C.A.).

abilities where a surveillance tape showed the employee receiving $100 from a customer that was not placed in the register.[77] At the end of the day, a sum of $100 was also missing from the register's till. Just cause for dismissal based on theft was therefore found to exist.

In another case, the court said an employer did not meet the required burden of proof where a parking lot attendant was accused of altering a number of parking tickets, thereby depriving his employer of revenue.[78] The court concluded that there was insufficient evidence to determine for certain who had altered the tickets and that the changes could very well have been made by customers. As a consequence, the attendant's termination was said to be wrongful because it was based on an unsubstantiated allegation of theft.

In some termination cases based on theft, it may be that criminal charges have also been laid with respect to the employee's conduct. However, courts are generally of the view that criminal findings are irrelevant for the purpose of determining whether an employer had just cause to dismiss the employee. This view is taken because the standard of proof in criminal proceedings is more onerous than that required to prove just cause. As a result, a case for cause based on theft can still be maintained even though criminal charges against the employee are ultimately dismissed. In one case, for example, a cashier was terminated because she failed to register all transactions and allowed customers to leave the store with unpaid merchandise.[79] Although criminal charges were brought against her, the cashier was subsequently acquitted in the criminal proceedings. Notwithstanding her acquittal, the court concluded that the employer had proven cause on a balance of probabilities and her dismissal was therefore warranted.

Where an employer attempts to establish that an employee has engaged in an act of theft, a court may find that termination is not justified if there is a reasonable explanation for the apparent misconduct. Nonetheless, it is up to the employee to establish the existence of such an explanation. Where the conduct is reasonably explained, a court will typically conclude that the employer has failed to properly meet the standard of proof required for just cause termination based on theft. In one case, a surveillance tape showed a store's supervisor picking up a package of screwdriver bits and putting it in his pocket.[80] He was subsequently confronted by a superior and did not deny possessing the bits. Instead, he explained that he intended to bring them to the returns department for proper processing. Notwithstanding this explanation, the supervisor was dismissed for allegedly attempting to steal company mer-

---

[77] *Meszaros v. Simpson Sears Ltd.* (1979), 19 A.R. 239 (Q.B.).
[78] *Jivrag v. Calgary (City)* (1986), 13 C.C.E.L. 120 (Alta. Q.B.), affd on this point 18 C.C.E.L. xxx (C.A.).
[79] *Murphy v. Canadian Tire Corp.* (1991), 39 C.C.E.L. 205 (Ont. Ct. (Gen. Div.)).
[80] *Cooper v. Sears Canada Inc.* (1991), 40 C.C.E.L. 225 (N.S.S.C.T.D.).

chandise. After viewing the surveillance tape and considering all other relevant evidence, the court concluded that the supervisor's explanation was a reasonable one and consistent with the proven facts. It also concluded that the supervisor had not intended to commit an act of theft and accordingly was wrongfully dismissed. One factor that helped persuade the court was that the supervisor was an employee of long standing who had always served the employer well.

Since the existence of a reasonable explanation will negate a finding of just cause, employers should give an employee the opportunity to explain an alleged act of theft before the employee is dismissed on this basis. A salesman in one instance was fired by an automobile dealer after being accused of assisting a co-worker to steal a small quantity of motor oil.[81] The termination occurred after the dealer's service manager saw the salesman holding a funnel over a container while the other employee poured oil into it. The court concluded that the employer had not made sufficient inquiries to establish the extent of the salesman's involvement in the incident nor had the salesman been given an opportunity to explain his version of the events. Because the saleman believed that the co-worker was not improperly taking waste oil, the court was unable to conclude that just cause for dismissal existed and was satisfied that the salesman's involvement in the incident was innocent.

Overview

An employer who reasonably believes that an employee has engaged in theft has grounds to dismiss the employee without notice if the theft can be proven on a balance of probabilities. The presence of some or all of the following factors serve to strengthen a termination on this basis:

1. A high degree of trust and integrity are paramount requirements of the position.
2. The employee benefited from the theft.
3. The employer suffered a loss as a result of the employee's conduct.
4. The employee cannot provide a reasonable explanation for the apparent misconduct.
5. Video surveillance and/or witnesses of the theft exist.
6. The employee was apprehended as the theft was taking place.
7. The theft involved goods with more than a nominal value.

---

[81] *Trask v. Terra Nova Motors Ltd.* (1991), 35 C.C.E.L. 208 (Nfld. S.C.), affd 9 C.C.E.L. (2d) 157 (C.A.).

7 ✧ INSUBORDINATION

Insubordinate behaviour can justify an employee's dismissal without notice in many circumstances. Because this behaviour is generally easier to demonstrate than other forms of misconduct, just cause tends to be easier to establish. In the employment context, insubordination refers to the failure to submit to the authority of an employer or superior. Insubordination encompasses two broad categories of workplace behaviour. The first is disobedience and the second is insolence or disrespectful and insulting behaviour towards an employer or superior.

(a) Disobedience

Disobedience relates to situations where an employee defies a superior's instructions or refuses to carry out a work order. The failure to obey instructions or orders can constitute a significant act of insubordination because it is inconsistent with the essence of most employment relationships. In these relationships, the employer has a general right to issue work-related orders and the employee has an obligation to follow them. As a consequence, refusing to follow a work order can be analogous to a rejection of the employment relationship. Whether this is actually so depends on a number of factors, including the nature of the disobedience.[82]

While a single incident of misconduct is not usually enough to justify dismissal without notice, disobeying a work order once can constitute just cause for termination where it amounts to serious insubordination. The facts and circumstances of each case must be considered to determine whether the employee's disobedience is an insubordinate act of sufficient seriousness that calls for summary termination. However, an excellent and lengthy service record with an employer is sure to mitigate against a finding of serious insubordination.[83]

An implied term of all employment contracts is that the employee will serve the employer honestly and faithfully. As such, employees have a general duty to accept and implement proper orders given to them by their employers.[84] While a more onerous duty is often imposed on employees who hold management positions, an employment contract can be breached in a fundamental way where any employee disobeys the instructions of an employer. This is the case unless circumstances surrounding the disobedience are influenced by mitigating factors. Such circumstances may exist if the employee has a legitimate reason for failing to implement the instructions, if

---

[82] For specific examples of disobedience, see discussions under Headings 8 to 11 of this Part.

[83] See *Dusconi v. Fujitsu-ICl Canada Inc.* (1996), 19 C.C.E.L. (2d) 143 (B.C.S.C.).

[84] *MacFarlane v. Westfair Foods Ltd.* (1994), 7 C.C.E.L. (2d) 75 (Alta. Q.B.).

the disobedience is not deliberate or if the instructions issued by the employer are unreasonable, unlawful, ambiguous or outside the scope of the employee's duties. Absent these circumstances, a dismissal without notice is likely to be justified based on the fact that the employment contract is breached by the employee's insubordinate behaviour. Further support for the termination exists where the employee has been warned that failure to obey will jeopardize his or her job.[85]

A termination based on the refusal to follow a work order can only be justified if the employee was in fact aware of the order. Otherwise, a legitimate reason for non-compliance will obviously exist. Similarly, just cause is unlikely to be established if the employee has a reasonable excuse for disobeying instructions. This will be the case, for instance, where an employee receives a verbal order that either contradicts a written order or conflicts with instructions received from a client.[86] The effect of a legitimate reason for disobedience was also demonstrated in a situation where an employee's termination was found to be unwarranted even though he had resisted changes and directives being implemented by management.[87] Because his resistance stemmed from a genuine concern for the company's best interests, the court concluded that the employee had a legitimate reason for not complying with the orders of management. Furthermore, it was found that in the past the employee had always been positive in implementing changes once he either agreed with them or failed to convince management that they should not be made. Accordingly, just cause for the employee's dismissal did not exist.

The general rule is that, absent a legitimate reason for non-compliance, the refusal to carry out a work assignment can amount to just cause for an employee's termination. However, unless it is wilful and deliberate, disobedience will not amount to serious insubordination and therefore just cause is not likely to be established. An example of deliberate and wilful disobedience is a situation where the employee initially agrees to carry out an order and then upon reflection refuses to do so without legitimate justification.[88] An employee's conduct is also deliberate and wilful if he or she takes a confrontational attitude when refusing to comply with an employer's request.[89]

The nature of the disobedience must be considered in order to determine whether termination without notice is justified. For example, the refusal to carry out instructions might take place outside of work hours or relate to mat-

---

[85] See, *e.g.*, *Mair v. Raymond and Heller Ltd.*, [2002] O.J. No. 563 (QL) (S.C.J.).

[86] *McNeil v. Burns International Security Services Ltd.* (1990), 11 C.C.E.L. (2d) 25 (Ont. Dist. Ct.).

[87] *Quinlan v. Bridgeport Self-Serve Carpet Clinic Ltd.* (1993), 2 C.C.E.L. (2d) 60 (B.C.S.C.).

[88] *Amos v. Alberta* (1995), 9 C.C.E.L. (2d) 69 (Alta. Q.B.).

[89] *Miguna v. African Canadian Legal Clinic* (1996), 18 C.C.E.L. (2d) 131 (Ont. Ct. (Gen. Div.)).

ters that are minor in nature. In these situations, a court is apt to say that the disobedience is not serious enough to support a summary dismissal. In other cases, a court may find that an employer's instructions are unreasonable and that failure to follow them is not an act of insubordination at all. Such a conclusion was reached in one case where the employee was told not to have sexual relations with female subordinates.[90] The court found this order to be unreasonable in today's contemporary society and therefore the employee's non-compliance did not amount to insubordination.

Similarly, just cause for termination is not likely to be established if the employee can show that a superior's instructions are rarely followed in the employer's workplace. A case for cause will also be more difficult to prove if an employer does not consistently impose discipline when employees fail to carry out an order. However, courts recognize that employers often expect a greater degree of compliance from a senior employee than from a junior one. The discrepancy in how an employer deals with disobedience might therefore be explained by differences in seniority and position.

Insubordinate conduct that did breach an employment contract was illustrated by the employee of a legal aid clinic who would not accept certain restrictions placed on her position.[91] The employee refused to work with or accept instructions from the clinic's director and board of directors. The court concluded that the employee's behaviour was severe enough to breach her employment contract in a fundamental way, thereby establishing just cause for her termination. Similarly, just cause existed where an employee failed to follow an order from his employer directing him not to take holidays during a particularly busy period.[92] The court said the employee breached a term of his employment contract by going on vacation during this period and the breach amounted to insubordination warranting termination.[93] In another case, a highway transport driver was dismissed after he refused to bid on peddle runs, which he felt were excluded by the terms and conditions of his employment.[94] The court found that he had avoided the peddle runs due to his seniority and his ability to bid on the better available runs. However, all highway drivers were still required to do peddle runs if necessary, and his refusal was just cause for termination.

---

[90] *Dooley v. C.N. Weber Ltd.* (1994), 3 C.C.E.L. (2d) 95 (Ont. Ct. (Gen. Div.)), affd 80 O.A.C. 234 (C.A.), leave to appeal to S.C.C. refused 197 N.R. 160n.

[91] *Stalker v. Community Legal Assistance Society* (1991), 37 C.C.E.L. 11 (B.C.S.C.), affd 27 W.A.C. 291 (C.A.).

[92] *Bratti v. F & W Wholesale Ltd.* (1989), 28 C.C.E.L. 142 (B.C. Co. Ct.).

[93] Such misconduct can also be categorized as an unauthorized absence from work: see discussions under Heading 12, "Absenteeism and Lateness", and Heading 13, "Leaving Work Without Permission", of this Part.

[94] *Battams v. S.L.H. Transport Inc.* (2002), 223 Sask. R. 222 (C.A.).

On the other hand, an employment contract is not likely to be breached if the failure to follow an employer's instructions does not lead to actual or potential harm. These were the circumstances when a private teacher was fired for allegedly failing to follow her principal's instructions.[95] The instructions included an order to keep confidential the fact that a particular student had head lice. Upon hearing all the facts, the court concluded that the teacher had not disobeyed the principal and that termination of her employment was therefore unwarranted. Even if there had been non-compliance with the instructions, the court said it would not have amounted to insubordination that justified summary dismissal. A dismissal without notice would have been unwarranted because the students of the school and their parents did not experience any negative repercussions. Furthermore, there were no adverse effects on the school's operations or the teacher's ability to carry out her responsibilities.

(b) Insolence

A display of insolence or disrespectful and insulting behaviour can constitute just cause for an employee's summary dismissal but only if it is sufficiently serious or severe in nature. This condition is frequently satisfied by proving that the insolent behaviour interferes with the safe or proper conduct of an employer's business. For example, an employee who undermines a superior's position and misbehaves during a staff meeting engages in serious insolence, and may be dismissed for cause.[96]

Many different workplace incidents qualify as examples of insolence. They can generally be characterized as falling within one or more of the following categories of misconduct.

(i) *Challenging Authority*

The safe and proper conduct of an employer's business will usually be prejudiced by an employee's actions that directly challenge the authority of an employer or other superior. For this reason, these actions are likely to constitute just cause for termination. A case for cause is further strengthened where the employee's actions amount to planned and deliberate behaviour, as opposed to an isolated and sudden reaction to a particular event or situation. This point is illustrated by the case of an employee who evoked conflict and directly challenged the authority of his superior.[97] In particular, the employee used strong and insulting language when he responded to a memo issued by

---

[95] *Greenwood v. Chilliwack Christian School Society* (1994), 8 C.C.E.L. (2d) 122 (B.C.S.C.).

[96] *Belliveau v. Dylex Ltd.* (1987), 79 N.B.R. (2d) 141 (Q.B.).

[97] *Neudorf v. Sun Valley Co-Op Ltd.* (1994), 6 C.C.E.L. (2d) 61 (Man. Q.B.).

his general manager. The employee also made several derogatory remarks about the general manager that included calling him a "drunken bum" and making negative comments in respect of his marital status. The court concluded that the employee's actions amounted to insubordination because they demonstrated a challenge to the general manager's directions and authority. This challenge interfered with the safe and proper conduct of the employer's business and constituted just cause for termination. The court also noted that the employee's conduct involved planning and foresight and could not be excused. By demeaning the general manager with disparaging comments and responding so aggressively to the memo, the employee had damaged the employment relationship beyond repair.

Issuing an ultimatum that serves to challenge one's employer is also inexcusable and incompatible with an employee's continued employment. Accordingly, just cause for termination will usually be established. For instance, a company in the business of developing and marketing travel tours was given an ultimatum by one of its employees who acted as a tour escort.[98] The employee threatened to abandon a tour scheduled to commence in four days unless he was immediately compensated for expenses that had been questioned and deducted from his pay. The demand was made even though the employee knew that the company had a practice of not issuing reimbursements until an adequate explanation of questionable expenses was provided. Despite this practice, the company gave into the employee's threat so that its business would not be disrupted by the tour's postponement or cancellation. However, the employee was subsequently fired upon completion of the tour and the company was able to satisfy the court that just cause for termination existed. The court concluded that the employee's conduct in challenging the company and its business amounted to insubordination warranting dismissal without notice.

However, in another instance of an ultimatum, the company's most senior technical employee who had been with the company for 19 years threatened to delete important computer files due to his disagreement with how they were being managed and stored. The court held that the employer must take the view of a reasonable employer and "assess the risk given all the circumstances of the employee, his employment contract, and the circumstances of his employment".[99] The court concluded that the reasonable employer would have communicated the perceived seriousness of the threat to the employee and ascertained his intentions before acting, and thus ruled

---

[98] *Clark v. Horizon Holidays Ltd.* (1993), 45 C.C.E.L. 244 (Ont. Ct. (Gen. Div.)).
[99] *Mothersele v. Gulf Canada Resources Ltd.* (2003), 24 C.C.E.L. (3d) 139 (Alta. Q.B.), at para. 18. For further discussion on this decision see Heading 4, "Dishonesty", in this Part.

that from the reasonable employer's point of view, there was no just cause for dismissal.

(ii) *Using Offensive Language*

The use of foul or offensive language towards an employer or other superior can constitute insolence in many circumstances.[100] If the language is destructive to an employment relationship, just cause for termination will be established. This is especially true where the offensive words are uttered in the vicinity of other employees. For example, in a case where an employee aggressively confronted his senior manager in the presence of co-workers, the court found just cause for his termination to exist.[101] During the confrontation, the employee belittled the manager both personally and professionally. He also belittled other employees, the company and the company's manufacturing abilities. All of this was done in a crude and offensive manner, with the employee using very profane language. The court concluded that termination was justified because the employee's insolence interfered with the proper conduct of the employer's business. In this respect, his behaviour was seen as a brutal verbal assault on a superior that amounted to unacceptable insubordination. Furthermore, the employee's relationships with his manager and employer were found to have been damaged beyond repair.

A case for cause can be maintained even where an employee does not swear at the employer in the presence of other employees. In one case, the employee called his employer a "fucking liar" while they were discussing the use of company credit cards.[102] Although no one else was present and the employee was upset at the time, the court concluded that his words amounted to just cause for termination because they were destructive to the employment relationship. However, if an employee can show that he or she was unreasonably provoked by an employer or superior, the use of profane language may be insufficient to constitute grounds for summary termination. Similarly, offensive language is likely to be excused if the court concludes that a company generally condoned its use among employees or between employees and superiors.[103]

Finally, a case for cause will fail unless the employee's use of offensive language amounts to conduct that could not possibly be tolerated by an employer concerned with running a well-disciplined business. In one case, the labour relations director of a company was terminated some time after dif-

---

[100] See, *e.g.*, *Blas v. Advance Glass and Aluminum Inc.*, [2003] A.J. No. 432 (QL) (Prov. Ct.).

[101] *Clare v. Moore Corp.* (1989), 29 C.C.E.L. 41 (Ont. Dist. Ct.).

[102] *Codner v. Joint Construction Ltd.* (1989), 27 C.C.E.L. 144 (Nfld. S.C.).

[103] See *E.C. & M. Electric Ltd. v. Alberta (Employment Standards Officer)* (1994), 7 C.C.E.L. (2d) 235 (Alta. E.S.C. Umpire).

ficulties began in his working relationship with a member of senior management.[104] The company said the director was terminated partly on the basis of his insolent behaviour. On one occasion, the director had incorrectly printed the manager's name as "Ass" rather than "Ash" on the cover sheet of a fax. However, the court concluded that the misprint was unintentional and therefore did not amount to insolence. Even if the director had acted intentionally, the court said his conduct was not indicative of insolence constituting just cause for termination. The court noted that a summary dismissal based on the use of offensive language would only be justified if what was said was intolerable and totally incompatible with continuance of the employment relationship. After all the facts were considered, the court found no evidence of conduct by the director that was intolerable by a company concerned with running a well-disciplined business. Accordingly, termination of the director was unwarranted.

(iii) *Criticizing Operations*

An employee's criticism of the organization or the employer for whom he or she works will support a dismissal for cause if it prejudices the organization's interests or is likely to harm its well-being. For example, where an employee makes derogatory comments and criticizes an employer in the presence of customers, just cause for termination will be established if the employer has no other way to control the employee's conduct and has legitimate concerns about the employee's behaviour.[105]

A case for cause based on an employee's criticism of the employer is also likely to succeed where the employee persists in taking a critical stance despite being told to do otherwise.[106] These were the circumstances of one case where a director of health records for a child treatment facility was fired for continuing to pursue a matter that her employer had said was resolved.[107] The director became concerned when she discovered that two staff members were exchanging intimate correspondence. She advised management that it was inappropriate to permit such conduct in a facility that treated children. Her employer seemed to agree and severely reprimanded the two staff members involved. In addition, there was an investigation that concluded that no actual or potential harm to the children within the facility existed. Accordingly, management declared that, having been appropriately dealt with, the matter was closed. Despite this declaration, the director engaged in a course of conduct that demonstrated her dissatisfaction with the facility's

---

[104] *Beja v. Titan Wheel International Ltd.* (1992), 45 C.C.E.L. 67 (Ont. Ct. (Gen. Div.)).
[105] See *Longaphie v. Newson Pharm-Care Ltd.* (1992), 104 Nfld. & P.E.I.R. 6 (P.E.I.S.C.).
[106] *Fraser v. Canada (Public Service Staff Relations Bd.)* (1985), 23 D.L.R. (4th) 122 (S.C.C.).
[107] *Nacey v. Arbutus Society for Children* (1990), 34 C.C.E.L. 216 (B.C.S.C.).

resolution of the matter. She was linked to letters and memoranda sent to professional societies, parents of the children treated by the facility and members of the facility's board of trustees. These materials described the incident involving the exchange of intimate correspondence and criticized how it had been dealt with by management. Once the facility acquired evidence that linked the director to the letters and memoranda, her employment was summarily terminated. The court agreed that there was just cause for dismissal because the director continued to criticize her employer after the concern had been addressed. Her behaviour was harmful to the facility's well-being and prejudicial to its interests.[108]

Just cause for termination is even more likely to be established where the employee engages in extreme condemnation of an employer's operations and its management. In a case cited earlier as an example of verbal abuse towards a superior, the employee also condemned and ridiculed both management's ability to manage and the employer's operations generally.[109] In particular, the employee said the manager was too stupid to perform his job effectively, that the company was unable to properly manufacture its products and that the policies of the company were unsound. While the employee's dismissal was justified on the grounds of verbal abuse and using excessively profane language, the court noted that termination could also have been supported by the employee's highly critical comments of his employer's operations. These factors were all inconsistent with his continued employment and served to repudiate the employment contract.

While an employee's criticisms can constitute just cause for termination, the same cannot be said of an employee's error in judgment. For this reason, employers should be careful not to characterize an error in judgment as insolence amounting to insubordination. A case on point concerns the summary dismissal of a private school employee.[110] Prior to being fired, the employee had expressed concerns about the fact that her salary had been reduced while her responsibilities remained the same. When these concerns were not addressed by the administration, she decided to write a letter to the parents of the school's students describing her dissatisfaction with the way she and other staff members were being treated. The employee was subsequently dismissed because her employer considered such a letter to be highly inappropriate, especially at a time when the school was having difficulty attaining full enrolment. However, the court concluded that termination was unwarranted as there was no evidence that the employee's conduct prejudiced the school or

---

[108] The termination was also justified on the basis of the director's refusal to comply with management's instruction that the matter not be pursued and her dishonesty in denying that she had anything to do with the letters and memoranda.

[109] *Clare v. Moore Corp.*, *supra*, footnote 101.

[110] *Clark v. St. Margaret's School* (1990), 34 C.C.E.L. 172 (B.C.S.C.).

its operations. In particular, the school had not suffered any losses and no parents had responded to the letter. The court also noted that the employee's intention had not been to harm the school. Instead, she was acting in good faith to protect her own interests since she reasonably thought that the reduction in her salary was an attempt to force her to resign. For these reasons, the court characterized the employee's conduct as an error in judgment rather than insubordination and as such just cause for termination did not exist.

Overview

Disobedience (*i.e.*, an employee's deliberate and wilful refusal to follow the orders and instructions of a superior) can amount to insubordination that warrants termination without notice. However, the employer must first establish that the employee was aware of the order or the instructions given. In addition, the case for cause will be strengthened where any or all of the following circumstances exist:

1. Work orders and instructions within the organization are consistently enforced.
2. The orders or instructions issued by the employer were clear and unambiguous.
3. The orders or instructions came within the scope of the employee's duties.
4. The employee knew or should have know that disobedience would result in disciplinary action and possibly termination of employment.
5. The orders or instructions were lawful and reasonable.
6. The employee had no reasonable excuse for refusing to obey.
7. The employer's operations were prejudiced by the employee's refusal to comply with the orders or instructions given.

Insolence amounting to insubordination can also constitute just cause for termination in the appropriate circumstances. Acts of an employee that support a case for cause on this basis generally fall within one or more of the following types of misconduct: challenging the employer or other superiors; verbal abuse, swearing and the use of profane language; and criticizing the employer or the employer's operations. A case for cause due to insolence is strengthened where any or all of the following circumstances exist:

1. The employee's conduct interfered with the safe or proper conduct of an employer's operations.
2. Negative repercussions were experienced by the employer's business as a result of the employee's conduct.
3. The employee's actions were planned, intentional and deliberate.
4. The misconduct took place in the presence of other employees or customers/clients.
5. The employee's actions were destructive to the employment relationship.

6. The employee's conduct was not provoked by the employer or a superior.
7. The misconduct could not possibly be tolerated by an employer concerned with running a well-disciplined business.
8. In the circumstances, the employee's actions were unreasonable and could not be characterized as a mere error in judgment.

8 ❖ BREACHING EMPLOYER POLICIES OR RULES

Most employers have policies or rules that govern their employees and their workplaces. While an employee's failure to follow these policies and rules can constitute just cause for termination, the following conditions must be satisfied:

1. The policy or rule must be clearly established and incorporated into the employee's contract of employment.
2. The employee must be aware and informed of the policy or rule.
3. The fact that termination is a consequence of not complying with the policy or rule must be known by the employee.

In determining whether a policy or rule has become a part of the employment contract (*i.e.*, a term of employment), courts recognize that there is often an imbalance of bargaining power between employees and their employers. As a result, policies and rules are not instantly incorporated into a contract of employment simply because they are not forcefully opposed by an employee. There must first be some evidence to show that the employee agreed to accept them as terms of employment. In this respect, the policies and rules of an organization should be clearly established in the workplace. Employers must also ensure that employees are informed of a policy or rule's existence and of the requirement that it be followed.

Some rules can become terms of employment by implication even though they are not formally established as such by an employer. These rules are often associated with standards of behaviour that govern particular professions such as the codes of ethics for doctors, nurses and social workers and the rules of professional conduct for lawyers and accountants. A case for cause based on noncompliance with such rules can succeed if the employer is able to demonstrate that they were expressly or impliedly accepted into an employment contract.

In contrast, failing to follow a policy or rule that is found to be unreasonable or that is not consistently enforced by an employer will seldom amount to just cause for termination. This is illustrated by the case of a mechanic who was fired for failing to follow his employer's billing manual when certain tasks were performed.[111] The court concluded that just cause for

---

[111] *Koonts v. Garf Baxandall Ford Mercury Sales Ltd.* (1996), 21 C.C.E.L. (2d) 259 (B.C.S.C.).

the mechanic's termination did not exist because the employer had permitted other workers to bill the tasks in a manner that contradicted the manual's instructions.

Another important component of a case for cause in this area relates to an employee's knowledge of a policy or rule. Without such knowledge, an employee cannot be dismissed without notice. In the case discussed previously, for example, the conclusion that just cause for termination did not exist was bolstered by the fact that the employer's workers were never advised of the proper billing procedures to follow.[112] It is generally the employer's responsibility to ensure that an employee is aware of the policy or rule's existence. However, senior or managerial employees are presumed to have knowledge of their employer's policies and rules and are more likely to be held accountable for non-compliance as compared to other employees. Notwithstanding the potential to treat senior and managerial employees differently, the general rule is that just cause for termination will not be established unless a policy or rule is clearly brought to an employee's attention.[113] In this respect, a company must make serious attempts to educate its staff on the policies of the organization. Providing a written statement along with several other documents at the time of hiring may not be sufficient to meet an employer's duty to inform employees about the existence of company policies and rules.[114]

The final condition for establishing just cause requires an employee to be aware of the consequences of not following a policy or rule. An employer must show that the employee knew serious consequences including the loss of employment would result from his or her misconduct in this respect.[115] Furthermore, a case for cause cannot succeed unless the policy or rule expressly or impliedly provides that non-compliance will justify dismissal without notice. For instance, an employee of a bank engaged in three cases of cheque kiting.[116] After the second instance the employee signed a memorandum agreeing to certain conditions, including that any future action by the employee representing a breach of trust could result in her immediate suspension or termination. After the third instance of cheque kiting, the employee was dismissed. The court concluded that the bank had just cause to terminate the employee because the employee was in a position of trust, she

---

[112] *Supra.*
[113] *Wright v. British Columbia Trade Development Corp.* (1994), 3 C.C.E.L. (2d) 254 (B.C.S.C.).
[114] *Supra.*
[115] *Forshaw v. Aluminex Extrusions Ltd.* (1988), 24 C.C.E.L. 92 (B.C.S.C.), affd 27 C.C.E.L. 208 (C.A.); *Mair v. Raymond and Heller Ltd.*, [2002] O.J. No. 563 (QL) (S.C.J.).
[116] *Komperda v. Hongkong Bank of Canada*, [2002] O.T.C. 619 (S.C.J.), affd 141 O.A.C. 373 (C.A.).

had been warned twice, and she was aware that a breach of policy could result in dismissal.

Satisfaction of the conditions just outlined, however, does not guarantee that just cause for termination will always be established. Various factors can strengthen or weaken a case for cause; thus, breach of a policy or rule may not warrant the same treatment in all situations. Whether a termination is justified often depends on the nature of the breach and the policy or rule in question. For instance, the violation of a policy relating to safety concerns or one that regulates the conduct of workers in life and death situations is going to be treated more seriously than other violations and a higher standard of compliance will generally be required.[117] A less serious breach or rule may call for a disciplinary response that is not as severe as the termination of an individual's employment. For example, the court concluded that a reprimand or some other form of discipline would have been more appropriate than dismissal where an employee failed to comply with a policy that required her to maintain separate accounts for cash donations.[118] This conclusion was partly based on the fact that the employee did not conceal the breach of policy or withhold any information from the employer. She also derived no personal benefit from her conduct and did not expose the employer to any financial loss. In addition, she had served the employer's organization for a long period of time and had made many important contributions over the years. All of these factors served to lessen the severity of the breach in question and as a result just cause for her dismissal was not made out.

Policy breaches are often distinguished because they were intended to serve different functions. In one case, an employee did not comply with the "chain of command" rules in his employer's company when he leapfrogged over two managers to contact the company's head of operations.[119] The court accepted that the employee had reasonable grounds for believing he was about to be discharged and that his sole purpose for violating the company rules was to have upper management hear his case. Based on the employee's purpose for breaching the policy, the court concluded that just cause for termination did not exist. The court also noted that a dismissal would not be justified if an employee violated a "chain of command" policy in order to expose a workplace fraud or conspiracy. The court did say, however, that just cause would likely be established if company rules were broken for the sole purpose of criticizing the employer's business or the administrative decisions of middle management.

---

[117] *Fox v. Souris Ambulance (1989) Ltd.* (1992), 45 C.C.E.L. 22 (Sask. Q.B.).

[118] *Rock v. Canadian Red Cross Society* (1994), 5 C.C.E.L. (2d) 231, supplementary reasons 7 C.C.E.L. (2d) 146 (Ont. Ct. (Gen. Div.)).

[119] *Bell v. Cessna Aircraft Co.* (1980), 19 B.C.L.R. 252 (S.C.), revd 131 D.L.R. (3d) 551 (C.A.), leave to appeal to S.C.C. refused 43 N.R. 167*n*.

Another factor mentioned earlier that can determine the seriousness of a policy's violation relates to whether or not the employee's conduct was prejudicial to a company's business. Where an organization has not suffered financial loss or significant prejudice, a court is less likely to conclude that a dismissal was justified on the basis of the violation of a policy or rule.[120]

The existence of a reasonable or legitimate explanation for not complying with a policy or rule is another reason why courts may find that a summary dismissal was not warranted. Similarly, just cause is not likely to be established where a policy or rule is breached as a result of an employee's honest mistake.[121] As noted in *Rock v. Canadian Red Cross Society*,[122] the courts will also take into account the fact that an employee did not personally benefit from the non-compliance with a policy or rule. This fact will tend to weaken an employer's case for cause.

While senior and managerial employees are more apt to be held liable for their conduct in breaching an employer's policy or rule, a good and lengthy service record may persuade a court to conclude that termination was too severe a response.[123] An employee's prior adherence to company policies is also persuasive and can weaken an employer's case for cause. A case for cause can also be rebutted if the breach does not undermine or seriously impair the employer's trust and confidence. This is especially true where an employee shows that he or she is open to instructions and has the ability to follow a superior's directive.[124] Such was the case where a store manager stopped breaching a company policy after being asked to do so by her area manager.[125] The store manager's dismissal some 13 days later was found to be without cause because she had shown herself to be amenable to direction. Moreover, the employee's behaviour had not undermined the employer's trust and confidence.

Companies should take note that caution must be exercised when implementing a policy or rule that unilaterally changes the terms of an individual's employment contract or modifies existing business practices and workplace relationships. An employee's failure to accept or follow the new policy or rule might not constitute just cause for termination. This is true even though an employer clearly warns that dismissal is the consequence of non-compliance. In one case, a company fired an employee who refused to sign a newly created code of conduct relating to the organization's policies and

---

[120] *Hill v. Dow Chemical Canada Inc.* (1993), 48 C.C.E.L. 254 (Alta. Q.B.).
[121] *Ennis v. Textron Canada Ltd.* (1987), 82 A.R. 260 (Q.B.).
[122] *Supra*, footnote 118.
[123] *Wiebe v. Central Transport Refrigeration (Man.) Ltd.* (1993), 45 C.C.E.L. 1 (Man. Q.B.), affd on this point 3 C.C.E.L. (2d) 1 (C.A.).
[124] See *Kakoske v. Carter Motors Ltd.* (1984), 6 C.C.E.L. 184 (Man. Q.B.).
[125] *Reeves v. Gap International Inc.* (1995), 10 C.C.E.L. (2d) 262 (Alta. Prov. Ct.).

practices.[126] A primary reason for the employee's refusal was that the new code changed an existing travel points policy which was included in his remuneration and benefits package. The policy had allowed employees who travelled on business to keep the travel points they accumulated. The court agreed that the policy had become a term of employment. By changing the policy without the employee's consent, the court found that the company had breached the employee's contract of employment, thereby giving him the right to make a claim for damages. In these circumstances, the court found that the employee's refusal to accept the new code of conduct did not amount to cause justifying his dismissal.

Clearly, employers are entitled to implement new corporate policies in their workplaces. However, where the policy alters a material term of employment, it can only be implemented by providing all affected employees with reasonable notice of the change. In such a situation, the employer cannot terminate or otherwise discipline an employee during the notice period for matters relating to the new policy. If an employee is dismissed, disciplined or not given proper notice of the change, a court may find that his or her employment contract was breached. As a consequence, the employer will not have cause to terminate the employee for failing to comply with the new corporate policy and the employee may be entitled to damages based on the employer's breach of the employment contract.

Overview

An employee's conduct in breaching an employer's policies or rules can amount to just cause for termination if certain conditions are satisfied. These conditions require that the policy or rule be well established and incorporated as a term of employment, that the employee have knowledge and be informed of the policy or rule's existence and that the employee appreciate that a consequence of non-compliance is dismissal without notice. In this regard, the presence of the following factors and circumstances will assist in satisfying the three conditions:

1. The policy or rule is clearly worded.
2. There is evidence that the employee agreed to accept the policy or rule as a term of employment.
3. The policy or rule is not unreasonable or unfair.
4. The policy or rule is consistently enforced by the employer.
5. The employer clearly brought to the employee's attention the existence of the policy or rule and the requirement that it be followed.

---

[126] *Adams v. Comark Inc.* (1992), 42 C.C.E.L. 15 (Man. C.A.).

6. The policy or rule expressly states that dismissal is a consequence of non-compliance or, alternatively, this consequence can be implied from the way in which the policy or rule is enforced in the workplace.

In addition, a case for cause will be strengthened where some or all of the following factors exist:

1. The nature of the breach was serious, such as the case of an employee violating a policy or rule relating to safety matters or emergency situations.
2. The employee who breached the policy or rule occupied a senior or managerial position.
3. The employee who breached the policy or rule did not have a lengthy or exemplary service record with the employer.
4. The "reason" for breaching the policy or rule was not reasonable.
5. The purpose of breaching the policy or rule was not to achieve some laudable or worthwhile objective but rather to enable the employee to do something harmful in character such as criticizing the employer's business.
6. The employee's conduct in violating the policy or rule had a prejudicial effect on the employer's interests and operations.
7. The employee who breached the policy or rule personally benefited from his or her conduct in this respect.
8. There was no legitimate excuse or explanation for the employee's conduct in breaching the policy or rule.
9. The employee had a history of not complying with the policies or rules of the employer.
10. Breaching the policy or rule undermined and impaired the employer's trust and confidence in the employee.
11. The employee who violated the policy or rule did not appear to be amenable to instructions or able to follow directives.
12. The policy or rule that was breached did not unilaterally change the terms of an employee's contract of employment or if it did the employee was given reasonable notice of the change.

9 ✧ FAILURE TO RELOCATE

From time to time, an employer may decide to transfer an employee to another branch or office within the same organization. In some circumstances, the employer can take the position that employees who refuse to relocate are in effect resigning or that failure to accept a transfer constitutes just cause for termination. Refusing to relocate may also be treated as an act of disobedience.[127]

---

[127] See discussion under Heading 7, "Insubordination", of this Part.

In most employment contracts, an employer will have an express or implied right to transfer employees. However, the reasons for a transfer should be consistent with good business practice and the employer must be acting in good faith. Just cause for termination based on the refusal to accept a transfer will not exist where a company has used relocation as an act of discipline. Similarly, a case for cause cannot be established if the company's decision to transfer an employee was not made in the ordinary course of its business. These were the circumstances in one case where a not-for-profit corporation had to reorganize and downsize in response to a decline in the house construction industry.[128] This resulted in a large reduction to the corporation's clerical staff and in field representatives having to perform clerical duties and begin using a new computer system. A field officer with a 10-year exemplary work record found the new duties difficult to master because he had no clerical skills. This was reflected in his performance review conducted after the corporation's reorganization. The employee opposed the poor evaluation he received and was subsequently advised of the corporation's decision to transfer him to another branch where he would have probationary status. The employee refused to relocate on these terms and the corporation took that to mean he was resigning from his job. The court concluded that transferring the employee without notice and with a reduction in employment status was an act of discipline. The court said such discipline was not warranted by his poor performance because the employee had not been given the means to achieve the skills now required for his position. The employee was therefore justified in resisting the corporation's attempt to have him relocated and his conduct in this regard did not constitute a resignation nor just cause for termination. However, the court noted that the employee would not have had reasonable grounds to refuse the transfer if the corporation had acted with notice and in the ordinary course of its business when deciding to have him transferred. Accordingly, a case for cause based on refusal to relocate will not succeed unless an employer provides adequate notice of the transfer and establishes that its decision to transfer the employee was made for legitimate purposes.

A termination based on the failure to accept a transfer tends to be easier to justify where the nature of a worker's job is such that relocation should be expected. In one case, the court accepted that relocation was a fact of life in the engineering profession and concluded that the company was justified in dismissing an engineer when he refused a transfer to another position and location.[129] The engineer was one of several employees who had been temporarily laid off due to the economic climate. After complaining about the

---

[128] *Poirier v. Ontario New Home Warranty Program* (1995), 9 C.C.E.L. (2d) 211 (Ont. Ct. (Gen. Div.)).

[129] *Stefanovic v. SNC Inc.* (1988), 22 C.C.E.L. 82 (Ont. H.C.J.).

layoff, the employee refused to accept either of two positions in other cities offered by the company. The court found that his refusal constituted just cause for termination because the employer had not acted in bad faith, because relocation was an accepted part of the employee's job and because neither transfer involved a demotion.

A similar conclusion was reached in a case where a company merged with an affiliate and moved its business to another city because of a downturn in the economy.[130] One of the company's managers became suspicious about his future employment with the organization, even though the company had offered all of its employees positions at the new location and said that moving expenses would be paid. The manager's suspicions first began when the company failed to provide specific and timely details about the actual expenses that would be paid. His concerns continued after the company refused to agree to an arrangement whereby the manager could work on a contracting-out basis and not have to move. The manager's suspicions were heightened when he learned that a part-time employee had apparently been hired at the new location to carry out duties similar to those that he was performing. As a result of his growing concerns, the manager quit and claimed that he was constructively dismissed because the company's decision to relocate had fundamentally altered the terms of his employment contract. The court rejected such a claim and said the manager's suspicions as to his future with the company were unfounded. Furthermore, the court concluded that an employer's decision to move its operations for practical business reasons did not constitute constructive dismissal and that employees had to expect and accept reasonable relocations if they wanted to remain with a particular employer. In this case, the court took the view that the company had acted reasonably in deciding to relocate its business and in notifying the manager of the move. While the company may have been tardy in providing the manager with details about the payment of moving expenses, the court recognized that such a delay was to be expected given the many problems an organization faces when effecting a merger and move. Accordingly, the terms of the manager's employment were not fundamentally altered by the company's conduct. On the other hand, the manager's refusal to relocate would likely have given the company just cause to dismiss him had he not chosen to resign on his own accord.

Generally speaking, an implied term of every employment contract is that an employee will accept all reasonable transfers that do not involve a demotion or undue burden and hardship.[131] This is so where the employee has previously demonstrated flexibility in terms of mobility and where the

---

[130] *Smith v. Viking Helicopter Ltd.* (1989), 24 C.C.E.L. 113 (Ont. C.A.).
[131] *Jim Pattison Industries Ltd. v. Page*, [1982] 5 W.W.R. 97 (Sask. Q.B.), revd 4 C.C.E.L. 283 (C.A.).

employer is a large or international organization. In this regard, courts have recognized that it would be very difficult for such companies to operate without having the right to require reasonable transfers. Even if the right to relocate an employee is not absolute, employers may be entitled to demand that an employee make a decision by a certain date in respect of a proposed transfer and just cause for termination could be established if the employee refuses to relocate or render a timely decision. However, a termination on either basis is not justified where the employer has merely urged the employee to accept the transfer and has not required the transfer to be accepted in a reasonable period of time.[132]

Whether a transfer is ultimately found to be reasonable depends upon a number of factors, including the size of the organization, its area of operations, the number and location of its branches and the number of people it employs. Also important is the nature of an organization's business, since relocation is very common in certain industries. An additional factor to take into account relates to the type of employee who is going to be transferred. An executive or managerial employee may be expected to accept a relocation more often than an employee occupying a lesser position. Finally, as already mentioned, the employer must be acting in good faith when making the decision to transfer an employee and the decision must be seen as advancing the company's best interests. The absence of a legitimate reason for the transfer or evidence of bad faith on the part of the employer will make a relocation unreasonable and a case for cause virtually impossible to establish.

Notwithstanding its reasonableness, an employee cannot be required to accept a transfer if acceptance would result in the employee suffering an undue burden or hardship. In these circumstances, a termination based on the refusal to relocate cannot be justified. Undue burden or hardship may be established in the following situations: where the employee has to pay all expenses related to relocation because the employer refuses to do so; where requiring the employee to relocate will cause the career of his or her spouse to be prejudiced; and where the employee's relocation will conflict with a familial obligation such as attending to and caring for an ailing relative. Whether or not a transfer will result in undue burden or hardship is usually determined after an individual's employment has already ended. To avoid surprises, the employer should discuss relocation plans with the employee to determine whether the employee might find a transfer particularly difficult. The employer will also be able to assess whether the employee's refusal to accept relocation could ultimately be justified because it would cause an undue burden or hardship.

In most cases of termination, employees are obliged to mitigate the damages they may suffer as a result of the loss of employment. Where a dismissal

---

[132] *Dho v. Patino Management Services Ltd.* (1984), 5 C.C.E.L. 11 (Ont. H.C.J.).

is based on an employee's refusal to accept a transfer, the duty to mitigate may require the employee to take the position offered until alternative employment can be obtained.[133]

Overview

Employees are generally required to accept reasonable transfers that do not involve demotion or result in undue burden or hardship. Where such a transfer is refused, just cause for an employee's dismissal may be found to exist. In this regard, a case for cause based on a refusal to accept relocation will be strengthened by the presence of the following factors and circumstances:

1. The employer is a large company that operates in several different locations.
2. The employee held a managerial or executive position.
3. The nature of the employer's business implies that there is a definite likelihood of transfer.
4. The employee had previously accepted transfers.
5. The proposed transfer did not involve a demotion or cause the employee to suffer an undue burden, excessive hardship or financial detriment.
6. The employer was prepared to pay for any and all relocation costs.
7. The transfer was proposed for *bona fide* business reasons.
8. The employee was given ample notice of the requirement to move.
9. The employee was provided with timely and detailed information concerning the nature of the transfer and any obligations owed by the employer.

10 ✧ REFUSING SHIFT WORK OR OVERTIME

Employers often ask employees to participate in a shift work schedule or to work more hours than usual. Depending on the circumstances, the refusal of either request can justify termination without notice.[134] A finding of just cause for termination may depend on whether the employer's request is fair and reasonable, whether proper compensation for the work is being provided and whether the employee would be substantially prejudiced by performing the work (*e.g.*, by having his or her income taxed at a higher rate).

---

[133] See also discussion under Heading 16, "Mitigation", of Part I, "General Concepts".

[134] Principles that relate to disobedience may also have application here: see discussion under Heading 7, "Insubordination", of this Part.

(a) Refusing to Perform Shift Work

The employer who wants to dismiss an employee for failing to accept shift work duties must first consider whether performing such duties is a term of that employee's contract of employment. Just cause for termination does not exist where participation in shift work is not a duty the employee is required to carry out. However, most employment contracts do not expressly set out each and every duty that an employee is obliged to perform. Some terms of employment arise out of necessity or by necessary implication. This is what happened in one case where a research technologist requested a transfer to a new manufacturing plant that his employer was constructing.[135] The plant was being designed so that it could eventually operate on a 24-hour basis, a fact known throughout the company and also noted in all employee handbooks. At some point after being transferred, the technologist refused to participate in rotating shift work when asked to do so by his employer. The court was satisfied that the employee knew such participation would likely be a job requirement when he asked for the transfer. Accordingly, just cause for termination was found to exist on the basis of the employee's refusal to accept the required shift work duties. In this situation, the court concluded that performance of these duties was a term of employment that arose by necessary implication.

On the other hand, there may be situations where the requirement to participate in shift work is not an expressly stated term of the employment contract and cannot be implied from the circumstances. In such cases, an employer will find it difficult to establish just cause for termination on the basis of an employee's refusal to carry out shift work duties.

(b) Refusing to Work Extra Hours

In some respects, an employee's refusal to work extra hours must be treated differently from a refusal to participate in shift work is treated. Where an express or implied term of employment requires an employee to work extra hours, refusal to do so does not necessarily constitute just cause for dismissal. Whether a dismissal is justified will depend on the circumstances and the number of extra hours at issue. It is generally the case that employers cannot force employees to work overtime nor can they fire or discipline an employee who refuses to work overtime. Such prohibitions are found in most employment standards legislation throughout Canada. The federal jurisdiction and all provinces and territories have laws that limit the number of regularly paid hours which an employee can work in a given day or week. Any hours worked in excess of these limits are treated as overtime hours and attract greater monetary compensation. Some jurisdictions go further and pro-

---

[135] *Ironmonger v. Moli Energy Ltd.* (1990), 32 C.C.E.L. 49 (B.C. Co. Ct.).

hibit employees from working more than a certain number of overtime hours without authorization from the appropriate governmental agency, department or ministry. On the other hand, much of the legislation in this area exempts certain employees from provisions that deal with maximum hours and overtime; that is, the maximum hours and overtime provisions do not apply to these particular employees. Although they vary between jurisdictions, categories of exempt employees include: professionals; students in professional training; supervisors; managers; certain sales people; and agricultural employees or farm labourers. Employers should refer to the legislation applicable to their jurisdiction for specific information about the lawfulness of requiring an employee to work more regular or overtime hours.

If requiring an employee to work overtime is not contrary to the law or subject to special approval, the employee's unreasonable refusal to work the extra hours may amount to just cause for dismissal. However, as with the case of refusing to perform shift work duties, this will only be true where working more hours is an express or implied duty of employment. Furthermore, employees do not generally have to commit on very short notice to work any and all future overtime that is required. In one case, this is exactly what an employer asked two employees to do.[136] The employees were involved in an ongoing pay dispute with their employer regarding compensation for overtime emergency work. On at least two occasions during the dispute, the employees threatened to be unavailable for emergency overtime. On each occasion, however, the employees did not carry out the threat and in fact made themselves available when directed to do so by their supervisor. Notwithstanding this fact, the supervisor demanded that the employees commit themselves on very short notice to be available for all future situations of emergency overtime. Although the demand was not made during an emergency situation, the employees were immediately fired for failing to provide such a commitment. The court said the dismissals were unjustified because in the past the employees had always performed their duties and were available despite the pay dispute. Just cause for termination was therefore not established by the employees' refusal to commit on very short notice to work any and all required future overtime.

Overview

Unreasonable refusal to perform shift work or work extra hours can constitute just cause for termination. The following factors serve to strengthen cases for cause on this basis:

---

[136] *Fraser v. Kelowna (City)* (1993), 1 C.C.E.L. (2d) 127 (B.C.S.C.).

1. An express or implied term of employment required the employee to carry out shift work duties or to work more hours when requested to do so by the employer.
2. The request for shift work or overtime was reasonable, fair and for *bona fide* business reasons.
3. The employer complied with all statutory obligations in respect of overtime hours.
4. The requirement that an employee work more hours than usual or participate in a shift work schedule was not being used as discipline.
5. The employee suffered no financial detriment as a result of being required to engage in shift work.
6. The employer had undertaken to provide proper compensation for overtime hours.
7. The employer had undertaken to provide proper compensation for shift work hours where they were to be compensated differently from the way regular or non-shift work hours were compensated.

11 ✧ REFUSING TO PERFORM UNSAFE WORK

While a refusal to follow an employer's order may amount to disobedience and can constitute just cause for termination, this is not true in cases of justified disobedience where the refusal is reasonable and the order is unlawful. Refusing to carry out work that is unsafe or dangerous is an example of a justified disobedient act that does not constitute grounds for summary dismissal. This is clearly recognized in the occupational health and safety legislation aimed at preventing workplace accidents and injuries. The legislation contains general health and safety provisions applicable to most work environments and provides employees with the right to refuse work where a refusal is warranted.

All occupational health and safety laws give employees the right to complain about unsafe workplace conditions and to refuse unsafe work. Refusing to work may be warranted where the equipment or conditions of a particular workplace are likely to endanger employees or where conditions are actually life-threatening. If the performance of a particular work assignment would cause an employee to suffer harm or injury or involves a risk of danger, refusing to carry it out will similarly be justified. Furthermore, employees in most jurisdictions can refuse to work where they reasonably believe that unsafe or dangerous workplace conditions exist, even if it turns out that such conditions are not actually present.[137]

---

[137] Because of differences between jurisdictions, employers are advised to check the occupational health and safety legislation applicable to them and to review the provisions that specify when an employee's refusal to carry out unsafe work is justified.

Employers in all jurisdictions are statutorily prohibited from disciplining or dismissing employees for exercising their rights to complain about and refuse work that may endanger their health and safety or the health and safety of others in the workplace. If an employee is disciplined on either basis, he or she may file a complaint with the applicable board or agency responsible for enforcing the legislation. Where the employee is actually fired, he or she has the option of registering a complaint or commencing an action for wrongful dismissal. Some boards or agencies have the power to order that an individual be reinstated where the employer is unable to show that dismissal was justified in the circumstances or, alternatively, to place sanctions on the employer for dismissing the employee improperly. If the employee has chosen to commence legal proceedings, the employer will be liable for wrongful dismissal damages.

Employers have a duty to investigate properly an employee's concerns about unsafe conditions in the workplace or conditions that are likely to endanger the employee's or others' health and safety. Employers are also obligated to inform employees about all avenues they may follow to have their concerns addressed. An employee who is not properly informed of his or her rights and is fired after refusing unsafe work may be entitled to damages for wrongful dismissal. In one case, for instance, an employee who worked for a fabric manufacturer advised his employer that he could not continue working in the company's dye plant because the fumes in that environment aggravated his bronchial condition.[138] When an alternative position in the company could not be found for the employee, he was dismissed without notice or pay in lieu of notice. The court concluded the termination of employment was wrongful because of the provisions in the relevant occupational health and safety legislation. Pursuant to the legislation, the employee was entitled to refuse work in his place of employment where he had reasonable grounds for believing it would likely endanger his health. In turn, the company was required to take certain steps to determine whether reasonable grounds for the employee's belief existed. In the particular circumstances, the court found that the employee had reasonable grounds to believe his health would be endangered if he continued to work in the plant. Further, the company did not carry out the steps it was required to take when health concerns were raised by the employee, nor had the company advised the employee that he could take his workplace complaint to the plant's safety committee and then to a provincial officer charged with enforcement of the health and safety legislation. Instead, the company acted unilaterally and dismissed the employee contrary to his statutory rights, rights that were also terms of employment. By virtue of these rights, the court concluded that the company

---

[138] *Crossman v. Scotia Textiles Ltd.* (1989), 27 C.C.E.L. 302 (N.B.Q.B.), vard 30 C.C.E.L. 318 (C.A.).

did not have just cause to dismiss the employee without having investigated the employee's workplace complaint or having given the employee an opportunity to pursue other means of redress.

Where an employee legitimately refuses to carry out a work order and subsequently leaves the workplace, employers should be careful not to treat the employee's conduct as a resignation. If employers do so, they may be held liable for wrongfully dismissing the employee. These were the circumstances in one case where a labourer's employment came to an end after she refused to perform a particular work assignment and went home.[139] The employee had advised her foreman that she could not operate a particular machine in the company's plant because of an arm injury she had sustained. When the employee was told that she had to work on that machine during her next shift, she refused and left the plant. Shortly thereafter, the company told the employee that she was no longer employed as she had quit her job. The court concluded that the employee did not quit or resign from her position. Furthermore, the employee's refusal to operate the machine and her conduct in leaving the workplace were not seen as interfering with or prejudicing the safe and proper conduct of the company's business. Accordingly, it was found that the employee had been wrongfully dismissed and was therefore entitled to damages for the company's failure to provide her with reasonable notice.

Finally, just cause for an employee's dismissal does not exist where an employee brings legitimate complaints against a company that stem from concerns of health and safety. In one case, for example, a labourer in a snack food plant complained to management about what she perceived to be a health risk to herself and others in the workplace.[140] In particular, the employee advised her supervisor that she would not work on the packing line beside another labourer who had "scabies", a highly contagious skin disease. The supervisor told the employee that she had to work with the labourer or go home. The employee chose to go home rather than work in conditions that she perceived as endangering her health. Some time later, the employee was assigned to work on a piece of machinery that caused her arms to become sore and blistered. Although she asked that she not be assigned to that machine again, she was forced to operate it on another occasion. As a result, she suffered further injury and was off work for five weeks. The employee applied for workers' compensation benefits but they were initially withheld because her employer disputed the claim. Shortly thereafter, the employee was laid off and not recalled to work. She subsequently filed a complaint with the appropriate agency for the employer's failure to provide her with statutory notice of termination. In addition, the employee commenced an action for wrongful

---

[139] *Warren v. Orlick Industries Ltd.* (1993), 47 C.C.E.L. 198 (Ont. Ct. (Gen. Div.)).
[140] *McLean v. Humpty Dumpty Foods Ltd.* (1994), 144 N.B.R. (2d) 63 (Q.B.).

dismissal. The court found that the supervisor was wrong to require the employee to work beside someone suffering from a transmittable skin disease or to require the employee to continue operating a machine that was harmful to her health. Because of provisions in the relevant occupational health and safety legislation, the supervisor's conduct was unlawful. The court confirmed that the legislation gave the employee an express right to refuse to perform an act that she had reasonable grounds for believing was likely to endanger her health or safety or the health and safety of others in the workplace. In turn, the employer was prohibited from disciplining or dismissing the employee for exercising her right to refuse unsafe work. Because the employee had lawfully refused to carry out work on both occasions, the court concluded that her dismissal was unjustified. The court also noted that employees could not be dismissed for bringing legitimate claims against their employers for statutory benefits to which they are entitled.[141]

It is clear that employees are entitled to refuse work if unsafe or dangerous conditions exist in the workplace. However, their refusals will only be justified if they have reasonable grounds for believing that their health and safety or the health and safety of others in the workplace is likely to be endangered. Some of the factors that may be considered when deciding whether an employee had reasonable grounds to refuse work include:

(a) the employee's apparent motives for refusing to carry out the work;
(b) the employee's experience with the job and workplace;
(c) the employee's knowledge of the circumstances at the time the work was refused; and
(d) whether anxiety associated with the employee's safety concerns affected his or her judgment at the time the work was refused.[142]

If it is found that an employee did not have reasonable grounds for refusing a work assignment, a case for cause could potentially be supported. Similarly, where unsafe conditions have been corrected, an employee may not be able to continue to refuse work. Once the problems have been investigated and remedied, an employee's continued refusal to work will be viewed with suspicion, especially where occupational health and safety investigators have concluded that unsafe conditions no longer exist.[143] In these circumstances, dismissal may be warranted, particularly where the employer's operations are prejudiced as a result of the continued work refusals.

---

[141] See also discussion under Heading 30, "Seeking Legal Advice or Initiating Claim Against Employer", of this Part.
[142] *Miller and Canadian National Railways (Re)*, [1980] 2 C.L.R.B.R. 344 (Can.).
[143] See, *e.g.*, *United Electrical, Radio & Machine Workers of Canada, Local 550 and Camco Inc. (Re)*, [1985] O.L.R.B. Rep. Oct. 1431.

The last point to be made on this subject relates to specific exemptions in occupational health and safety legislation that do not permit employees to refuse work in certain circumstances.[144] For instance, in some jurisdictions the right to refuse work is limited where the circumstances which give rise to the employee's refusal are an inherent part of the employee's work activity or constitute normal conditions of employment. The right to refuse work is also limited where a refusal would directly endanger the life, health or safety of another person. In these circumstances, an employer would have more success establishing just cause for termination where an employee refused to carry out work.

Overview

An employee's legitimate refusal to carry out unsafe work does not constitute just cause for termination. In fact, a dismissal on this basis violates occupational health and safety legislation. However, it is sometimes possible to establish a case for cause where an employee's refusal to work interferes with or prejudices the safe and proper conduct of an employer's business and where the following factors and circumstances exist:

1. The employee did not have reasonable grounds for believing that his or her health and safety was likely to be endangered by certain workplace conditions.
2. The employee continued to refuse work, even after an investigation was carried out and investigators concluded that the workplace posed no safety risk.
3. There was an improper motive behind the employee's decision to refuse work.
4. The employee's refusal to work posed a serious health and safety risk to others.
5. The employee refused work in circumstances that are an inherent part of the work activity or that constitute normal conditions of employment.

12 ✧ ABSENTEEISM AND LATENESS

One of the basic elements of an employment contract is the requirement that an employee attend work regularly and on a timely basis. In most employment relationships, the hours an employee is expected to work are specified by the employment contract. Where times are not specified and unless otherwise stated, it is implied that the employee will work in accordance with the company's normal business hours or as dictated by the nature of the particular job. Being absent during the required work period without a reasonable or

---

[144] Once again, employers are advised to review the provisions of the occupational health and safety legislation applicable in their jurisdiction.

legitimate excuse will typically amount to a breach of the employment contract. Similarly, consistently failing to report to work at the required time may amount to behaviour that allows an employer to end the employment relationship. In this regard, absenteeism and lateness may be viewed as examples of employee misconduct that can constitute grounds for just cause termination. In determining whether dismissal is justified, the employer will generally have the right to ask why an employee was absent or late and to require that medical documentation be provided for absences of long duration.

(a) Absenteeism

In the context of cause for termination, absenteeism refers to an absence from work that is not the product of a specific serious illness. Absence resulting from a temporary illness does not constitute cause for dismissal, but where it results from a permanent illness, a dismissal could be justified if the employment contract becomes frustrated.[145]

In general, one isolated unauthorized absence does not constitute just cause for termination.[146] However, a single occurrence may justify dismissal if it occurs at a critical time for the employer. Where, for example, an employee is told that his or her presence on a particular day is crucial and that non-attendance will lead to the termination of employment, an employer has sufficient cause to dismiss the employee for failing to attend without a reasonable excuse.[147] On the other hand, if an absent employee was unaware of how important it was to be in attendance on a critical day, a single absence will only justify termination if it is combined with other misconduct.[148]

Courts consider all the circumstances when determining whether an unauthorized absence amounts to just cause for termination. For instance, it is generally true that an employee on a leave of absence has an obligation to advise the employer if he or she will not be back at work on the scheduled day of return. Even so, failure to meet this obligation does not automatically give rise to just cause for termination. In one case, for instance, a dismissal on this basis was not justified where the employee was on a doctor-recommended rest leave following the death of her mother and an extended period of long stressful work days.[149] Given that the employee was fairly senior and that the employer was aware of the circumstances surrounding the leave of absence, including the doctor's recommendation, the court concluded that it was not proper to dismiss the employee.

---

[145] See also discussion under Heading 14, "Illness and Disability", of this Part.

[146] *Bowie v. Motorola Canada Ltd.* (1991), 44 C.C.E.L. 307 (Ont. Ct. (Gen. Div.)).

[147] *Aeichele v. Jim Pattison Industries Ltd.* (1992), 44 C.C.E.L. 296 (B.C.S.C.).

[148] *Nossal v. Better Business Bureau of Metropolitan Toronto Inc.* (1985), 19 D.L.R. (4th) 547 (Ont. C.A.).

[149] *Baxter v. Hallmark Ford Sales Ltd.* (1995), 17 C.C.E.L. (2d) 71 (B.C.S.C.).

A court will often be influenced by evidence that an organization's business was prejudiced by the unauthorized absence of an employee. In one instance, an employee unilaterally and without approval took a holiday and made no arrangements for the continuance of her employer's services in her absence. The court held that this went to the root of her employment contract and amounted to just cause.[150] Even when a business has not actually been harmed, sufficient prejudice may be shown by demonstrating that the employee's conduct had the potential of putting the company's operation at risk. In one case, the employee took a vacation at a time when the company specifically said he was not to take holidays.[151] The employee was told he was needed because the company was short-staffed and had to handle a very large contract. Moreover, the employee was specifically warned that if he did leave, he would have no job to come back to upon his return. The employee chose to take his vacation despite the warning, thereby prejudicing the company's business and putting its operations at risk. The court held that his conduct amounted to cause for dismissal. In contrast, it can seldom be said that an employer will seriously be prejudiced by an absence where the employee arranges for a replacement to cover his or her duties. In that situation, it is doubtful that just cause for termination will be established.[152]

(b) Lateness

Lateness or frequent tardiness refers to a pattern of arriving or reporting to work after the required start time. In certain circumstances, lateness will amount to just cause for termination. However, the employer must clearly and unequivocally warn the employee that lateness as defined is not going to be tolerated and may lead to dismissal. Bringing this fact to an employee's attention in an offhand manner is insufficient, especially where an organization has a very relaxed atmosphere and a laid-back working environment.[153] On the other hand, an intolerance for lateness may be evident in some workplaces, as in cases where the success of a company's business depends heavily on the punctuality and attendance of its employees. In an industrial plant, for instance, production lines are often organized in a way that makes it crucial for employees to be on time. Where an employee's failure to be on time results in delay and disruption to the organization's production, it is usually easier to prove cause, particularly if the employer can also demonstrate a loss

---

[150] *Gilman v. Society for Information Children* (2003), 27 C.C.E.L. (3d) 165 (B.C.S.C.).
[151] *Bratti v. F & W Wholesale Ltd.* (1989), 28 C.C.E.L. 142 (B.C. Co. Ct.).
[152] See *Warren v. Super Drug Markets Ltd.* (1965), 54 D.L.R. (2d) 183 (Sask Q.B.); *MacDonald v. Richardson Greenshields of Canada Ltd.* (1985), 12 C.C.E.L. 22 (B.C.S.C.).
[153] *Andover & Perth United Farmers' Cooperative Ltd. v. Skaarup* (1987), 18 C.C.E.L. 63 (N.B.C.A.).

in profits.[154] Similarly, the case for cause is stronger where the tardiness damages existing harmonious relationships between co-workers, harms customer relations or is seen as an example of wilful disobedience.[155]

A company must be careful not to condone chronic lateness if it wants to dismiss an employee on this basis. An organization cannot rely on past instances of tardiness that were initially overlooked and not acted on. In other words, an employer will not have legal grounds or cause to dismiss an employee where it has a history of tolerating tardiness. A court will usually conclude that lateness was condoned if an organization does not take action when one would reasonably expect action to be taken. For example, if instances of lateness are severe in a particular year, one would expect the employer to address the issue and impose disciplinary measures against the employee at that time. Failure to do so implies that the organization is prepared to accept the employee's behaviour notwithstanding continued episodes of tardiness.[156] However, persistent lateness will typically amount to just cause if the employer takes responsive action when the conduct occurs.[157]

(c) Absenteeism and Lateness as Grounds for Termination

Several instances of either tardiness or unauthorized absences are likely to be sufficient to justify a termination where the employer has spent the prerequisite time and effort warning the employee about the conduct and advising the employee that his or her job will be in jeopardy if the conduct does not improve.[158] Failing to warn an employee about absenteeism or chronic lateness often leaves an employer unable to prove a case for cause because the employee's conduct in this respect is seen as having been condoned. It is for this reason that warnings to the employee should be explicit, clear and in writing.

There are some factors that mitigate in cases of dismissal thus preventing a court from finding cause on the basis of absenteeism or tardiness. Two such factors are a strong work record without a history of absenteeism or lateness, and the existence of a legitimate reason for an absence or instance of tardiness. Where medical reasons are provided and depending on the employee's ability to perform his or her job, human rights legislation may create an obligation on the employer to accommodate the employee. In such

---

[154] *Cardenas v. Canada Dry Ltd.* (1985), 10 C.C.E.L. 1 (Ont. Dist. Ct.).

[155] *Riley v. Crown Trust Co.* (1977), 5 A.R. 1 (S.C.); *Millett v. Saint John (City)* (1986), 70 N.B.R. (2d) 233 (Q.B.).

[156] See *Pagnotta v. Read Jones Christoffersen Ltd.* (1990), 29 C.C.E.L. 5 (Alta. Q.B.).

[157] The preceding comments on condonation are equally relevant to absenteeism as a ground for dismissal.

[158] *Andover & Perth United Farmers' Cooperative Ltd. v. Skaarup, supra,* footnote 153.

a case, lateness or absenteeism could be an aspect of the illness the employer has to accept.[159] Another mitigating factor exists where employees have fairly wide latitude in setting their own hours. This will typically be the case if the employee is in a more senior or executive position. It therefore tends to be more difficult to prove a case for cause against such an employee on the basis of absenteeism and lateness.

A number of considerations that facilitate a case for cause have already been mentioned but are worth repeating. They include evidence that the employer's interests are prejudiced by an employee's absenteeism or lateness and clear warnings by the employer that further absences or instances of tardiness will not be tolerated. Another factor that makes just cause for termination easier to establish is the deliberate intention of an employee to be absent or late.

When building a case for cause on the basis of absenteeism or lateness, it is very important for the employer to document all occurrences of absenteeism and lateness, and to use a progressive pattern of warnings in disciplining the employee. Written warnings are best for proving just cause because the court can rely on them to conclude that the employee was told that further occurrences of absenteeism and/or lateness would lead to dismissal and that opportunities were given to the employee to change his or her behaviour.

The effects of an employee's absenteeism or lateness on an organization should also be well documented. In particular, the employer should note whether production is affected, whether the company has to pay another employee overtime to cover for the absent employee and whether the work schedule is affected. As already noted, the more adverse the effects experienced by an organization, the stronger will be the case for cause.

Finally, a company would be wise to implement a clear policy on absenteeism and lateness. The policy should set out the protocol and procedures an employee must follow when advising the employer about anticipated absences or late arrivals to work. The policy must also be applied consistently, otherwise a court may find that the employer tolerated or condoned absences and occurrences of lateness.[160]

Overview

While single instances of absenteeism or chronic lateness will usually not justify summary dismissal, they can be grounds for just cause termination

---

[159] See discussion under Heading 14, "Illness and Disability", of this Part.
[160] See also discussion under Heading 8, "Breaching Employer Policies or Rules", of this Part.

in certain circumstances. The presence of the following factors and circumstances strengthen a case for cause based on absenteeism or lateness:

1. The employee was frequently absent or late.
2. The employer was substantially prejudiced by the employee's absenteeism or lateness.
3. The employee did not occupy a senior position in the organization.
4. The many occurrences of absenteeism or lateness are well documented in the employee's file.
5. The employer provided unambiguous warnings about an employee's absenteeism or lateness that clearly informed the employee that further conduct in this respect would result in the loss of employment.
6. The employee did not have a legitimate reason for being late or absent and made no attempt to find a replacement to cover his or her duties.
7. The absenteeism or lateness of the employee was intentional.
8. The absenteeism or lateness was not caused by an illness or disability.

13 ✧ LEAVING WORK WITHOUT PERMISSION

An employer will understandably take issue with an employee's decision to leave work prematurely and without authorization. However, such misconduct will not likely amount to just cause for termination unless it interferes with or is extremely prejudicial to an employer's interests and operations. Where an employer's business suffers damage or faces a risk of potential harm as a direct result of a worker's unauthorized departure, the case for cause is easier to prove.

The requirement of prejudice or potential harm to an employer's interests was satisfied in a case dealing with the dismissal of an employee who operated dangerous electrical machinery used to manufacture and design expensive mold products.[161] The employee was fired for going home before his shift was over and leaving his machine unattended. Annoyed with a supervisor, the employee failed to notify anyone of his departure and in so doing exposed his employer to potentially serious damage and showed disregard for the welfare of his co-workers. In particular, the employer was able to show that leaving the machinery unattended could have damaged the mold that was being worked on, which could have caused the employer to incur substantial repair costs or other losses related to selling a defective product. In addition, a fire could have developed from sparks generated by the equipment and since no one was in the area it would probably not have been extinguished quickly. Such a fire would thus have endangered the safety of those in the

---

[161] *Rankin v. Active Mold and Design (1987) Ltd.*, 92 C.L.L.C. ¶14,007 (Ont. Ct. (Gen. Div.)).

workplace and further increased the risk of harm to the employer's operations. The court concluded that in the circumstances the employee had repudiated his employment contract because his conduct had seriously prejudiced the safe conduct of the employer's business. Just cause for termination was established on this basis alone, although there was other evidence of employee misconduct that could have been relied upon as well.

Even if an employer suffers no substantial pecuniary loss, a dismissal may be justified on the basis of an employee's failure to obey an order relating to when time can be taken off.[162] In one case, for instance, a production manager was dismissed for taking a leave of absence in order to take a one-week trip to Germany made available to him by his son.[163] The manager had specifically been told by his supervisor that authorization for the leave was being denied because two employees were already scheduled to take their holidays during that week. In addition, the supervisor made it clear to the manager that his presence was required and that his decision to take the leave of absence would be treated as his resignation. Notwithstanding this warning, the manager took the week off and his employment was terminated upon his return when he refused to sign a letter of resignation. The court concluded that, by leaving as he did, the manager's conduct was tantamount to resigning from his position. Even if this were not the case, the court said that his actions amounted to just cause for termination despite the fact that the employer had suffered no substantial pecuniary loss. In reaching this decision, the court was primarily influenced by the fact that the manager had specifically been told not to leave and was warned about the consequences he would face if he did. As such, the manager's conduct could be seen as wilfully disobeying the order of a supervisor despite having knowledge of the repercussions.

To decide if just cause for termination has been established, a court will consider whether the dismissed employee acted reasonably in being absent from work without authorization. In one case, for example, it was concluded that just cause for the termination of a hotel's lounge manager did not exist because the manager had not acted in an unreasonable manner.[164] The manager had advised his employer that he needed a week off as he was "whipped" from working 40 days straight. While the employer did not really believe the manager, he was told that he could take a couple of days but not during the upcoming weekend. Despite these instructions, the manager took the weekend off and his employment was terminated as a result. The court concluded that just cause for the manager's dismissal did not exist. Given the fact that

---

[162] See also discussion under Heading 7, "Insubordination", of this Part.
[163] *Ehmcke v. Penetang Bottling Co.* (1992), 41 C.C.E.L. 251 (Ont. Ct. (Gen. Div.)).
[164] *MacNeil v. Ronscott Inc.* (1988), 22 C.C.E.L. 89, supplementary reasons 13 A.C.W.S. (3d) 4 (Ont. H.C.J.).

he had worked 40 days straight without a break, the court regarded his conduct in absenting himself from work on the weekend as reasonable. The following factors were also relied upon to support the court's finding that the employee had acted reasonably:

1. The manager had arranged for his co-worker to look after the lounge in his absence.
2. The employer had no rules in place with respect to the taking of holidays.
3. The manager had taken only one other weekend off during his one year of employment.
4. The manager was never warned that he might be terminated.

Overview

An employee's conduct in absenting himself or herself from work without authorization may amount to just cause for termination in certain fact situations. A case for cause based on such behaviour is strengthened by the existence of the following factors and circumstances:

1. The employee's conduct in leaving work without authorization was harmful or prejudicial to the employer's interests and operations.
2. The employee's absence was in defiance of a specific order by the employer not to leave.
3. The employee was warned of the consequences of leaving without authorization.
4. The employee did not act reasonably by leaving as he or she did.

14 ✧ ILLNESS AND DISABILITY

Although it is possible to justify a termination on the basis of an employee's illness or injury/disability, the task is often an onerous one. To establish just cause for termination, not only must an employee's behaviour be inconsistent with his or her duties and generally prejudicial to the employer's interests, it must also be wilful or deliberate. This last requirement will rarely be satisfied where the essential duties of an employee's job cannot be performed on account of illness or disability. Having said this, an employer may still be able to dismiss an individual based on the "doctrine of frustration". Application of this principle provides that an employment contract will be frustrated if it cannot be performed as a result of some unplanned incident, namely an employee's illness or disability. In this respect, subject to compliance with human rights and workers' compensation legislation (whose provisions may impose onerous obligations on the employer), a termination can be justified where an illness or disability makes it impossible for the employee's duties to be discharged. It is important for an employer to deal appropriately with an employee's disability during employment as well as at the time of dismissal, as a dismissal conducted in bad faith can lead to an employee's entitlement to *Wallace* damages.[165]

(a) Establishing Just Cause

It is difficult to prove a case for cause on the basis of a sick or disabled employee's inability to perform. This is true because most illnesses and disabilities lack the element of wilfulness that is necessary to establish just cause for termination. However, there may be circumstances where an illness or disability is caused by deliberate conduct on the part of an employee and just cause can therefore be established. For example, consider the employee who chooses to participate in motorcycle racing or a similarly dangerous activity. If the employee is repeatedly injured as a result and is often absent from work for prolonged periods, the employer may have grounds to dismiss the employee summarily. The important point to note is that just cause for termination will not exist unless the employee has engaged in wilful or intentional conduct that impairs the proper discharge of employment duties and prejudices the employer's business.

While a case for cause will not succeed if an employee's misconduct is explained by illness or disability, this is only true where the employer is aware of the illness or disability. This knowledge will be inferred where the facts clearly show that the employee is suffering from some ailment but, generally speaking, employees are responsible for advising the employer of any problems affecting their performance or behaviour. Failure to do so may prevent them from relying on the existence of an illness or disability to excuse their behaviour. In one case, for instance, an employee was dismissed when he left the workplace without completing his shift and without shutting off his machinery.[166] He did this despite being fully aware of the potential danger it posed to other workers and the employer's place of business. The employee had also refused to carry out the instructions of a superior and on a number of occasions did not report for work. In his wrongful dismissal action, the employee suggested that his conduct had been caused by emotional and stress-related difficulties. The court refused to accept this explanation because there was no evidence of the employee going to management to discuss his condition or to ask for time off in order to deal with his alleged problems. Accordingly, it was concluded that the employee's conduct amounted

---

[165] *Zorn-Smith v. Bank of Montreal* (2003), 31 C.C.E.L. (3d) 267 (Ont. S.C.J.). See also Heading 8(a), "Wallace Damages", of Part I, "General Concepts", for a more detailed discussion.

[166] *Rankin v. Active Mold and Design (1987) Ltd.*, 92 C.L.L.C. ¶14,007 (Ont. Ct. (Gen. Div.)).

to just cause and that dismissal was warranted since there was no legitimate excuse for his actions.

Where employees become ill or disabled through no fault of their own, a termination can still be justified if there has been frustration of the employment contract. The concept of frustration differs from that of just cause for termination. While the existence of cause warrants a dismissal on the basis of an employee's misconduct, frustration of the employment contract brings the contract to an end without laying blame on either the employer or employee. When a contract is frustrated, the employer is not held liable for dismissing the employee without cause nor will a court conclude that the employee was dismissed for having engaged in misconduct.

A contract of employment will be frustrated when an unforeseen event makes performance of the contract either impossible or fundamentally different than originally contemplated. Subject to human rights and workers' compensation legislation,[167] employers may be able to treat an employee's contract as at an end if the employee loses the capacity to perform required job duties because of illness or disability. However, only an illness or disability that is permanent in nature can frustrate an employment contract and justify dismissal. In this context, the term "permanent" is used to describe a condition that frustrates the object of an employer's and employee's engagement, thereby putting an end (in the business sense) to their relationship.[168] In order to determine whether an illness or disability is sufficiently permanent and whether the employment contract has been frustrated by an employee's incapacity, the overall context of the particular employment situation should be assessed. In this respect, one essential question must be answered. Has the employee been incapacitated to such a degree that further performance of the employee's obligations are impossible or would be substantially different from the performance initially contemplated?[169] If this question is answered in the affirmative after considering a number of cumulative and interrelated factors, it is likely that the employment contract has been frustrated and that dismissal of the employee is therefore justified.

One of the first things an employer should do in any illness or disability case is examine the terms of the employment contract, including any provisions that relate to sick pay. Courts have agreed that contracts dealing with weekly employment are more easily frustrated than those dealing with

---

[167] See discussion under Heading 14(b), "Employees' Statutory Protections", *infra*.

[168] Paraphrasing from *Jackson v. Union Marine Insurance Co.* (1874), L.R. 10 C.P. 125 (Ex. Ch.), as referred to in *Yeager v. R.J. Hastings Agencies Ltd.* (1984), 5 C.C.E.L. 266 (B.C.S.C.), at pp. 288-9.

[169] This question was asked in the English case *Marshall v. Harland & Wolff Ltd.*, [1972] 1 W.L.R. 899 (N.I.R.C.), which also identifies many of the factors currently used by Canadian courts in deciding whether an illness or disability is sufficiently permanent to frustrate an employment contract.

monthly, annual or indefinite employment. Furthermore, a contract will not be frustrated in situations where sick pay is provided and the employee is able to resume his or her duties before the period expires. A contract might also contemplate leaves of absence or expressly provide an employee with the right to take time off work. In one case, for instance, such a contract applied to a company's president and chief operating officer.[170] It specifically entitled him to take time off with pay as he saw fit, as long as the business was operating efficiently. After serving the company for a couple of years, the president took an immediate leave of absence when his doctor told him that his blood pressure was "off the scale". Shortly thereafter, the president was told that his association with the company was being terminated for cause. Although a number of grounds for termination were advanced by the company, one of them related specifically to the president's absence on account of illness. It was ultimately concluded that the president's dismissal was wrongful and, in particular, the court noted that the president had a contractual right to take time off as there was no evidence of the company being unable to function effectively during his absence.

Another factor to consider is the length of time an employee would likely have been employed in the absence of illness or disability. An employment contract is more apt to be frustrated on account of illness or disability if the employment in question is inherently temporary in nature. It is less likely to be frustrated where employment is expected to be long term or for life. A related consideration is the length of the employer-employee relationship. Employment contracts involving long-standing employees are not as readily frustrated as those that relate to employees who have served the employer for a short time. In this respect, it is presumed that longer periods of sickness will have to be tolerated as the employee continues to serve the employer over the years.

The employer should also assess the nature of the sick or disabled employee's position and duties. Where an employee is one of many in the same category, his or her employment contract is likely to survive a longer period of incapacity than that of the employee who occupies an essential and vital position. In one case, for example, the service manager of a car dealership was dismissed after he began to suffer from a stress-related illness that prevented him from adequately performing his many duties.[171] This illness had substantially affected his performance for about 18 months prior to his dismissal. The court concluded that the manager had a permanent disability that brought an end to his employment contract. A primary factor leading to this conclusion was the nature of the manager's employment. In essence, he

---

[170] *Thom v. Goodhost Foods Ltd.* (1987), 17 C.C.E.L. 89, supplementary reasons 5 A.C.W.S. (3d) 329 (Ont. H.C.J.).

[171] *McRae v. Dodge City Auto (1984) Ltd.*, 94 C.L.L.C. ¶14,036 (Sask. Q.B.).

was found to occupy a key position in the organization that was very demanding and involved much more than working "nine to five". Furthermore, it was held that dismissing the manager and replacing him with someone else on a permanent basis was warranted since his employment contract had ultimately been frustrated.

By way of contrast, the court in another case concluded that an employee's incapacity and absence due to illness did not frustrate his employment contract because there was nothing particularly special about his position that required a permanent replacement.[172] The employee was a salesman who handled several accounts for the agent of various clothing manufacturers. Presumably, a number of salespeople worked for the manufacturers' agent and there were other means available to handle the employee's duties during his prolonged absence.

Additional elements to consider are the nature of an employee's illness or disability, the length of time it has already continued and the prospects for recovery. An employment contract will be frustrated more easily where the employee's incapacity because of illness or disability is severe and has persisted or is likely to persist for a substantial period of time. Having said this, be aware that the length of time a disability has persisted will not alone determine whether an employment contract has been frustrated. Instead, the term of incapacity due to illness or disability must be compared to the length of the particular employment relationship. As noted earlier, employers are generally expected to tolerate a longer period of incapacity if the employment contract was intended to be long term and had in fact endured for a substantial amount of time. In *Yeager v. R.J. Hastings Agencies Ltd.*,[173] the employee was "incapacitated" due to illness for two years. During this period, the employee was unable to perform adequately the duties of his job. The court concluded that two years of incapacity did not frustrate the contract of employment because it was intended to be of long duration. The permanency of the employment relationship was demonstrated by the fact that it had survived 30 years. Furthermore, the employee had become a shareholder in the employer's business because it was expected that he would continue working there for a substantial period of time. A contract of employment may likewise not be frustrated by an illness or disability of long duration where the employer knew from the start that the employee's illness was going to be lengthy. This will especially be true if the sick employee was never told throughout his prolonged absence from work that his job might be in jeopardy.[174]

---

[172] *Yeager v. R.J. Hastings Agencies Ltd.*, *supra*, footnote 168.
[173] *Supra*.
[174] See *Zelisko v. "99" Truck Parts & Equipment Ltd.* (1985), 8 C.C.E.L. 201 (B.C.S.C.).

Finally, the effect of an employee's illness or disability on an employer's operations will play a role in deciding whether the employment contract has indeed been frustrated. A court is more likely to conclude that frustration has occurred if the workplace or business of an organization is significantly prejudiced.

As a practice point, employers should note that they can retroactively rely on an employee's permanent disability as justification for dismissal even though the fact that the disability was permanent was not known at the time the employee was dismissed. These were the circumstances in a case involving an employee who was dismissed by a general contracting company while off work on account of an ankle injury.[175] The employee's injury and absence from work were not initially the reasons for his termination. Rather, the employee was dismissed because the company was experiencing financial difficulties. Although the employee was offered termination pay, he did not consider it to be enough and chose to sue the company for wrongful dismissal. After considering the facts, the court concluded that at the time of his dismissal, the employee's injury constituted a permanent disability that left him incapacitated and frustrated the employment contract. The employee's disability was found to be permanent rather than temporary because he was continuing to receive disability benefits and had been receiving them since his dismissal. Further, the employee was still unable to work at the time the wrongful dismissal action was being heard by the court. Accordingly, termination based on frustration of the employment contract was justified notwithstanding that the company was unaware of the employee's permanent disability when the decision was made to terminate his employment.

An employment contract can only be frustrated by a permanent disability where it results in the employee being unable to discharge an essential feature of the job in question. Incapacity on account of illness or disability will not act to frustrate the employment contract if the task that cannot be performed is superfluous in nature and not an occupational requirement. A case on point deals with a residence counsellor who was terminated by his employer who ran a residential school for handicapped children up to 21 years of age.[176] The counsellor developed osteoarthritis during his employment and as a result was unable to lift more than 20 to 30 pounds without difficulty. The school eventually terminated the counsellor when it became clear that he no longer had the capacity to lift and support some of the disabled students. The court concluded that dismissal was justified because the counsellor was suffering from a permanent disability that frustrated his employment contract. The disability was found to be permanent on the basis of objective

---

[175] *MacLellan v. H.B. Contracting Ltd.* (1990), 32 C.C.E.L. 103 (B.C.S.C.).
[176] *Parks v. Atlantic Provinces Special Education Authority Resource Centre for the Visually Impaired* (1991), 87 D.L.R. (4th) 369 (N.S.S.C.A.D.).

medical evidence and the counsellor's own admission that he was "totally disabled" and "unable to perform the substantial duties" of his employment. The employment contract was therefore frustrated since the counsellor's disability had left him permanently incapable of doing any substantial lifting, an essential requirement of his occupation.

(b) Employees' Statutory Protections

The factors in cases of illness and disability that determine whether a termination can be justified must be considered in light of the statutory protections afforded to employees by workers' compensation and human rights legislation. When dealing with a sick or disabled employee, the employer may be required to follow a legislated workers' compensation scheme and always has to comply with human rights legislation. Failure to do either can result in significant legal liability to the employer.

Each of the provinces and territories has workers' compensation laws for the benefit of its jurisdiction's employees. Within some jurisdictions, however, the legislation does not apply to certain exempted employees such as farm labourers, domestics and casual workers. Employers should therefore examine the laws that apply to them and their employees to determine whether any of their employees are excluded from workers' compensation coverage.[177] In any event, where an employee is protected under workers' compensation legislation and suffers a work-related injury (illness and/or disability), the employer must comply with the requirements imposed by the applicable legislation. Some of these laws require employers to reinstate an injured employee where it is possible to do so. Employers may also have an obligation to accommodate an employee's injury or disability up to the point of undue hardship. Changes to the workplace or job may be needed to bring a disabled employee back to work. Although the duty to accommodate is not imposed by all workers' compensation schemes, it will still exist in the appropriate circumstances as a result of the common law and the human rights legislation in certain jurisdictions.

As is the case with workers' compensation laws, human rights legislation exists at the provincial, territorial and federal levels.[178] These laws prohibit employers from discriminating against employees on the basis of a

---

[177] It should be noted that provincial and territorial legislation does not apply to individuals employed by the federal government. Rather, these employees are governed by federal jurisdiction law, namely the *Government Employees Compensation Act*, R.S.C. 1985, c. G-5.

[178] The *Canadian Human Rights Act*, R.S.C. 1985, c. H-6, is federal legislation applicable to employers in federally regulated areas such as banking, aeronautics and railways, while, *e.g.*, in Ontario, the *Human Rights Code*, R.S.O. 1990, c. H.19, applies to all other employers who carry on business in the province.

handicap, regardless of whether or not it arose in the course of employment. However, the prohibition only applies to ongoing and significant impairments. A condition that is temporary in nature does not constitute a handicap for this purpose. Where an employee is terminated on the basis of a physical or mental disability that falls within the ambit of human rights legislation, the employee is entitled to file a complaint of discrimination with the appropriate human rights agency or tribunal. An employer will then have to justify the discrimination and, if the justification is not acceptable, the employer could be required to reinstate the employee. Furthermore, an order may be made requiring the employer to compensate the terminated employee for lost wages, to pay the employee general damages for emotional upset and/or to provide other remedies designed to promote human rights public policy.

In human rights law, the defences available to employers as justification for a termination based on handicap or disability depend on whether the discrimination is characterized as being direct or indirect. Direct discrimination occurs if an employee is dismissed strictly because he or she has a handicap. Where an employee claims that termination is an example of direct discrimination, the employer can attempt to assert that absence of the particular handicap is a "*bona fide* occupational requirement or qualification" ("BFOR"). To establish a BFOR defence, the employer must show that absence of the handicap or disability/illness is a requirement imposed honestly, in good faith and with the sincerely held belief that it is in the best interests of adequate, safe and economical work performance. Further, the employer must show that the requirement is directly related to the performance of the employment concerned, that is, the requirement must be seen as being reasonably necessary to ensure efficient, economical job performance that does not endanger the employee, other workers or the general public. If the employer successfully establishes a BFOR defence, the termination may be justified even though it technically amounts to direct discrimination on the basis of a handicap. In some jurisdictions, however, the employer may be obligated to show that accommodation was not possible.

In many illness and disability cases, the employer's conduct in dismissing an employee involves discrimination that can be characterized as indirect in nature. For instance, termination often occurs because the employee is absent from work and/or lacks the capacity to carry out the duties of a job effectively. This is not direct discrimination since the decision to dismiss the employee is not specifically based on his or her disability. Instead, the decision is based on consequences of the disability and therefore amounts to indirect discrimination. In such circumstances, the BFOR defence is not available to employers. However, a claim of indirect discrimination can be defended if the reason for the employee's dismissal is logically connected to job performance and the employer can demonstrate that the employee could not be accommodated without incurring undue hardship. This duty to accommodate an employee may also be imposed on employers by the common law or the workers' compensation legislation in some jurisdictions.

The duty to accommodate requires employers to accommodate the needs of an employee who is protected from discrimination on the basis of handicap. The purpose of this duty is to give the employee an equal opportunity to perform a job he or she is otherwise qualified to do. However, the law recognizes that the employee's right to be treated without discrimination should be balanced against the employer's right to operate a business in a safe, efficient and economical manner. Accordingly, the employer is required to accommodate an employee only up to the point of "undue hardship". What amounts to undue hardship has not been completely settled by the courts. It largely depends on the circumstances of each case but, practically speaking, employers may have to meet a fairly onerous standard in order to discharge their obligation to accommodate a particular employee.

A number of factors and guiding principles can assist employers in determining the extent of hardship they are required to endure in accommodating an employee. It is clear that some hardship on the part of the employer is expected. In this respect, larger companies or organizations will generally have to endure more hardship than smaller ones before they can successfully demonstrate that accommodation of an employee is not possible. Although the costs of accommodation are considered in calculating an employer's hardship, they must be substantial in order to displace an employer's duty to accommodate. Furthermore, some degree of risk must be accepted by employers in discharging their duty to accommodate. Accordingly, any health and safety risks to the employee or other workers must be clear and significant in order to argue that accommodation is not feasible. Another element to consider is the effect of the accommodation on the morale of other employees. However, more than minor inconvenience to the workplace must be proven before this factor will be given substantial weight. Employers should consider whether interchangeability of the workplace and its facilities is available and in particular whether or not another job for the disabled employee exists within the organization. In the end, the duty to accommodate may require an employer to do one or more of the following things: physically adjust the workplace to assist an employee; tolerate shorter work hours or a certain level of absenteeism; modify work schedules; re-assign job duties; offer the employee an assistance or rehabilitation program; hire an assistant for the employee; and create a new job for the employee.

It has also been recognized that employees have certain obligations in this area. First and foremost, an employee must advise the employer of the need to be accommodated unless the circumstances are such that the need is obvious. Secondly, the employee has an obligation to tell the employer what is required and to co-operate with the employer in order to arrive at a mutually acceptable level of accommodation. In this regard, some hardship may have to be accepted by the employee and, where accommodation to the point of undue hardship is offered, the employee has a reciprocal duty to accommodate the employer or risk the loss of employment. Accordingly, once an employer is able to demonstrate that an employee was dismissed for reasons reasonably connected to job performance and that either the employee was accommodated or that accommodation was impossible to achieve without undue hardship, termination will be justified even though it amounts to indirect discrimination.

Overview

In cases of illness and disability, employers must exercise care and caution if the decision is made to dismiss an employee. Just cause for termination will rarely be established because most illnesses and disabilities lack the necessary element of wilfulness. The better option is to rely on the frustration of contract principle when justifying an employee's dismissal whose illness or disability is permanent in nature. An employee's contract of employment is more likely to be frustrated where any or all of the following factors and circumstances exist:

1. The illness or disability made performance of the employment contract impossible or fundamentally different than originally contemplated.
2. The employment contract dealt with employment for a specified term.
3. The employment contract did not contemplate leaves of absence or expressly provide an employee with the right to take time off work.
4. The employment in question was inherently temporary in nature.
5. The employee had only served the employer for a short period of time.
6. The employee occupied an essential and vital position in the employer's organization that must be filled on a permanent rather than a temporary basis.
7. The employee's incapacity on account of illness or disability was severe and persisted or was likely to persist for a substantial period of time.
8. The employee's illness or disability prejudiced the employer's workplace and/or operations.
9. As a result of the illness or disability, the employee was unable to discharge job duties that are necessary and essential in nature.

For terminations in cases of illness or disability, employers must also consider the effects, if any, of the common law, workers' compensation laws and human rights legislation. An employer may be obliged to reinstate an employee whose injury arose in the course of employment. Moreover, the employer may have a duty to accommodate the needs of any disabled employee up to the point of undue hardship. Where the duty exists, an employer must demonstrate that reasonable accommodation was offered to the employee or that the employee could not be accommodated without the employer incurring undue hardship. A termination can therefore be justified only if the employee refused to accept a reasonable accommodation proposal or if the employer can demonstrate that no reasonable accommodation is available.

15 ✧ UNDERMINING CORPORATE CULTURE

A company can attempt to justify a summary dismissal by claiming that an employee's behaviour has undermined or disrupted its "corporate culture". Generally speaking, corporate culture considerations relate to the smooth functioning of an organization's operations and the attempt to maintain a workplace with minimum conflict and maximum productivity. Whether or not a termination based on these considerations is warranted depends on the degree of disruption to the employer's operations and the employee's discharge of duties, and to the adequacy of warnings given to the employee about the disruptive conduct.

Examples of misconduct that have been recognized as potentially impairing an organization's corporate culture are attitudinal problems, such as unco-operative behaviour, and personality conflicts.[179] However, any behaviour that is wholly inconsistent with the proper discharge of an employee's duties or that is unduly prejudicial to the interests of an employer can be detrimental to a company's make-up and can therefore justify a dismissal without notice.

Just cause is likely to exist where a company can show that the employee is totally incapable of getting along with others and that, as a result, there is constant conflict in the workplace. In one case, it was found that a dismissed employee had great difficulty in dealing amicably with his co-workers during the course of his employment.[180] In particular, the individual was extremely rude and overbearing to those who were not his superiors, belittling them in an abusive manner. As a result, the employee became a disruptive force in his department and was the reason for a substantial drop in morale. Several complaints were made and grievances filed about the employee's behaviour and he was told to change his ways. Despite these directions, the employee's conduct remained the same and he was subsequently dismissed without notice. The court ultimately concluded that just cause for termination existed even though the employee had not specifically been warned that his job was in jeopardy. This conclusion was reached on account of the prejudicial effect

---

[179] See reviews of these grounds for termination under Heading 18, "Unco-operative Behaviour", and Heading 21, "Personality Conflicts", in this Part.

[180] *Fonceca v. McDonnell Douglas Canada Ltd.* (1983), 1 C.C.E.L. 51 (Ont. H.C.J.).

that the employee's conduct and personality had on his employer's operations and because both were incompatible with the proper discharge of the employee's duties.

In most instances, just cause for termination exists if a managerial employee behaves in a manner that jeopardizes the morale of the employer's workplace and could detrimentally affect the proper conduct of the employer's operations. In one case, the branch manager of a bank was dismissed because he berated and reprimanded his staff daily and treated his customers rudely.[181] The bank was able to demonstrate that the manager had a major problem in handling staff and customers and that he was extremely overbearing and intimidating. As a direct result of his behaviour, the morale in the branch deteriorated substantially and there was a very high employee turnover rate. After considering the many complaints filed in respect of the manager's conduct, he was confronted by the bank with its concerns. On two separate occasions, he was warned that his behaviour had to improve and on the second of these occasions he was told that it was the last chance he would be given to show that his behaviour had changed. After a reasonable period of time had passed, the manager's conduct and management style continued in the same manner as before and his employment was therefore terminated. The court concluded that termination was justified because the manager's misconduct was detrimental to the proper conduct of the bank's operations and was likely to result in the lessening of services, a loss of customers and fewer transactions. Simply put, the bank was entitled to act before its business was destroyed and rightly dismissed the manager summarily for cause.

Although behaviour that jeopardizes the morale and efficiency of an employer's business can warrant a termination without notice, this will not be true if the employer has condoned or sanctioned the employee's misconduct. In one case, for instance, a company's corporate controller was extremely abusive to his staff and to the employees of other departments.[182] When subordinates made errors either big or small, the controller would reprimand them in a loud and obnoxious manner by using graphic, offensive and foul language. This kind of abuse was unleashed several times a week and made his staff feel uncomfortable, embarrassed, tense and distressed. In effect, the controller's staff and surrounding employees were totally intimidated by him. Three staff members eventually walked out on their jobs and resigned in protest of the controller's abuse. Even after this incident, the company continued to employ the controller until a representative from the company's British office recommended that he be fired. Following termination, the controller commenced an action for wrongful dismissal and the company responded by asserting that just cause for his termination existed. The court

---

[181] *Perham v. Canada Trust Co.* (1988), 23 C.C.E.L. 277 (B.C.S.C.).
[182] *Miller v. Wackenhut of Canada Ltd.* (1989), 31 C.C.E.L. 245 (Ont. Dist. Ct.).

agreed that the controller's abuse of and disrespect for his subordinates was inappropriate behaviour, especially for someone in a managerial position. Furthermore, the court said the cumulative effect of the controller's conduct on the company's morale and make-up would ordinarily have justified dismissal. In this case, however, the company had condoned the manager's abuse and denigration of employees. In particular, management had allowed such conduct to continue unabated and had specifically approved of it by rejecting the controller's offer to resign after the walk-out of the three staff members. The court also found that, despite his "boorish and obnoxious manner", the controller had been rewarded with promotions and raises. Because his abusive behaviour had been accepted and even encouraged, the court concluded that the company was precluded from relying on it as grounds for summary dismissal.

Another type of behaviour that can potentially affect the corporate culture of an organization is an employee's overzealous ambition. Although ambition is usually a positive trait, if it disrupts the smooth functioning of a company's management, it may constitute just cause for termination. For example, in *Green v. Confederation Life Insurance Co.*,[183] the assistant vice-president and in-house lawyer of a life insurance company was dismissed summarily because of his ambitious tendencies. There, the company was able to show that the employee was intent on eventually becoming president of the organization and that he would not allow anything to stand in his way. While on his quest, the employee threatened the head of the company's legal department in respect of a colleague's proposed promotion that was harmful to his own aspirations. In addition, the employee threatened to ruin the careers and reputations of three junior lawyers if they did not support his plans for advancement. After considering all the facts, the court concluded that the company had ample and just cause to terminate the employee because his ambition was counter-productive to the smooth management of the company.

Overview

Matters relating to the "corporate culture" of a company can constitute just cause for termination as long as they are not condoned or sanctioned by the employer. Where an employee's conduct disrupts the smooth functioning of an organization's operations and causes conflict in the workplace, a termination is likely to be justified. The case for cause will be strengthened by any or all of the following factors and circumstances:

1. The actual or potential disruption to the employer's operations was substantial.
2. The employee was warned that his or her conduct had to improve.

---

[183] (1985), 10 C.C.E.L. 109 (Ont. H.C.J.).

3. The alleged misconduct was detrimental to the proper discharge of the employee's duties.
4. The misbehaviour was caused by personality traits of the employee that were unlikely to change.
5. The employee was totally incapable of getting along with others in the workplace.
6. The misconduct involved extreme abuse or denigration of subordinate staff members by a managerial employee.

16 ✧ CONFLICTS OF INTEREST

Employees are expected to refrain from engaging in conduct that conflicts with the interests of their employers. A conflict of interest in the employment context generally refers to an employee doing something for his or her own benefit that runs counter to the best interests of the employer's business. To a certain degree, the common law has defined what constitutes a conflict of interest. However, specific situations that would, as far as the employer is concerned, create conflicts can be detailed in the policies and guidelines that an employer establishes.

Both real and potential conflicts of interest can be grounds for just cause for termination. In cases where a policy relating to the specific type of conflict was established by the employer, employers will likely have an easier time establishing just cause for termination when the conflict involved situations where employees: were competing with their employer; had acquired some benefit or advantage to which they were not entitled; had personal involvement or dealings with clients; or were involved in some "miscellaneous" conflict situation.

(a) Competing with Employer

A condition imposed on all employees is that they not compete with their employers' business unless they are given permission to do so. Generally speaking, the most common way in which an employee can breach this condition is by creating a company that operates in the same industry as that of the employer. A conflict of interest will be found to exist in this situation. An employee is expected to be attentive, diligent and loyal while carrying out his or her employment duties and this is rarely possible where an employee owns a business similar in nature to that of the employer; the personal interests and employment duties of the employee are bound to conflict with each other.

The principle that competition with an employer will amount to conflict and justify termination was demonstrated in the case of a senior management officer who incorporated a company that competed with his employer's business.[184] The company was created so the officer could bid for work on a project being planned by one of the employer's customers, and the services provided by the new company were the same as those of the employer's business; therefore, the officer was directly competing with his employer. To make matters worse, the officer acted dishonestly by giving the customer the impression that he was acting in the interests of the employer and not his own. When his actions were discovered, the officer was fired on the basis that his behaviour constituted a conflict of interest and a breach of his duty of loyalty owed to the employer. The court concluded that the officer had shown disloyalty by competing with his employer's business and attempting to acquire an opportunity to the employer's exclusion. Furthermore, the court noted that proof of an actual conflict of interest was not required because an employee's dismissal could be justified where the potential for conflict is proven. In the circumstances of this case, the officer's disloyalty revealed a potential for conflict and therefore justified his dismissal.

Competition with an employer is even more likely to exist where the employer has established a clear policy against such conduct. In one case, for instance, a salesman started his own company to operate in the same general industry as that of his employer.[185] This violated the employer's conflict of interest policy which provided that no salespersons were to represent any products or services other than those of the employer. When the existence of the salesman's company was discovered, he was dismissed without notice. The court concluded that the dismissal was justified because the salesman's conduct constituted a conflict of interest. In particular, the court found that the salesman had been carrying on a full-time business that was not wholly outside the scope of his employment duties. Further, by secretly carrying on this business during the course of his employment, the salesman was seen by the court as breaching the employer's conflict of interest policy and his employment contract. Accordingly, a case for cause based on conflict of interest was successfully proven.

Even if an employer's business is in the process of being shut down, a conflict of interest can still arise if the employee establishes a company that operates in the same industry. This is especially true where the employee acts in a deceitful manner as in one case where a publishing company decided to close its "direct book sales" division.[186] The employee who acted as the division's president assisted in the shutting down process. While doing this, the employee started a business in the same field and began to transfer books

---

[184]   *Duguay v. Maritime Welding and Rentals Ltd.* (1989), 28 C.C.E.L. 126 (N.B.Q.B.).
[185]   *Edwards v. Lawson Paper Converters Ltd.* (1984), 5 C.C.E.L. 99 (Ont. H.C.J.).
[186]   *Aasgaard v. Harlequin Enterprises Ltd.* (1993), 48 C.C.E.L. 192 (Ont. Ct. (Gen. Div.)), affd 70 A.C.W.S. (3d) 80 (C.A.).

from the employer's company to his own. When the books were ultimately sold, the employee attributed only their original cost to the employer's business while the rest of the proceeds were allocated to his company. Not only were the transactions not authorized by the employer, they were intentionally concealed by the employee's reporting methods. The court concluded that the employee had put himself in a position of conflict by establishing his business while still working for the employer, by not disclosing the existence of the business and by misappropriating the employer's inventory.

It also appears that an employee can be put in a conflict of interest position by family members who compete with the employer's business. This will especially be true where the employee is an integral part of the employer's organization. These were the facts in a case that involved a sales manager who was employed by a plating line company.[187] The manager was the organization's only salesperson and she soon became a key employee acquiring substantial knowledge about the company and the plating industry. At some point after her employment began, the manager's common law spouse started an enterprise that eventually evolved into a plating company. When the employer learned that the manager's spouse operated a competing business and that the manager's son was one of its employees, she was fired for being in a position of actual or potential conflict of interest. The court concluded that the circumstances amounted to a potential conflict and agreed with the principle that marriage or cohabitation with a particular person can create just cause for termination in some circumstances. The facts of the situation at hand showed that the manager herself did nothing to direct business away from her employer's business and that it had suffered no harm in this respect. However, the employer was able to show that potential conflict or prejudice existed since it was reasonable to assume that the manager was somewhat informed about her spouse's commercial and competing activities. It was therefore found that the manager's knowledge in the employer's company and her active role in its business were inconsistent with her continued common law relationship. Accordingly, although the facts seemed to indicate a second possible ground for termination, the manager's dismissal could be justified solely on the basis of potential conflict of interest.

Some early cases on conflicts of interest suggested that competing with one's employer was grounds for summary dismissal regardless of the degree of competition involved. This principle has been somewhat moderated in Ontario, particularly in the absence of a conflict of interest policy. It now appears that a conflict will only exist if the employer can establish that there was in fact actual or planned competition. Furthermore, the competition must be objectively clear and not just the employer's unfounded perception. Finally, the success of a case for cause based on competition will usually

---

[187] *Laverty v. Cooper Plating Inc.* (1987), 17 C.C.E.L. 44 (Ont. Dist. Ct.).

depend on the degree of actual or potential interference with the employer's interests, together with the character of the employee's "competitive" conduct and the nature of his or her employment duties. In this regard, the following factors should be considered: the nature of the work performed by the employee outside the course of employment; the employee's position in the employer's business; whether the employer specifically prohibited outside work or activities; whether there was any dishonesty on the part of the employee; whether the outside work was actively pursued by the employee; and whether the employee used the employer's resources to obtain or perform the work.

All of these factors were considered in the case of an engine mechanic who was fired for performing engine repair work on his own time.[188] The employer took the position that the mechanic was competing with him and that dismissal without notice was therefore justified. The court, however, concluded that the outside work performed by the mechanic did not constitute just cause for his termination. The court noted that the work was minor in nature since it consisted of engine repairs for the mechanic's family, friends or acquaintances on a few occasions and with only modest compensation being received. The court also noted that the mechanic did not hold a management or sales position and that the employer had never explicitly prohibited him from engaging in outside work. Furthermore, there was no evidence of dishonesty on the part of the mechanic and he had not used the employer's resources to do the repairs performed on his own time. As a consequence of these factors, the employer's case for cause based on competition was unsuccessful.

In another case, just cause for termination based on competition was also not established when it was held that the employer had a duty to warn the employee that his conduct was being perceived as a conflict of interest.[189] The employee worked for a newspaper as an advertising salesman. One of his hobbies was bass fishing and he established an association for bass fishermen. To promote the sport and the association, the salesman published a newsletter, the costs of which were covered by selling advertisement space to local businesses. The newspaper took the view that both the publication and the soliciting of advertisers were clear conflicts of interest that justified the salesman's dismissal. However, the court concluded that just cause for termination did not exist and noted the following factors:

1. The salesman was not a managerial employee.
2. He had no intention of competing with the newspaper for advertisers but was simply promoting a recreational activity on his own time.

---

[188]   *Segin v. Hewitt* (1993), 1 C.C.E.L. (2d) 5 (Ont. Ct. (Gen. Div.)).
[189]   *Atkins v. Windsor Star* (1994), 2 C.C.E.L. (2d) 229 (Ont. Ct. (Gen. Div.)).

3. He had not used the employer's resources or interfered with the newspaper's advertising revenue.
4. The newspaper had no policy about extracurricular activities or conflicts of interest.

The court added that the newspaper should have provided its employees with express directions about its views on outside activities and conflicts. In effect, the court concluded that publishing a newsletter on one occasion did not amount to actual or potential conflict. The court did recognize that a potential for conflict would have existed if the newsletter had been published on a recurring basis. Because it was published only once and the employer had no policy against such activity, the court said the salesman should have been warned that his job would be lost if the newsletter continued.

Although planned competition with the employer's business constitutes a conflict of interest, this is only true where it is the employee's intention to compete in the course of his or her employment. In this regard and unless an employment contract prohibits it, individuals can take some steps in preparation for a post-employment business that will ultimately compete with their employers. However, if confidential information acquired in the course of employment is used to prepare for such a business, the employer does have just cause to terminate the employee.[190] Similarly, just cause for dismissal exists if the employee is in a fiduciary position.[191]

Another way that employees have been found to compete with their employers is by soliciting their clients for personal benefit as occurred in a case concerning an employee who was the sole consultant of an employee-benefits consulting firm.[192] The consultant solicited a number of the firm's clients for the purpose of persuading them to appoint him rather than the firm as their agent. The court concluded that there was clearly just cause for termination because the consultant had breached the obligations he owed to be loyal to the firm and to act in good faith. In so doing, the consultant had placed himself in a conflict of interest where his personal ambitions were pursued to the firm's detriment.

As in all cases of employee misconduct, just cause for termination based on attempts to compete with the employer's business will fail if the employee's actions have been condoned. Nonetheless, the courts have said that employers may take a reasonable period of time to decide whether an employee should be terminated for competing with the employer's business.

---

[190] See *Leith v. Rosen Fuels Ltd.* (1984), 5 C.C.E.L. 184 (Ont. H.C.J.); *Billows v. Canarc Forest Products Ltd.* (2003), 27 C.C.E.L. (3d) 188 (B.C.S.C.).

[191] See discussion under Heading 17, "Breaching Fiduciary Duties", of this Part.

[192] *Coughlin, Welton Beauchamp Inc. v. McAlear* (1996), 61 A.C.W.S. (3d) 289 (Ont. Ct. (Gen. Div.)).

In a case already examined,[193] for example, the employer waited almost six months before firing a senior management officer for incorporating a company that competed with the employer's business. When the competing company's existence was discovered by the employer, the officer was told that the matter would be fully investigated before any steps were taken. After approximately six months, the officer was ultimately dismissed. The court concluded that the employer could not be faulted for exercising caution and investigating the extent of the officer's misconduct to be sure that it warranted termination. The officer had served the employer's company well for many years and the employer wanted to be certain that his misconduct did in fact warrant termination. Accordingly, the court did not infer that the actions of the officer had been excused. Having said this, it should be noted that in most instances and unless legitimate reasons for a delay exist, a case for cause will likely fail if an employer waits too long before dismissing the employee.

(b) Acquiring an Advantage or Benefit

Conflicts of interest often arise where employees acquire some advantage or benefit from their position of employment to which they are not entitled. A common situation that falls into this category of conflicts involves accepting gifts or favours from those who do business with the employer. Such conduct tends to raise an impression of partiality, thereby constituting a conflict and justifying termination since an employer has the right to demand employee impartiality and loyalty. Just cause for termination on this basis is especially likely to exist where the conduct of accepting gifts or benefits is hidden from the employer and is expressly prohibited by an actively enforced company policy. In one case, for instance, a manager obtained free tickets to Las Vegas without his employer's knowledge from an advertiser doing business with the company.[194] The manager's conduct breached a clear company policy on conflicts because the company's regional manager was supposed to decide whether "trade" tickets offered by advertisers should be accepted and, if so, to whom they would be given. The court concluded that the manager's unauthorized and deceptive acceptance of the tickets created a potential conflict because the employer's position with the advertiser could be compromised. This conclusion was supported by the fact that the manager was in a position to influence the company's advertising activities. In this regard, the manager might feel obliged to prefer the advertiser over others in return for having obtained the benefit of a free trip. The court also found that the employer's trust and confidence in the manager had been impaired. For all of

---

[193] *Duguay v. Maritime Welding and Rentals Ltd.*, *supra*, footnote 184.
[194] *Durand v. Quaker Oats Company Canada Ltd.* (1990), 32 C.C.E.L. 63 (B.C.C.A.).

these reasons, just cause for termination on the basis of potential conflict was established.

A case for cause will likely not succeed, however, if it is common practice in an industry for employees to receive promotional gifts directly from suppliers or clients. This is especially true in the absence of a company policy on the matter and where the employee accepts such a gift without intending to deceive the employer.[195]

Another way in which a conflict can arise occurs when an employee acquires an advantage or benefit that should otherwise have been enjoyed by the employer. This will amount to just cause for termination in most circumstances. In one case, for example, a car dealership was deprived of the benefit of a sale by its sales manager.[196] Earlier, the manager had personally guaranteed the loan for a customer's purchase of a new car from the dealership. The purchaser became dissatisfied with the car soon afterward and returned it to the manager who was able to sell it to another customer. Since it was the manager and not the dealership who owned the car at that point, the dealership gained no benefit from the transaction. Rather, it was the manager who benefited because his liability for the car loan was reduced and he received a modest amount of cash as a result of the second sale. The court concluded that the manager had breached his employment contract by putting his personal interests before those of the dealership, thereby placing himself in a conflict of interest position. Accordingly, the decision to terminate the manger's employment without notice was justified.

A conflict of interest also exists when an employee's position is used to gain some advantage not contemplated or authorized by the employer. The conflict is created by the fact that the employee intentionally uses his or her position to acquire a greater amount of compensation than the employer originally agreed to provide. This is exactly what happened in the case of a plant supervisor who was fired for misusing his position and deceiving his employer.[197] The supervisor devised a scheme whereby he rented a warehouse from his employer at a very low rent. He did this under the name of a friend in order to disguise the arrangement. The court concluded that the supervisor had caused his interests to conflict with those of the employer by using his position to secretly rent the warehouse and to set the monthly amounts that he would be required to pay. As a consequence, the employer had just cause to terminate the supervisor's employment summarily.

---

[195] See *Kreager v. Davidson* (1992), 44 C.C.E.L. 261 (B.C.C.A.).
[196] *Andrew v. Kamloops Lincoln Mercury Sales Ltd.* (1994), 7 C.C.E.L. (2d) 228 (B.C.S.C.).
[197] *Smith v. Reichhold Ltd.* (1989), 26 C.C.E.L. 229 (B.C.C.A.), leave to appeal to S.C.C. refused 103 N.R. 398.

A similar type of conflict that can justify termination occurs where an employee uses his position to convey an undeserved and fraudulent benefit upon a third party. A stationary engineer in one case was terminated for this reason.[198] He worked in a city works department and was involved in the execution and supervision of job contracts awarded by tender. The city alleged that the engineer had improperly influenced the tendering process so that his friend's contracting company would be awarded certain jobs. The engineer was seen as having fraudulently preferred his friend's company at the city's expense. Furthermore, it was alleged that the engineer had not properly supervised the company in its execution of the contracts it was granted. The court agreed that an employee's planned and fraudulent preference of a friend's company at his employer's expense places the employee in a conflict position and is just cause for termination. However, it was concluded that the city had not proven its allegations. At the very most, the city had been able to establish that the engineer had given his friend more allowance in terms of how the contracts were performed than he should have. After considering the engineer's long and satisfactory service record, the court concluded that this conduct warranted a reprimand and not dismissal.

The court also noted the doctrine of near cause, but did not adopt it. The appeal court ruled that there was authority for applying the principle of near cause and, therefore, the trial judge was correct in reducing the employee's notice. The Supreme Court of Canada, however, rejected all arguments relating to near cause and remitted the case to the trial court to determine the appropriate amount of notice.

(c) Having Personal Involvement or Dealings with Employer's Clients, Customers or Suppliers

Conflicts of interest often exist as a result of an employee's personal involvement or dealings with the employer's clients, customers or suppliers. Many situations in this category of conflicts are similar in nature to circumstances that involve the taking of gifts or favours from those who do business with the employer. In one case, for instance, a maintenance supervisor who was having personal financial difficulties borrowed money from one of his employer's suppliers.[199] This conduct was contrary to the conflicts of interest policy that the employer had established, particularly because the supervisor did not disclose the loan to management before it was accepted. Since the supervisor had become indebted to the supplier, the court agreed that his conduct could result in a distortion of company business practices or create a per-

---

[198] *Dowling v. Halifax (City)* (1995), 15 C.C.E.L. (2d) 299 (N.S.S.C.), affd 136 D.L.R. (4th) 352 (C.A.), revd 158 D.L.R. (4th) 163 (S.C.C.).

[199] *Connolly v. General Motors of Canada Ltd.* (1993), 50 C.C.E.L. 247 (Ont. Ct. (Gen. Div.)).

ception of distortion in the minds of the supplier, the employer, other workers or the general public. The chances of this were increased in the circumstances because the supervisor was in a position to influence the timing, quantity and choices of products provided by the supplier. However, even if the supervisor's influence had been limited, the court concluded that his conduct would still have constituted a conflict of interest justifying summary dismissal. Moreover, it was clear in this case that the employer had regularly reminded employees of the company's policy and had warned that failure to follow it would jeopardize their continued employment. As a consequence, it was established that the supervisor knew his conduct was wrong and therefore the fact that he may have underestimated its seriousness was not a mitigating factor.

Just cause for termination can exist when an employee acquires some advantage from dealing with the employer's clients, even though the employer is not harmed. This point was demonstrated in a case involving a bank's credit officer who was dismissed for entering into certain transactions with customers of the bank.[200] The bank had specific rules governing the relations between its employees and customers, including a prohibition against accepting financial assistance from any customers without approval from the bank's supervising office. Such approval was also required if an employee wanted to make an investment with a customer or invest in a customer's enterprises. The officer breached these guidelines by accepting loans from at least three of the bank's customers without authorization. The guidelines were further breached when the officer did not seek or obtain approval before purchasing shares in companies owned by customers of the bank. With respect to the financial assistance he received, it was found that the officer had put himself in a position of conflict because there was a chance that he might discharge his personal obligations to the customers at the expense of his obligation to protect and advance the interests of the bank. The officer created a further conflict by investing in customers' enterprises because he might be inclined to place his own interests before those of the bank. While there was no evidence of the bank having suffered any direct harm, the court concluded that the officer's dismissal was justified since the transactions at issue had placed him in a position where his interests and personal obligations conflicted with those of the bank. Not only did the officer violate the bank's policies, he also failed to meet the higher standard of conduct imposed on employees in the banking industry. In this industry, employees are expected to exercise maximum caution and be completely candid and honest in the course of their employment. Accordingly, bank officers will generally face a greater risk of conflict as compared to other employees.

---

[200] *Ennis v. Canadian Imperial Bank of Commerce* (1986), 13 C.C.E.L. 25 (B.C.S.C.).

In a similar case, the dismissal of a bank's branch manager was justified because he did not disclose his financial dealings with customers of the branch, thereby violating a policy on conflicts of interest.[201] In particular, the manager invested in business ventures operated by branch customers and was the guarantor of a loan given to one of the ventures. The court agreed that the manager had disregarded the bank's policy and that his involvement with the customers potentially interfered with the independent exercise of his professional judgment.

In another case, an employee who was charged with administrating an international student program was dismissed for cause for failing to disclose the private business he was running, and for misrepresenting the nature of his business to third parties.[202] A school vice-principal's employment was centred on administering an international student program that included student recruitment, registration, evaluation and student housing. He also ran private programs of recreational and instructional activities for foreign students that were offered between the programs run by the school district. The court held that the employee had made inadequate disclosure regarding these programs to the school district. The employee failed to clarify that the programs were being carried out for the employee's own benefit and profit rather than as a marketing device to encourage enrolment in the international student program. The court stated that in this situation it is the employee's obligation to "disclose fully and to seek approval and confirmation that it was in order for him to carry on this private program for his own benefit".[203] Also, when corresponding with agents, parents, students, immigration authorities and a Canadian Embassy, the employee used the international student program's letterhead. The court found this to be a misrepresentation of his private programs to third parties, exposing the school district to a serious risk of liability. The inadequate disclosure and misrepresentation, coupled with the court's finding that the employee held a senior position with significant freedom, led the court to conclude that the implied term of the employment contract, namely that the employee would faithfully perform his duty, had been breached and, therefore, the school district had cause for termination.

In some circumstances, an employee's intimate relationship with his or her employer's client can place the employee in a conflict of interest position. This is particularly so in the social services context where employees are often bound by codes of ethics that prohibit them from having sexual relationships with clients. In such a case, as with other kinds of conflict, actual prejudice to the employer is not required to justify termination. Just cause for

---

[201] *Rowe v. Royal Bank of Canada* (1991), 38 C.C.E.L. 1 (B.C.S.C.).
[202] *Rupert v. Greater Victoria School District No. 61*, 2002 C.L.L.C. ¶210-001 (B.C.S.C.), affd 315 W.A.C. 212 (C.A.).
[203] *Supra*, at para. 36 (S.C.).

dismissal tends to be established if the employer can show that there was likely to be prejudice. In most circumstances, whether the actual or potential conflict will justify termination depends on the nature of the employee's responsibilities and the nature and status of the employer's business. For example, a case for cause is easier to establish where the employer's organization depends on government and public funding and operates in a sensitive area such as providing services and counselling to sexual offenders. A potential conflict was found to exist under these circumstances when a social worker became intimately involved with an offender who was being counselled by her employer's organization.[204] Just cause for termination was found to exist, particularly because the employee had concealed her relationship. She then refused to end the relationship, refusing to acknowledge that it could cause harm to her employer's organization.

Finally, there may be situations where an employee is intimately involved with a person who, although not a client, nevertheless poses a security threat to the employer's property. In one case, an assistant branch supervisor of a bank was living with a convicted bank robber who had recently been charged in another armed robbery.[205] While the court did not find that co-habitation with such an individual amounted to a conflict of interest, it did conclude that by living with him, the supervisor's conduct was incompatible with her managerial duties. The supervisor's dismissal was therefore justified on the basis that her partner's illegal activities constituted a standing threat to all financial institutions, including those of her employer. Furthermore, at least in the circumstances of this case, the supervisor's conduct outside the workplace had caused her to lose a characteristic that the court said might reasonably be regarded as necessary for carrying out her duties. As a consequence, the employer's confidence in the supervisor was lost and the employment relationship could not continue.[206]

(d) Miscellaneous Conflicts

There are many situations that do not fall neatly into the categories of conflicts already canvassed. Nonetheless, they may also amount to conflicts of interest that justify the termination of an individual's employment without notice. Although it is impossible to discuss every possible type of conflict, what follows are some examples of "miscellaneous" conflicts that could warrant an employee's summary dismissal.

---

[204] See *Smith v. Kamloops and District Elizabeth Fry Society* (1996), 136 D.L.R. (4th) 644 (B.C.C.A.).

[205] *Canadian Imperial Bank of Commerce v. Boisvert*, [1986] 2 F.C. 431 (C.A.).

[206] See also discussion under Heading 25, "Off-work Criminal or Improper Conduct", of this Part.

One situation that may result in a conflict of interest relates to an employee's commitment of his or her time. When an individual agrees to work for an employer, it is assumed that the work will be done during the employer's normal business hours unless the contrary is specified or is obvious from the nature of the work to be done. Accordingly, the general rule is that an employee cannot allocate any of this time to some other commitment without the employer's authorization. Once an employee is committed to work for a company or organization during its normal business hours, the employee cannot subsequently arrange to work for someone else during these same hours.[207] To do so would constitute a conflict of interest and a breach of the employment contract unless the subsequent arrangement is approved by the employer.

In contrast, a conflict of interest is not created by an employee's attempt to secure other work before giving the employer notice of his or her intention to resign.[208] If a case for cause is based on a time conflict, it will fail where the employee can demonstrate the existence of an intention to leave his or her position once alternative employment was arranged.

A conflict of interest can arise where an employee's loyalties shift from the employer's company to some other organization or enterprise. Just cause for termination is also likely to exist if the employee becomes preoccupied with another company's best interests to the disadvantage of the employer's business. This can occur where the employee gives the other company a substantial amount of preferential treatment or where the employer's property or resources are used without authorization for this other company's benefit.[209] A case for cause is likely to succeed if an employee's shift in loyalties and preoccupation with another company's interests are found to have caused prejudice to the employer's business and a loss of trust in that employee. Even so, one court held that to have just cause, the employer must discuss the expectation of confidentiality and loyalty with the employee, and warn the employee that a breach of confidentially will result in his or her termination for cause.[210]

Conversely, in dealing with the question of disloyalty, a court held that there was no just cause where an employee sought "a negotiation for corporate restructuring and a more central role for himself in [the company] . . . As

---

[207] See *Wells v. Newfoundland and Labrador Nurses' Union* (1986), 12 C.C.E.L. 205 (Nfld. S.C.).

[208] See *Donovan v. New Brunswick Publishing Co.* (1996), 17 C.C.E.L. (2d) 51 (N.B.Q.B.), affd 184 N.B.R. (2d) 40 C.A.).

[209] See *Chipley v. Saskatchewan Oil and Gas Corp.* (1990), 30 C.C.E.L. 313 (Sask. Q.B.).

[210] *Mann v. Northern B.C. Enterprises Ltd.*, [2003] B.C.J. No. 2408 (QL), supplementary reasons [2004] B.C.J. No. 151 (QL) (S.C.).

a shareholder, he had every right to ask for a negotiation on a proposal to purchase more shares."[211]

Conflicts often arise where the interests of an employee as a customer of the employer's business clash with his or her employment obligations. These conflicts are more commonly associated with employees who hold management positions, as in the case of a department store manger whose purchases were seen as causing a conflict between his personal interests as a customer and his duties as a manager.[212] However, even if a conflict of interest is established, just cause for termination may not exist unless a company provided clear directions about what it expected from managerial employees in such circumstances. Similarly, a long and satisfactory service record with an employer may entitle an employee to corrective discipline rather than to dismissal.

The final "miscellaneous" case that will be considered involves the conflict that can arise when the duties of managerial employees conflict with their membership in a non-managerial association. In one case, for instance, the court concluded that a newspaper's editor had put himself in a conflict of interest position by joining an association that was formed for the purpose of addressing a number of staff concerns.[213] The newspaper's publisher took the position that managerial personnel could not perform their duties if they were members of the association because these individuals were expected to carry out the paper's policies and to communicate them to the rest of the staff. This was viewed as being impossible to do if they were also acting as staff spokespersons. Accordingly, the editor was given the option of removing himself from the association and keeping his management position, or remaining a member of the association and resigning from management. The editor refused to resign and was therefore demoted. He treated the demotion as a termination without cause and sued the newspaper. The court concluded that the editor had placed himself in a position of conflict by joining the association and that such a conflict constituted just cause for termination. Even if he did not realize it at the time, the court said the editor became aware of this conflict when his employer pointed it out to him and gave him the choice of resigning from management or leaving the association.

Overview

A conflict of interest arises when an employee's conduct clashes with the interests of an employer's business. The common law has defined what constitutes a conflict of interest, but situations that amount to conflicts are

---

[211] *Hoffman v. VRP Web Technology Inc.* (2001), 12 C.C.E.L. (3d) 255 (Ont. C.A.), at para. 8.

[212] See *Schmidt v. Sears Canada Inc.* (1995), 12 C.C.E.L. (2d) 261 (Alta. Q.B.).

[213] *Walker v. Canadian Newspapers Co.* (1985), 6 C.C.E.L. 209 (Alta. Q.B).

also contemplated by the specific policies established by employers in their workplaces. Although it is not an exhaustive list, the following situations and circumstances are indicative of actual or potential conflicts in the employment context:

1. During the course of employment, an employee is engaged in a business that competes with that of the employer.
2. An employee's partner or spouse operates a company that competes with the employer's business.
3. There is actual competition with an employer's business or a real intention to compete with it while an employee still works for the employer.
4. An employee uses confidential information acquired in the course of employment to prepare for a post-employment competing business.
5. An employee solicits the employer's clients to advance his or her personal interests.
6. An employee acquires an advantage or benefit to which he or she is not entitled.
7. The taking of a particular benefit or gift is not a practice that is common in the employer's industry and the fact that such a gift or benefit was accepted is concealed by an employee.
8. An employee enjoys a benefit or opportunity that would otherwise have been enjoyed by the employer.
9. An employee's position is used to convey a fraudulent or undeserved benefit on a friend to the detriment of the employer's business.
10. An employee has undisclosed personal dealings with those who do business with the employer.
11. An employee's intimate relationship with a client of the employer's organization is concealed and the employee will not end the relationship when it is discovered by the employer.
12. An employee arranges to work for someone else and such an arrangement conflicts with the time commitment made to the employer.
13. An employee's interests as a customer of the employer's business clash with his or her employment obligations.
14. An employee's membership in a particular organization or association conflicts with his or her employment duties.
15. An employee's loyalties shift from the employer's business to some other company or enterprise.

The existence of an actual or potential conflict of interest can provide the employer with grounds for termination without notice. Where any or all of the following factors are present, a case for cause based on a conflict of interest will likely be successful if the employee is dismissed:

1. The employee's misconduct is clearly and specifically prohibited by a company's policy on conflicts.
2. The employer has not condoned the circumstances giving rise to the conflict.
3. The employee continues to engage in certain conduct even though the employer has warned that it constitutes a conflict of interest.
4. The situation of conflict involves an employee who holds a managerial position.
5. The conduct that constitutes the conflict of interest is engaged in secretly and in a deceitful manner.
6. The employer's resources are used by the employee for his or her own benefit.
7. The employer's company or organization operates in an area that imposes a particularly high standard of conduct on its employees such as the social services domain or the banking industry.
8. The situation of conflict involves an employee who does not have a long and exemplary service record.

17 ✧ BREACHING FIDUCIARY DUTIES

Where an employee breaches or fails to satisfy the requirements of a fiduciary duty, just cause for termination exists. In the employment context, fiduciary duties are those duties owed by an employee with fiduciary status. Such an individual is distinguished from the non-fiduciary or regular employee and the distinction can be important because stricter obligations and higher standards of conduct are imposed on employees who are fiduciaries.

An all-inclusive definition of the fiduciary employee does not exist. An individual is usually treated as such if he or she holds a high managerial, senior or key position in an employer's organization. While the most common examples of fiduciary employees are corporate directors and officers, it is the nature of an employee's position and responsibilities that determine whether fiduciary status exists. Courts consider the role that an employee serves in an employer's organization and not a job title when deciding if the employee is a fiduciary.[214] For example, individuals who exercise a policy-making function, executive authority and/or a high degree of control over the employer's business are usually seen as fiduciary employees.[215] It has also been sug-

---

[214] See *Tomenson Saunders Whitehead Ltd. v. Baird* (1980), 7 C.C.E.L. 176 (Ont. H.C.J.).
[215] See *Mercury Marine Ltd. v. Dillon* (1986), 30 D.L.R. (4th) 627 (Ont. H.C.J.); *Empire Stevedores (1973) Ltd. v. Sparringa* (1978), 19 O.R. (2d) 610 (H.C.J.), leave to appeal to C.A. refused 39 C.P.R. at p. 178; *R.W. Hamilton Ltd. v. Aeroquip Corp.* (1988), 65 O.R. (2d) 345 (H.C.J.); *Mitchell v. Paxton Forest Products Inc.* (2002), 286 W.A.C. 205 (B.C.C.A.).

gested that fiduciary duties will be imposed in employment relationships where the employee has the authority to exercise some discretion or power, where the employee can unilaterally exercise the discretion or power so as to affect the employer's legal or practical interests, and where the employer is particularly vulnerable to or dependent on the employee.[216] While these characteristics are not absolutely determinative, a court may refuse to treat an employee as a fiduciary where no evidence of employer dependency or vulnerability exists in the employment relationship.[217]

Fiduciaries are held to higher standards of behaviour than regular employees with respect to avoiding conflicts of duty or self-interest and the obligations of loyalty and good faith.[218] Furthermore, many obligations imposed on fiduciary employees after their employment has ended are not generally imposed on other employees. While non-fiduciary employees are subject to a general duty of good faith in the course of their employment, a greater degree of misconduct is usually required to establish just cause for termination. Even if a non-fiduciary employee's conduct conflicts with an employer's interests, the success of a case for cause will be determined by the particular circumstances of the situation.[219] In contrast, just cause for termination will immediately arise whenever a fiduciary duty owed by an employee is breached in the course of employment.

The case law dealing with fiduciary employees demonstrates the nature and extent of these fiduciary duties. Most of the cases consider post-employment obligations, including the fiduciary employee's duty to avoid competition against the business of a former employer. This particular obligation continues for some time after the employee has left a position.[220]

Taking a "corporate opportunity" from one's employer is a common breach of a fiduciary duty. The general rule is that employees in a fiduciary position with an employer cannot, either secretly or without approval, obtain for themselves any property or business advantage belonging to their employer. Fiduciary employees are also prohibited from taking opportunities that the employer is trying to acquire. For example, if an employer is actively pursuing a contract for work in respect of a development project, a fiduciary employee cannot attempt to take or divert the contract for his or her personal

---

[216] See *International Corona Resources Ltd. v. LAC Minerals Ltd.* (1989), 61 D.L.R. (4th) 14 (S.C.C.); and cited therein, *Frame v. Smith* (1987), 42 D.L.R. (4th) 81 (S.C.C.).

[217] See *Crain-Drummond Inc. v. Hamel* (1991), 35 C.C.E.L. 55 (Ont. Ct. (Gen. Div.)), affd 36 C.P.R. (3d) 163n (Div. Ct.).

[218] See *Canadian Aero Service Ltd. v. O'Malley* (1973), 40 D.L.R. (3d) 371 (S.C.C.).

[219] For a discussion of the factors that affect the determination, see Heading 16, "Conflicts of Interest", *supra*.

[220] A consideration of post-employment misconduct is not within the scope of this book. Accordingly, the discussion here will focus on those imposed fiduciary duties that, if breached during the term of employment, give rise to just cause for termination.

gain. To do so will normally constitute a breach of fiduciary duty, especially where the employee was very much involved in pursuing the contract on the employer's behalf.[221] For the purpose of determining whether the conduct of an employee is a breach of his or her fiduciary duty, several factors must be considered. They include:

(a) the position or office occupied by the employee;
(b) the nature of the corporate opportunity taken;
(c) how much the employee knew about the opportunity;
(d) whether or not the employee was involved in pursuing the opportunity for the employer; and
(e) when in fact the opportunity was taken.

If the employee's fiduciary duty has been breached and the breach occurs while the employee is still working for the employer, then termination for cause is justified. However, it is often the case that former employees will take opportunities or advantages away from the employer after the employment relationship has ended. In these circumstances, the court's task is to ascertain whether a post-employment duty has been breached and, if so, how much to award the employer in damages as compensation for the loss of the business opportunity.[222]

If a fiduciary employee intercepts an opportunity that is first offered to the employer or one that arises from his or her employment, a breach of fiduciary duty will likely exist. In contrast, there is no breach where the nature of the business advantage taken is such that it belongs to the employee and not to the employer. This was the situation when a development company alleged that its project manager, a key employee in the organization, breached his fiduciary duty by pursuing a business opportunity for his own gain.[223] In the company's opinion, just cause for the manager's dismissal was established on this basis even though there were no problems with his work performance. In particular, the company asserted that the manager had deprived it of an opportunity to acquire certain parcels of land for development purposes. The court found that the advantage taken by the manager was one that belonged to him before he began working for the company and that he had not intercepted an opportunity first offered to the company or one that he became aware of from his employment. Rather, the land that the manager attempted to purchase in the course of employment belonged to an individual with whom the manager

---

[221] *Canadian Aero Services Ltd. v. O'Malley, supra*, footnote 218.
[222] Where a business opportunity belonging to the employer is inappropriately taken by an employee in breach of his or her fiduciary duty, the employer is usually entitled to compensation for the loss, regardless of when it was taken. In this respect, the breach of fiduciary duty constitutes grounds for a separate action against the employee for damages.
[223] *Ivanore v. Bastion Development Corp.* (1993), 47 C.C.E.L. 74 (B.C.S.C.).

had a previous existing business and social relationship. Furthermore, it was found that the manager had initially disclosed and offered the land opportunity to the company before he decided to take advantage of it himself. The court ultimately concluded that the manager had not acted in breach of his fiduciary duty. He was entitled to pursue the opportunity because it was one that he had brought to the company and one that the company was not interested in taking. Moreover, the evidence showed that the company usually permitted employees to engage in personal land development projects in which it had no interest as long as the employees disclosed their involvement to the company and the involvement did not detrimentally affect their work performance. For these reasons, just cause for the manager's termination based on the taking of a business opportunity could not be established.

In a similar vein, a case for cause based on the breach of fiduciary duties will fail if an employee did not obtain an opportunity because of his or her position and made no attempt to compete with an employer's business. This will particularly be true where the employer does not contemplate taking advantage of the opportunity and is not entitled to do so in any event.[224]

Employees do breach a fiduciary obligation if they make plans in the course of their employment to buy a company that competes with the employer's business. While a non-fiduciary employee can take some steps in preparation for a competing post-employment business, the same cannot be said of fiduciaries. This was illustrated in one case where two senior employees occupied high managerial positions in the subsidiary company of a major clothing line.[225] While holding these positions of trust and confidence, the individuals began to negotiate and plan for the purchase of a business that competed directly with the company for which they worked. Some of the preparatory work for the transaction was done in their offices and on company time. Further, several long distance calls relating to the purchase were billed to the company's telephone account. Both employees were eventually dismissed after their plan and activities were discovered, even though they had not yet acquired the competing business. The appellate court concluded that just by planning to purchase the business the employees had breached their fiduciary duty to refrain from competition with the employer's company and just cause for termination therefore existed.

An obligation often imposed on fiduciary employees is the duty to disclose certain kinds of information to an employer in a timely manner. The extent of the duty can require employees to warn superiors that corporate opportunities are in danger of being lost. In one case, for instance, a senior officer of a corporation's consulting division was told that three valued

---

[224] See *Sanders v. Children's Aid Society of Rainy River (District)* (1995), 9 C.C.E.L. (2d) 87 (Ont. Ct. (Gen. Div.)).

[225] *Wilcox v. G.W.G. Ltd.* (1984), 4 C.C.E.L. 125 (Alta. Q.B.), revd 8 C.C.E.L. 11 (C.A.).

employees were planning to gain control of the division's operations, either by purchase of its assets or through competition.[226] This plan posed a real threat to the corporation's future because it was likely to result in the loss of clients and business. After considering the evidence, the court concluded that the officer was a "prime mover" and "business getter" in the organization and therefore occupied a fiduciary position. Accordingly, he was obligated to advise the corporation's directors of the employees' plan to acquire control of the division. By failing to do so immediately, the officer was in breach of his fiduciary duty. This duty was breached further when the officer failed to notify the directors of his subsequent intention to join the employees in forming a competing enterprise. The court was not required to decide whether just cause for the officer's dismissal existed because he left the corporation on his own accord. However, it was clear that the officer had breached a fiduciary obligation and a case for cause on this basis would have succeeded.

In some circumstances, retaining counsel and taking a legal position that is incompatible with that of the employer may amount to a breach of one's fiduciary duty.[227] In one case, for instance, the vice-president and general manager of a company was dismissed for asserting ownership of the patent of an item he had created in the course of his employment.[228] The appeal court concluded that the employee's dismissal was justified because he had taken a position that was entirely inconsistent with that of his employer. The court held the employee was in a fiduciary position and that his persistence in claiming ownership over the newly created product constituted a breach of fiduciary duty. Just cause for termination was therefore established.

Employees typically are in breach of a fiduciary duty when they fail to follow a company policy established by the employer.[229] This is especially true where the policy is clearly articulated in writing, where it relates to an area specific to the employee's position or where the non-compliance shows that the employee failed to appreciate the nature of his or her duties and obligations. In one case, a trust company's senior financial officer was fired on account of several instances of misconduct, including his violation of a company policy.[230] In particular, the officer purchased a number of employee term deposits for family members, a practice specifically prohibited by a written policy of the trust company. The court recognized that the highest propriety of conduct is demanded from executives, particularly a financial executive

---

[226] *DCF Systems Ltd. v. Gellman* (1978), 5 B.L.R. 98 (Ont. H.C.J.).

[227] See discussion under Heading 30, "Seeking Legal Advice or Initiating Claim Against Employer", of this Part.

[228] *Helbig v. Oxford Warehousing Ltd.* (1983), 1 C.C.E.L. 217 (Ont. H.C.J.), revd 20 D.L.R. (4th) 112 (C.A.), leave to appel to S.C.C. refused [1985] 2 S.C.R. vii.

[229] See also discussion under Heading 8, "Breaching Employer Policies or Rules", of this Part.

[230] *Ma v. Columbia Trust Co. Ltd.* (1985), 9 C.C.E.L. 300 (B.C.S.C.).

dealing in an area of finance in his or her own field of expertise. The court viewed the officer's conduct as a breach of the fiduciary duty he owed to his employer and found that the officer had failed to appreciate the duties and obligations associated with his position. The court concluded that on its own, the breach of fiduciary duty caused by non-compliance with the company's policy constituted just cause for the officer's dismissal.

Employees are also in breach of a fiduciary duty if they blatantly abuse the positions they occupy. In one case for instance, the superintendent of a correctional centre misused an inmates' welfare fund and entered into contracts with inmates for the making of various carvings.[231] This conduct was seen as inconsistent with his position because he was trustee of the fund and a public officer entrusted with the inmates' care and custody. The court concluded that the superintendent had abused his position and that his actions were incompatible with his fiduciary duties. On this basis, just cause for termination existed and the superintendent was not entitled to reasonable notice of his dismissal.

On the other hand, breach of a fiduciary duty based on misappropriation and mismanagement of an employer's funds is not established where the employer's funds were not used for the fiduciary employee's personal benefit, a strict accounting of all money generated by the employee's activities was kept and the employer benefited from the employee's conduct and management. Where these circumstances are found to exist, a court will likely conclude that the employee did not breach any fiduciary duty and the employee's dismissal was unwarranted.[232]

Finally, an employee's fiduciary duty is often breached where the employee discloses confidential information acquired in the course of employment. However, it is not every disclosure that will constitute a breach of the duty and justify summary termination. Rather, the facts of each situation and the seriousness of the information disclosed must be considered. After such a consideration in one case, the court concluded that just cause for termination did not exist.[233] In the case, a comptroller of a department store was dismissed for revealing information about the store's recent decline in sales to a former employee. The store's president was of the view that the comptroller had acted in breach of his fiduciary obligation to keep confidential all financial information that related to the store's operations. The court considered all the facts and concluded that a case for cause based on the disclosure of confidential information did not exist. While the comptroller had

---

[231] *Dennis v. Northwest Territories (Commissioner)* (1989), 28 C.C.E.L. 54, supplementary reasons [1990] N.W.T.R. 97 (S.C.).

[232] See *Rock v. Canadian Red Cross Society* (1994), 5 C.C.E.L. (2d) 231, supplementary reasons 7 C.C.E.L. (2d) 146 (Ont. Ct. (Gen. Div.)).

[233] *Warnes v. Army & Navy Dept. Store Ltd.* (1996), 22 C.C.E.L. (2d) 11 (Sask. Q.B.).

disclosed such information, the court said the seriousness of the information had to be assessed in the context of the circumstances and noted that the information was not likely to be used in a harmful manner. Furthermore, the comptroller readily admitted that what he had done was wrong and that it would never happen again. The comptroller also had an otherwise unblemished record and the incident was an isolated one. Accordingly, the comptroller had not acted in breach of any fiduciary duty he owed to the store and his conduct in disclosing the information was insufficient to constitute just cause for termination.

Overview

An employee's breach of a fiduciary duty will amount to just cause for dismissal, thereby removing the need for an employer to provide reasonable notice of termination or pay in lieu of notice. To establish a case for cause, however, employers must demonstrate that the employee had fiduciary status and engaged in conduct that constituted a breach of fiduciary duty. In this regard, the following factors are likely to support the finding that an employee is a fiduciary and not a regular employee:

1. The employee occupies a high managerial, senior or key position in the employer's organization.
2. The employee is a director or officer.
3. The employee exercises a policy-making function, executive authority and/or a high degree of control over the employer's business.
4. The employee has authority to exercise some discretion or power.
5. The employee can unilaterally exercise a discretion or power so as to affect the employer's legal or practical interests.
6. The employer is particularly vulnerable to or dependent upon the employee who is able to exercise power or discretion.
7. The employee is considered a "prime mover" or "business getter" in the employer's organization.
8. The employee occupies a position of trust and confidence.
9. The employee is a public officer.

Once an employee is seen as having fiduciary status, he or she can be held to higher standards of behaviour with respect to avoiding conflicts of duty or self-interest and the obligations of loyalty and good faith. While it has not been possible to identify every situation and type of misconduct that constitute a breach of fiduciary duty, some of the factors and circumstances that will strengthen a case for cause on this basis are:

1. The employee secretly or without approval obtained for personal benefit a property or business advantage that belonged to the employer.

2. A business opportunity that was first offered to the employer or that arose in the course of employment was intercepted or taken advantage of by the employee in a secretive or unauthorized manner.
3. The employee took or diverted an opportunity that the employer was trying to acquire.
4. The business advantage taken by the employee was one that he or she initially pursued on the employer's behalf.
5. A business opportunity that the employer was contemplating and entitled to take was acquired by the employee as a result of his or her position.
6. The employee planned to purchase or start up a company that would compete with the employer's business.
7. The employee acquired information relating to the employer's operations and did not disclose it to the employer in a timely manner.
8. The employee persisted in taking a legal position that was wholly incompatible with that of the employer.
9. The employee failed to comply with an employer's policy.
10. The policy not followed by the employee was clearly articulated in writing and consistently enforced.
11. The policy not followed by the employee related to his or her position and area of expertise.
12. The employee's non-compliance indicated a failure to appreciate the nature of his or her duties.
13. The employee abused his or her position in the employer's organization for personal gain (as in the case of a trustee who misappropriates the trust money over which he or she has control).
14. The employee engaged in conduct that appears to be wholly inconsistent with his or her position and obligations.
15. The employer did not condone nor benefit from the employee's actions.
16. The employee disclosed confidential information about the employer's business to someone (like a competitor) who is likely to use it to the employer's detriment.
17. The employee's disclosure of confidential information was not an isolated incident of misconduct.

18 ✧ UNCO-OPERATIVE BEHAVIOUR

Unco-operative behaviour refers to an employee's unwillingness or refusal to work together with the employer, management or other staff members. Such conduct by an employee can sometimes form the basis for a just cause termination.

In certain circumstances, an employee's lack of co-operation can support a case for cause based on disruption of the corporate culture.[234] Similarly, lack of co-operation in the workplace is occasionally categorized as insubordination because it may involve disobedience or refusal to carry out an employer's directives.[235] For instance, a newspaper editor was dismissed by his employer when he adopted a negative and unhelpful posture in response to changes that the new managing director wanted to implement.[236] Not only did the editor disagree with the changes and the newspaper's new format, he sneered at them and was antagonistic about carrying them out. The court said the editor showed a lack of co-operation by proceeding slowly and unwillingly in implementing the changes. His behaviour was particularly unacceptable in light of the encouragement he had received from the director who wanted the editor's support and had tried hard to obtain it. The court concluded that by refusing to co-operate with management and by refusing to properly implement the directives he was given, the employee breached his employment contract. In reaching this conclusion, the court noted that a term implied in every contract of employment is that an employee will serve honestly and faithfully. Employees have a general duty to accept proper orders given to them because of this implied term of employment. As a result, the editor's dismissal was justified since his unco-operative and disobedient behaviour demonstrated his inability to serve the employer properly and uphold his end of the employment contract.

However, just cause for termination will not be established in every case of unco-operative conduct by an employee. Even though an employee's lack of co-operation can contribute to the failure of working relationships, the employer may be partially to blame. Accordingly, a termination will not be justified where an employee can show that his or her lack of co-operation was not the sole reason for deterioration of the working relationship with fellow employees or the employer.[237]

Employers are generally required to warn unco-operative employees about the consequences of continued misconduct. Employees should be told specifically that their unco-operative behaviour must stop or that more co-operation is required from them. The employer should also clearly state that failure to follow this direction can or will result in dismissal.

A case for cause on the basis of unco-operative conduct is made out where co-operation is a fundamental aspect of an employee's position and the employee fails to demonstrate the amount and type of co-operation required. However, just cause is not necessarily established by an employee's failure to

---

[234] See discussion under Heading 15, "Undermining Corporate Culture", of this Part.

[235] See also discussion under Heading 7, "Insubordination", of this Part.

[236] *Ogle v. Canadian Newspapers Co.* (1984), 5 C.C.E.L. 162 (Alta. Q.B.).

[237] See *Macdonald v. Richardson Greenshields of Canada Ltd.* (1985), 12 C.C.E.L. 22 (B.C.S.C.).

be co-operative in an overly enthusiastic manner, so long as specific work orders or company polices are not actually disobeyed.

There is a greater onus on senior and managerial personnel to be co-operative. A case for cause may thus be easier to establish where the employee occupies a management or executive position. In one case, for instance, a plant manager displayed argumentative and unco-operative behaviour in the workplace.[238] The court said that in normal circumstances this kind of conduct by a manager would have been enough to constitute just cause for termination, except that the manager in this case had a lengthy service record. The court concluded that the manager should have been warned that his conduct could lead to dismissal.

Overview

There will be cases where an employee's unco-operative behaviour can amount to just cause for termination. The following factors and circumstances will strengthen the employer's case for cause on this basis:

1. The employee's lack of co-operation involved disobedience or a refusal to carry out a reasonable work order.
2. The employee's unco-operative behaviour was coupled with other instances of misconduct that together were prejudicial to the employer's interests or showed that the employee was unable to serve the employer properly.
3. The employee was specifically told to demonstrate more co-operation and that failure to do so could or would result in termination of employment.
4. The employee occupied a management, senior or executive position.
5. The employee did not have a lengthy or exemplary work record.
6. Co-operation was an integral part of the employee's job.
7. The employee's unco-operative conduct was the sole cause of failed working relationships or other disruptive events in the employer's workplace.

19 ✧ SUBSTANCE ABUSE

The use of alcohol and other drugs can in some circumstances constitute just cause for an employee's dismissal. Employers must consider a number of factors before firing an employee without notice on this basis. One of the reasons why caution must be exercised in this area is that an employee's abuse of alcohol or other drugs may be the consequence of an addiction illness. Summary dismissal on the basis of illness alone is generally not justified and

---

[238] *Degelman v. Anderson Industries Ltd.* (1987), 61 Sask. R. 85 (Q.B.).

may violate human rights legislation.[239] In this area, onerous obligations are imposed by law on employers when dealing with an alcoholic employee or one addicted to drugs.

(a) Alcohol Consumption

Several factors determine if a case for cause based on an employee's intoxication can be maintained, particularly:

(a) whether the employee's ability to perform his or her duties has been impaired;
(b) whether the workplace has been detrimentally affected;
(c) whether there have been any risks to the employee's safety or to the safety of others; and
(d) whether an employer's business has suffered harm or prejudice.

Other important considerations include the type of position held by the employee and the nature of the work in question. Evidence of a company's tolerance for alcohol consumption or the existence of a "no drinking policy" is also relevant. Finally, the general rule is that employees should be warned that their drinking behaviour could lead to the loss of employment.

Just cause for dismissal is most likely to exist where alcohol consumption prevents an employee from effectively carrying out his or her responsibilities and where the employer has provided sufficient warning about the consequences of the employee's continued poor performance.[240] A dismissal without notice will rarely be justified unless the evidence shows that alcohol consumption has significantly impaired job performance. In one case, it was the absence of such evidence that prompted the court to conclude that an employee's dismissal was unwarranted.[241] Although the employee often had the smell of alcohol on his breath, he had continued to perform his duties in a satisfactory manner.

If the safety of an employee or of others in the workplace is endangered by an employee's drinking habits, just cause for termination is more apt to be established. This is also the case where a company can show that its interests have been or are likely to be harmed on account of the employee's conduct while under the influence of alcohol. On the other hand, an isolated incident of intoxication is generally insufficient to warrant summary dismissal. This is especially true where an employer's business has not been prejudiced and the employee's duties are carried out in a satisfactory manner.[242]

---

[239] See discussion under Heading 14, "Illness and Disability", of this Part.
[240] See *Cox v. Canadian National Railway Co.* (1988), 84 N.S.R. (2d) 271 (S.C.T.D.).
[241] *Johnston v. Algoma Steel Corp.* (1989), 24 C.C.E.L. 1 (Ont. H.C.J.).
[242] See *Buchanan v. Continental Bank of Canada* (1984), 58 N.B.R. (2d) 333 (Q.B.).

In contrast to situations where summary dismissal can be justified, a case for cause will not be easy to support if a company has encouraged social activities with clients and alcohol is consumed during those activities. That is, once the duties of an employee include participation in this type of activity, it is more difficult to establish just cause on the basis of alcohol consumption in the course of employment. This is especially true in the case of a business that fosters a fair amount of drinking among its salespeople. In these circumstances, a court is likely to conclude that the employer should expect that alcoholic beverages will be consumed during business lunches, dinners or functions arranged for the benefit of clients.[243]

An employer will also have difficulty proving a case for cause based on intoxication where an employee's drinking habits have been condoned or pardoned. If an employee is not reprimanded for drinking incidents when they occur, they will be deemed to have been condoned by the employer. There will likewise be condonation if an employee is promoted notwithstanding drunken behaviour. This is what happened in one case where a company's manager would often stay behind after board meetings to have a few drinks.[244] The manager often drank to excess and his behaviour would sometimes become inappropriate and embarrassing. However, the manager was only reprimanded once for engaging in such conduct. On that occasion, the manager became intoxicated and insulted the company's president who had been drinking as well. The manager apologized for his behaviour and subsequently the company prohibited alcohol consumption after all meetings and the manager complied with this direction. Some 16 months later, his driver's license was suspended for driving while impaired by alcohol. Although the manager failed to advise every board member about his suspension, they were all aware of it by the next board meeting. At that meeting, the manager's employment contract was reviewed to ensure that it properly reflected a promotion he had been given. The manager's employment was terminated several weeks later. The company maintained that the manager was fired on account of his drunken behaviour in the past and because he had failed to advise all board members about his impaired driving charge. After considering the facts, the court took the view that the company had condoned the manager's drinking habits. Similarly, the manager's failure to advise board members about the criminal charge was seen as having being condoned and, in any event, the court said the charge was not relevant because it dealt with conduct outside the course of the manager's employment. Ultimately, the court concluded that grounds for just cause termination did not exist and the manager was therefore entitled to damages for wrongful dismissal.

---

[243] See *Hardie v. Trans-Canada Resources Ltd.* (1976), 71 D.L.R. (3d) 668 (Alta. C.A.).
[244] *Pelletier v. Caisse Populaire Lasalle Sudbury Ltd.* (1984), 5 C.C.E.L. 1 (Ont. H.C.J.), affd 56 O.R. (2d) 784 (C.A.).

Condonation can also be implied if a company maintains a very relaxed and permissive working environment. In these circumstances, just cause for dismissal is likewise difficult to prove. This was the situation in one case where an employer had never said anything about employees' occasional use of alcohol or marijuana during work hours.[245] The court concluded that the employer was not entitled to fire an employee without notice based on his moderate drinking and drug habits because such conduct had always been tolerated.

Many companies have policies in place that prohibit alcohol consumption during work hours. Whether the breach of such a policy warrants an employee's termination will depend on whether the policy was a term of employment and there must be evidence to demonstrate that the employee had agreed to be bound by the policy's provisions. Where a policy against drinking on the job is clearly an employment term, a case for cause on the basis of intoxication can be supported more easily. This will be particularly true where the intoxicated employee holds a supervisory job of considerable responsibility and where several employees must report to the employee on a given work shift.[246] In this respect, termination of a supervisor or managerial employee on the basis of intoxication tends to be easier to justify than other terminations because these employees are often held to a higher standard of conduct. On the other hand, if an employer is unable to show that a "no drinking policy" was a condition of employment, just cause for termination based on a breach of the policy will not exist.[247] However, a case for cause based on intoxication might still be established if an employee's consumption of alcohol prejudiced the employer's business and affected the performance of an employee's duties.

A factor that must always be considered in this and perhaps all cases of employee misconduct is whether the employee is experiencing any personal or emotional problems that might serve to explain his or her behaviour.[248] A court will consider mitigating circumstances to determine if the employee's intoxication can be justified and possibly excused. In this regard, the employee's service record can also act to mitigate against a termination for cause. An employer is usually expected to be more tolerant towards those who have always been satisfactory employees and who have been with an organization for a significant period of time. This can be true even where the

---

[245] *Andover & Perth United Farmers' Cooperative Ltd. v. Skaarup* (1987), 18 C.C.E.L. 63 (N.B.C.A.).

[246] See *Rose v. Marystown Shipyard Ltd.* (1985), 6 C.C.E.L. 220 (Nfld. C.A.).

[247] See *Wiebe v. Central Transport Refrigeration (Man.) Ltd.* (1994), 3 C.C.E.L. (2d) 1 (Man. C.A.). See also discussion under Heading 8, "Breaching Employer Policies or Rules", of this Part.

[248] See *Robinson v. Canadian Acceptance Corp.* (1973), 43 D.L.R. (3d) 301 (N.S.S.C.), affd 47 D.L.R. (3d) 417 (C.A.).

employee's behaviour has breached a well-established company policy. A case on point involves the dismissal of a sales executive employee who had recently been demoted to a non-sales position in the company for which he worked.[249] The employee met a sales client for lunch to say good-bye and thank him for his loyalty and business over the years. After both men consumed a large quantity of alcohol, they got into a verbal and physical fight that apparently began when the client made a disparaging remark about the employee's wife. As a result of his conduct, which was contrary to a company policy, the employee was fired. After reviewing the facts, the court concluded that in the circumstances the company owed the employee a response of loyalty and support, particularly because he was close to retirement age and had served the company in an exemplary manner for 27 years. Furthermore, the court noted that losing his job was like a death sentence for the employee and that instead of dismissing him over an isolated incident the company should have offered to provide the employee with counselling. Accordingly, the court found the dismissal to be wrongful and awarded the employee damages.

The requirement to provide greater latitude or accommodation on account of an employee's service record is not, however, an absolute rule. A case for cause is apt to succeed if an employee's drinking habits continue to impair his or her job performance, even after the employee was given ample opportunity to improve and has been warned that failure to do so would result in dismissal.

(b) Use of Other Drugs

Cases of terminations because of substance abuse are mainly based on misconduct that relates to an employee's alcohol consumption. The principles derived from these cases apply whether the employees make use of illicit drugs, prescription drugs or "over-the-counter" products. As a consequence, the factors that are relevant in determining whether an employee's use of drugs will amount to just cause for termination are the same as those that assist in determining whether a dismissal on account of an employee's alcohol consumption is justified.[250]

Furthermore, possessing or using illegal drugs in the workplace can amount to just cause for dismissal if proven by the employer.[251] The termination of employment in such circumstances is generally warranted on the basis that the employee has engaged in criminal conduct during normal work hours and on work premises.[252]

---

[249] *Ditchburn v. Landis & Gyr Powers, Ltd.* (1995), 16 C.C.E.L. (2d) 1 (Ont. Ct. (Gen. Div.)), var'd on other grounds 29 C.C.E.L. (2d) 199 (C.A.).

[250] See Heading 19(a), "Alcohol Consumption", *supra*.

[251] See *Billingsley v. Saint John Shipbuilding Ltd.* (1989), 23 C.C.E.L. 300 (N.B.Q.B.).

[252] See discussion under Heading 24, "Criminal Conduct While Working", of this Part.

(c) Addiction Illnesses

If an employee's alcohol or drug use is properly characterized as an illness or if it develops into an illness, a company will typically be obliged to provide the affected employee with the option of taking a leave of absence in order to obtain treatment. As noted earlier, most human rights statutes prohibit the termination of employment on the basis of an illness or disability. However, notwithstanding the employer's duty to give employees an opportunity to get help for their addiction, persistent drinking or drug use that results in continued poor job performance may finally amount to just cause for dismissal. In one case, for example, a gas company told one of its field operators that he should consider using the organization's employee assistance plan in order to obtain treatment and counselling for his alcoholism and other personal problems.[253] The suggestion to seek help was made after deficiencies in the operator's work were noticed. Although he did receive some counselling, the employee ultimately chose to cope with the alcoholism and personal problems on his own. As a consequence, his drinking problem and his performance did not ameliorate and he was warned on several occasions that failure to improve would lead to disciplinary action, up to and including termination. The employee subsequently agreed to commence a treatment program for alcoholism but was eventually expelled from the program and failed to follow up on further treatment. In the meantime, the company continued to express specific concerns about the employee's poor performance. The employee was warned that a real effort to deal with his problems was required and that his job would be lost unless his work performance improved. When no changes in his performance were noticed, the company finally dismissed the employee following an incident in which his safety and that of others was jeopardized. On that occasion, the employee failed to use correct safety procedures when handling a gas leak. In an action for wrongful dismissal, the court recognized that the employee suffered from alcoholism and that it was a permanent illness. At the same time, the court held that alcoholism was treatable but that the employee was not committed to controlling it. Just cause for termination was therefore found to exist based on the employee's alcoholism, his failure to persevere in a course of treatment and his persistent poor performance which culminated in an incident that jeopardized both his and other employees' safety.

Overview

The mere use of alcohol or other drugs will not by itself constitute just cause for an employee's dismissal. Just cause for termination on this basis can, however, be established by the employer in some circumstances. In this

---

[253] *Visentin v. Shell Canada Ltd.* (1989), 29 C.C.E.L. 65 (Alta. Q.B.).

regard, a case for cause is more likely to succeed if one or more of the following elements exist:

1. The employee's job performance was impaired and the employee was warned that failure to improve would lead to dismissal.
2. The employer's business or reputation had been or would likely have been harmed.
3. The employee's safety and/or that of others was threatened.
4. The employee breached a company policy in respect of alcohol or drug use that was a term of employment.
5. The employee held a supervisory or management position with significant responsibilities.

Notwithstanding the presence of any one or more of these elements, the following factors can serve to mitigate against a finding of just cause and make it more difficult to justify dismissal without notice:

1. The employer had earlier condoned the employee's use of alcohol or drugs.
2. The employee had a strong service record with the employer.
3. The employee was experiencing personal or emotional problems that would explain and perhaps excuse the alcohol or drug use.
4. The employee suffers from a drug or alcohol addiction. Where the employee acknowledges the addiction and is willing to seek assistance, an employer is required to provide accommodation by granting the employee sufficient time to enrol in a treatment program. A termination in these circumstances is usually prohibited by the human rights legislation applicable to the employer's jurisdiction.

20 ✧ PARTICIPATION IN HARASSMENT

Sexual harassment in the workplace is an example of discrimination either expressly or impliedly prohibited by the human rights legislation of all Canadian jurisdictions. Also prohibited in employment is harassment connected to characteristics such as race, marital status or handicap (*i.e.*, any ground of discrimination prohibited by law). In this context, harassment refers to any demeaning or offensive conduct. An employee's participation in harassment based on a prohibited ground of discrimination can give rise to grounds for just cause termination. While this issue has come before the courts mainly in cases of alleged sexual harassment, the principles that stem from these cases apply with equal force to other forms of harassment. For example, whether a ground for cause is established in any case necessarily depends on whether an employee has engaged in behaviour that actually constitutes harassment. However, a court's inquiry is not limited to this question alone. Other factors will be considered to determine if summary dismissal was warranted. In contrast, firing employees for refusing to accept workplace harassment or because they sought redress for having been harassed can never be justified. If these reasons are influential in an employer's decision to summarily dismiss an employee, the employee will likely be entitled to wrongful dismissal damages or to remedies provided by the applicable human rights statute.

Sexual harassment has been defined as "unwelcome conduct of a sexual nature that detrimentally affects the work environment or leads to adverse job-related consequences for [its] victims".[254] Examples of such harassment can include coerced intercourse, unsolicited physical contact, persistent propositions or comments of a sexual nature, gender-based insults or taunting and express demands for sexual favours. While these acts often occur together with threats of adverse job consequences, tangible economic awards do not have to be attached to the behaviour for sexual harassment to exist. In this respect, harassment might also take the form of a "poisoned workplace" or "hostile environment".

The type of behaviour that will constitute just cause for termination based on harassment will vary from case to case, largely due to the fact that harassment presents itself in many forms and degrees. In any event, several factors play a role in determining whether just cause exists in any particular fact situation. For instance, courts recognize that a termination based on an employee's harassing behaviour can be warranted because an employer may be held accountable and liable for the actions of that employee.[255] Where liability is imposed, the employer may have to assume the costs of damages, legal fees and negative publicity associated with harassment complaints. Furthermore, employers have a duty to keep the work environment free of harassment and will therefore be held liable for such conduct where reasonable steps were not taken to stop it. Other adverse effects that the employer might suffer in these circumstances include low morale in the workplace, a decrease in productivity and the loss of good employees who choose to resign rather than tolerate a poisoned environment. For all these reasons, just cause for termination is often established where employers can show that they fired a harassing employee to protect others in the workplace and to protect themselves from the adverse effects of a human rights complaint. Such a termination can even be justified in the case of a long-serving employee.[256]

---

[254] *Janzen v. Platy Enterprises Ltd.* (1989), 59 D.L.R. (4th) 352 (S.C.C.), at p. 375.

[255] Where a claim of workplace harassment is made and confirmed, liability for the harassment may be imposed on the employer pursuant to the human rights legislation of some jurisdictions. Employers should review the law applicable in their jurisdiction to determine when they could be held personally liable for harassment committed by their employees.

[256] See *Tellier v. Bank of Montreal* (1987), 17 C.C.E.L. 1 (Ont. Dist. Ct.).

A primary challenge in establishing a case for cause on the basis of an employee's harassing behaviour is proving that the behaviour actually constitutes harassment. In one case, the court concluded that a supervisor's comments, even if he had made them, were not so obscene or disgusting as to constitute sexual harassment.[257] Similarly, where an employee does not continue to engage in conduct that another employee finds offensive, that conduct will not amount to harassment. These circumstances arose in one case where an employee made a sexual advance towards a co-worker but did not persist when the co-worker told him that his attention was not welcomed.[258] The court concluded that the actions of the employee did not constitute sexual harassment and, accordingly, just cause for his dismissal did not exist.

However, if the employee's behaviour reveals a pattern of sexually harassing conduct, even while not directed at the same person, it may provide just cause for termination. This was the case where an executive director engaged in multiple incidents of sexual harassment aimed at a number of female employees. The incidents involved engaging an employee in sexual discussions and unwanted touching. The court held that when the incidents were viewed objectively in their totality, they constituted sexual harassment and cause for termination.[259]

When deciding if certain behaviour constitutes harassment and just cause for termination, a factor often considered is the character of the business run by the employer. A dismissal may prove justified where the nature of the organization is such that the impugned actions of an employee are particularly prejudicial to its reputation. In one case, for instance, the employer was a private co-ed boarding school entrusted with the moral, physical and educational upbringing of about 175 youths.[260] The school decided to fire its bursar after complaints by his secretary of sexual harassment were investigated and confirmed. In particular, the bursar had made lewd comments to the secretary, had occasionally brushed his hands against her breasts and on one occasion had attempted to corner her in a stairwell. The court agreed that just cause for termination existed because the bursar had engaged in offensive sexual acts that amounted to sexual harassment. The court also noted that failure to dismiss the bursar would have been akin to moral degradation in light of the nature and responsibilities of the school. This would have adversely affected the school's reputation and was further support for finding that just cause for termination existed.

---

[257] See *Brick v. Bell Communications Systems Inc.* (1989), 27 C.C.E.L. 118 (Ont. H.C.J.).
[258] *Shiels v. Saskatchewan Government Insurance* (1988), 51 D.L.R. (4th) 28 (Sask. Q.B.).
[259] *Simpson v. Consumers' Assn. of Canada* (2001), 209 D.L.R. (4th) 214 (Ont. C.A.), leave to appeal to S.C.C. refused 214 D.L.R. (4th) vi.
[260] *Himmelman v. King's Edgehill School* (1985), 7 C.C.E.L. 16 (N.S.S.C.).

The nature of the workplace environment is not a consideration that courts may assess when deciding if a case for cause based on harassment has been established. For example, where employees have fostered and accepted a workplace atmosphere of sexual innuendos and off-colour jokes, a court may still find that conduct of this nature was unwelcome. As a consequence, such behaviour may amount to sexual harassment constituting just cause for termination. In one case, the supervisor of a company's security department was accused of sexual harassment by some of his female subordinates.[261] His employment was terminated on this basis and for failing to comply with the company's non-discrimination policy as it related to harassment. In its decision (reversed later on appeal) the divisional court found the context or fabric of the workplace to be significant in determining whether a policy concerning sexual harassment had in fact been incorporated into the security department's day-to-day working relationships. After reviewing the evidence, the court was convinced that many of the elements that constitute sexual harassment were everyday occurrences in the department. In particular, the court found that interactions between male and female employees had created a workplace atmosphere where inappropriate language and jokes of a sexual nature were the norm. Moreover, those who had made the harassment complaints were seen as having tolerated and engaged in coarse language and inappropriate behaviour themselves. In light of the workplace atmosphere that was fostered and permitted to exist in the security department, the court concluded that the company had not in fact implemented its policy against sexual harassment and that just cause for the supervisor's dismissal did not exist.

The Court of Appeal reversed this decision, holding that management in this case was entitled to have a supervisor who would ensure the work environment was void of objectionable conduct. Furthermore, the court held that the supervisor was not entitled to act as he did merely because everyone else conducted him or herself in a similar fashion. The supervisor's termination with cause was found to be fully justified on the basis that a supervisor who permits an atmosphere to develop that is conducive to inappropriate behaviour, and then participates in such conduct, is a supervisor who is not performing his or her duties properly.

While a court will not be influenced by the atmosphere of a workplace in every case,[262] misconduct that is not too severe is frequently interpreted according to the environment in which it occurs. In one case, for instance, a manager was dismissed for his role in a Valentine Day's prank that was con-

---

[261] *Bannister v. General Motors of Canada Ltd.* (1995), 8 C.C.E.L. (2d) 281 (Ont. Ct. (Gen. Div.)), revd 164 D.L.R. (4th) 325 (C.A.).

[262] See, *e.g.*, *Hutchinson v. St. Leonard's Society of Brant* (1993), 46 C.C.E.L. 306 (Ont. Ct. (Gen. Div.)).

ceived by a co-worker.[263] The co-worker purchased "G-strings" for three female employees, wrapped them and signed to them the names of three other male employees. Although the manager expressed reservations about this prank, he put the items in interoffice mail at his co-worker's request so that they would be delivered to the intended recipients. While agreeing that the prank was ill-conceived, the court saw the manager's conduct in carrying out the prank to be minor and noted that the manager had not denied or concealed his involvement. Further, the court said the manager's activities had to be interpreted in light of the environment in which they took place. Accordingly, the employer's policy on standards of conduct was reviewed. While the policy contained guidelines prohibiting sexual harassment including "practical jokes which cause awkwardness or embarrassment", no attempt had ever been made to advertise the guidelines or to educate staff members about them. In addition, the policy did not state that non-compliance with these guidelines would result in dismissal. Finally, there was evidence to suggest that the prevailing attitude in the workplace toward sexual jokes was fairly relaxed. For these reasons, together with the fact that the employee had apologized for his conduct, the court concluded that the manager's conduct did not constitute just cause for dismissal.

The nature of an employee's work can also play a role in determining whether there was just cause for dismissal. Generally speaking, the standard of personal conduct is quite high for employees who work primarily with the general public. The standard of conduct is also quite high if the employee's position requires the public to have trust and confidence in the employee. This is true in the case of bus operators, for instance, since their misconduct can adversely affect public confidence in the transportation system that employs them.[264] Where a higher standard of conduct is imposed due to the nature of an employee's work activities, a case for cause based on the employee's harassing behaviour may be easier to establish.

The role of the employee in creating a workplace free of sexual harassment is also a factor in determining sexual harassment. For example, in a case where an employee was involved in a pattern of sexual harassment aimed at female employees, the court held that because the employee was "the executive director of the Association and the supervisor to whom the employees reported, his obligation to the Association was to ensure that sexual harassment did not occur, and to set the standard of a workplace which protected both the employees and his employer from complaints of offensive con-

---

[263] *Wright v. British Columbia Trade Development Corp.* (1994), 3 C.C.E.L. (2d) 254 (B.C.S.C.).

[264] See *Brantford (City) Public Utilities Commission and ATU, Div. 685 (Ferrante) (Re)* (1991), 22 L.A.C. (4th) 326 (Ont.).

duct".[265] Having failed to live up to this standard, the court held that there was just cause for the supervisor's termination.

While harassing behaviour can be a ground for just cause termination, employers must be careful not to act too quickly in terminating an employee on the basis of a harassment complaint. Allegations of improper conduct should always be properly investigated before they are relied on to terminate an individual's employment. The failure to conduct such an investigation or to speak with the employee accused of harassment will result in an improper firing if the allegation of misconduct is ultimately found to be unfounded.[266] The consequence of such a finding is that the employer will be liable for wrongful dismissal damages.

An employee's dismissal will likewise be improper where the employee is fired for engaging in conduct that was corrected or that the employer has condoned or forgiven. These were the circumstances of one case where an employee complained that she was being sexually harassed by a company's branch manager.[267] The employee specified that she was not seeking the manager's dismissal but simply wanted the improper conduct to stop. The manager was warned about his behaviour and subsequently "cleaned up" his act. There were no further complaints with respect to his conduct from the employee or from anyone else in the workplace. However, the manager was summarily dismissed many months later when a former employee alleged that the manager had sexually harassed her while she was still employed. The company decided to terminate the manager's employment on the basis of this and the earlier complaint. The court concluded that the former employee's allegations were unfounded and therefore did not warrant the manager's dismissal. Furthermore, the court said the company could not rely on the earlier complaint of sexual harassment as cause for termination because it had been dealt with at the time it was made and the manager had resolved the problem by correcting his behaviour.

Credibility is usually a key consideration in cases where employees are dismissed on the basis of their alleged harassing behaviour. A court is not apt to find just cause for termination where the complainant (*i.e.*, the individual claiming to have been harassed) is not believable or where the court does not accept the complainant's evidence over that of the employee dismissed on grounds of harassment. In contrast, if complainants are found to be credible and accurate in their recollections, a case for cause will succeed where the alleged harasser's conduct, as demonstrated by the evidence, constitutes harassment. In one case, for example, the court accepted the testimony of two

---

[265] *Simpson v. Consumers' Assn. of Canada, supra,* footnote 259, at para. 83.
[266] See *Murrell v. Burns International Security Services Ltd.* (1994), 5 C.C.E.L. (2d) 123 (Ont. Ct. (Gen. Div.)), affd 33 C.C.E.L. (2d) 1 (C.A.).
[267] *Supra.*

complainants and found that a service station manager had engaged in acts that included patting or pinching the buttocks of female employees, touching or rubbing up against their breasts, putting his arm around their waists and making obscene remarks.[268] The court did not believe the manager's testimony or his denials and concluded that his conduct amounted to sexual harassment and just cause for his termination. In reaching this conclusion, the court held that the harassment demonstrated a serious defect in the manager's character and was highly prejudicial to the employer's operations. The misconduct was further aggravated by the fact that it occurred frequently over a long period of time and persisted even after the manager had been spoken to by a superior.

In addition to the credibility of a complainant, a court may also be influenced by the complainant's apparent motive for alleging sexual harassment. In one case, for instance, the assistant manager of a company's customer service department was dismissed when an employee complained that he sexually harassed her by subjecting her to off-colour remarks.[269] The court's view was that the complainant was not disturbed by the manager's comments until he began to find fault with her performance. In addition, the complainant was found to have used off-colour language herself and very often repaid the manager's comments in kind. For these reasons, just cause for the manager's termination was not established.

A court may refuse to find that an employee's harassing conduct constitutes just cause for termination where it is totally inconsistent with the employee's character and can be reasonably explained.[270] These were the circumstances of one case where a supervisor was dismissed after allegations of sexual misconduct were made against him. While some of his actions were found to constitute sexual harassment, the court determined that the supervisor's conduct was completely out of character. The court concluded that his misbehaviour was the result of an illness he was suffering from at the time and, accordingly, it fell short of constituting just cause for termination. To further support its conclusion, the court noted that the employer had not conducted a fair investigation of the harassment complaints nor had the supervisor been given an opportunity to respond to the allegations made against him.

While harassing behaviour can amount to just cause for termination, victims of workplace harassment cannot be summarily dismissed for complaining about the misconduct. This means that a case for cause will not succeed where an employee is dismissed for seeking redress after being subjected to harassment. In one case, tensions developed between an employee who worked as a hospital's business manager and her immediate supervisor after

---

[268] *Neigum v. Wilkie Co-operative Association Ltd.* (1987), 55 Sask. R. 210 (Q.B.).
[269] *Brick v. Bell Communications Systems Inc.* (1989), 27 C.C.E.L. 118 (Ont. H.C.J.).
[270] *Quirola v. Xerox Canada Inc.* (1996), 16 C.C.E.L. (2d) 235 (Ont. Ct. (Gen. Div.)).

their sexual relationship of 15 years came to an end.[271] In particular, the supervisor reprimanded the employee about alleged deficiencies in her work performance and caused her salary to be reduced $50.00 a month. When the employee complained that the reprimand and salary cut were unwarranted, the hospital's chairman said there was nothing he could do and suggested that she see a lawyer. The employee did this and the lawyer subsequently sent a letter to the supervisor on her behalf. Because the letter expressed the employee's intention to pursue a legal remedy if things could not be resolved, her employment was terminated. The court concluded that termination was not justified because the reprimand and reduction to the employee's pay were unwarranted and stemmed from the break-up of her sexual relationship with the supervisor. Accordingly, the employee had legitimate reasons to complain about the supervisor's conduct and to retain legal counsel since she had no other means to deal with the problem. Furthermore, the court saw the letter as a good faith attempt to settle the differences between the manager and supervisor and to resolve the disputed issues related to the manager's employment. Because the letter was not improper, it did not amount to just cause for dismissal.

Human rights legislation prohibits employers from dismissing or otherwise retaliating against employees for exercising their right to employment free from discrimination or harassment. This is the main reason why a termination based on the making of a complaint is not justified. In this respect, an employee who alleges that he or she was dismissed for complaining about harassment can file a human rights complaint with the appropriate agency or commence an action for wrongful dismissal. While the employee may be entitled to do both concurrently, some courts have said that the wrongful dismissal action should be stayed (*i.e.*, postponed) until the human rights complaint is dealt with and resolved. In any event, employers should note that the consequences of improperly firing an employee for complaining about workplace harassment are not limited to damages for wrongful dismissal. Most human rights legislation contemplates any one or any combination of the following remedies:

(a) reinstatement of the employee to his or her former position;
(b) payment of lost wages;
(c) general damages as compensation for the harassment; and
(d) a monetary award of damages where the employer's conduct was wilful or where the employee suffered humiliation and/or a loss of self-respect.

---

[271] *Gagne v. Smooth Rock Falls Hospital* (1991), 39 C.C.E.L. 281 (Ont. Ct. (Gen. Div.)), affd [1997] O.J. No. 835 (QL) (C.A.). See also discussion under Heading 30, "Seeking Legal Advice or Initiating Claim Against Employer", of this Part.

In light of the potential consequences, employers should be extremely wary of dismissing employees who complain of harassment.

Overview

An employee's harassing behaviour in the workplace can constitute just cause for termination. This is true whether the harassment is sexual in nature or based on other prohibited grounds of discrimination. While employers should act carefully whenever alleged "harassers" are dismissed on this basis, they can feel more confident about proving a case for cause where the following factors or circumstances exist:

1. The employee engaged in conduct that included coerced intercourse, unsolicited physical contact, persistent propositions or comments of a sexual nature, gender-based insults, taunting or demands for sexual favours.
2. The employee's conduct led to a poisoned or hostile work environment.
3. The employee's harassing behaviour was severe in nature and/or persisted over a long period of time.
4. The employee refused to acknowledge allegations of harassment or to apologize for harassing behaviour.
5. The employer can demonstrate that the employee's dismissal was necessary in order to protect others in the workplace and to protect the employer from the liability of a potential human rights complaint.
6. The employee continued to engage in harassing behaviour even after co-workers made it clear that the conduct was unwelcome and offensive.
7. The employee was warned that if the harassing behaviour persisted, termination would result.
8. Given the nature of the employer's organization, the employee's actions were particularly prejudicial to its reputation.
9. The workplace of an employer's organization is not one in which employees have tolerated and engaged in coarse language, off-colour jokes or inappropriate behaviour.
10. The employer has imposed a clear policy prohibiting workplace harassment that is actively observed, employees have been educated about the policy's content and the policy provides that non-compliance is likely to result in the termination of employment.
11. A high standard of conduct has been imposed on the employee because the nature of the work activity involves working with the general public or requires the public's trust and confidence.
12. The employer conducted a fair and thorough investigation of the harassment complaint made against the employee.
13. The employee was given a fair opportunity to respond to the allegations of harassment.

14. The employee's harassing behaviour cannot be explained by illness.
15. Those who made complaints about the employee's conduct did not appear to have ulterior motives for doing so.
16. The complainant and any witnesses were credible.
17. The employee's conduct had not already been dealt with or forgiven by the employer.

21 ✧ PERSONALITY CONFLICTS

There may be many cases where an employee has difficulty getting along with others in the workplace. These situations are often referred to as personality conflicts. On occasion, such conflicts may amount to just cause for termination, but only if they give rise to difficulties that are sufficiently serious and prejudicial to the employer. In this regard, personality conflicts can also be seen as impairing an employer's ability to foster a productive and conflict-free atmosphere in the workplace.[272]

A dismissal based on an employee's inability to get along with co-workers will likely be justified where the employee is also abusive and rude to them. In one extreme case, for example, an engineer belittled those in the workplace who were not his superiors and his obnoxious nature eventually served to decrease the morale of his fellow employees.[273] A number of grievances with respect to specific incidents had been formally filed against the employee and numerous general complaints were made by individuals who worked with him. The employee's conduct continued over a long period of time despite the employer telling him on several occasions to change his ways. Just cause for the employee's termination was established by the behaviour of the employee even though the employer had never expressly warned him that his job was at risk if his behaviour did not improve. The court relied on the following factors in holding the termination justified:

1. The difficulties arising from the employee's character were serious in nature.
2. The high number of grievances and complaints against the employee demonstrated how unacceptable the personality conflict had become.
3. The employee had ignored all instructions to co-operate and work better with others.

The court also said the employee should have known dismissal was likely if he did not change his ways and in any event a specific warning would have

---

[272] See also discussion under Heading 15, "Undermining Corporate Culture", of this Part, where an employee's personality and personality conflicts are discussed in relation to disruptions to an employer's "corporate culture".

[273] *Fonceca v. McDonnell Douglas Canada Ltd.* (1983), 1 C.C.E.L. 51 (Ont. H.C.J.).

been futile because of the employee's inherently difficult personality and his refusal to accept criticism about his conduct.

In less extreme circumstances, just cause for termination may be more difficult to establish despite conflicts in personality between an employer and an employee. This was the case where a bookkeeper was fired after a period of tension and animosity with a new employer, although no legitimate complaints had been made in respect of his work performance or competence.[274] The court accepted that the new employer viewed the employee as being defiant and that they mutually resented each other. However, this was not found to constitute just cause because the employee carried out his duties in a more than a satisfactory manner. Therefore, the summary dismissal was unjustified and the employee was entitled to damages.

Similarly, the fact that an employee may not be a "proper fit" for an organization does not in and of itself justify termination.[275] Although a company has the right to dismiss an employee whose personality is dissimilar to that of other employees, reasonable notice or pay in lieu of notice must be provided. Just cause is apt to be established, however, if the employee's personality alienates all his sales staff to such a degree that they are prepared to move to a competitor.[276] In this situation, the personality conflict can serve as grounds for summary dismissal because the business interests of the employer are being prejudiced.

Overview

While mere differences in the personalities of those in an employer's organization are not likely to justify termination, a case for cause may succeed where an employee's personality or the conflict it creates gives rise to difficulties in the workplace that are serious in nature. In this regard, the case for cause will be stronger where the following factors and circumstances exist:

1. The employee was abusive and rude to others in the employer's workplace.
2. The employee was told to change his or her ways but failed to do so.
3. There was evidence that the employee was an inherently difficult person to get along with.
4. Several complaints were made or filed against the employee in respect of his or her personality and conduct.
5. The employee's personality or the conflict it created alienated others in the workplace.

---

[274] *Blackburn v. Coyle Motors Ltd.* (1983), 3 C.C.E.L. 1 (Ont. H.C.J.).
[275] *Levi v. Chartersoft Canada Inc.* (1994), 8 C.C.E.L. (2d) 10 (Man. Q.B.).
[276] *Woolley v. Ash Temple Ltd.* (1991), 36 C.C.E.L. 257 (B.C.S.C.).

6. As a result of the employee's personality and the conflict it created, workers threatened to resign or in fact did so.
7. The employer's interests were prejudiced or harmed by the employee's personality or the conflict it created.
8. The personality conflict was coupled with poor performance or other misconduct.

22 ✧ PHYSICAL FIGHTS OR ALTERCATIONS

There may be situations where a workplace conflict eventually results in a physical altercation between employees. Depending on the particular facts of a case and certain factors, just cause for termination may be established where an employee physically fights with or assaults a fellow employee.

A single incident of fighting may be insufficient to justify termination. Yet, in one case an employee arrived one hour late for work, following which a confrontation took place with his supervisor.[277] After repeated inquiries by his supervisor as to the reason for his lateness, the plaintiff responded with profanity, pushed his supervisor and left the work site. The next day the employee was given notice of termination. The trial judge found that there was no just cause for dismissal and the Court of Appeal agreed. The Court of Appeal cited *McKinley v. B.C. Tel*[278] in support of the proposition that an employee's misconduct should be judged in the context of his overall employment relationship. In this case, the context "included the respondent's employment history with his employer, his relationship with . . . his immediate supervisor . . . [his immediate supervisor's] role in the relevant events, the actual nature of the misconduct, and the effect, if any, of the misconduct on the employer's business".[279] The trial judge also noted that the altercation "did not demonstrate that [the plaintiff] constituted a danger or threat of violence to other employees in the workplace".[280]

However, when a single incident of fighting is combined with other less serious episodes of conflict, just cause is likely to exist. In one case, an employee of a plywood plant was fired for physically fighting with a co-worker.[281] The altercation arose when the co-worker attempted to assist the employee in a teamwork task. The employee subsequently lost his temper, used foul and abusive language and then charged the co-worker. The fight was fairly serious, causing the co-worker to suffer back injuries that kept him from work for three months. The dismissed employee was injured as well but

---

[277] *Thompson v. Lex Tec Inc.*, [2000] O.T.C. 130 (S.C.J.), affd 149 O.A.C. 106 (C.A.).
[278] (2001), 200 D.L.R. (4th) 385 (S.C.C.).
[279] *Thompson v. Lex Tec Inc., supra*, footnote 277, at para 1 (C.A.).
[280] *Supra*, at para. 43 (S.C.J.).
[281] *Gurvit v. Richmond Plywood Corp.* (1979), 10 B.C.L.R. 141 (S.C.).

to a lesser degree. The evidence indicated that the employee who had been the aggressor had a prior history of conflicts with workers in the plant. Moreover, the court accepted that the employee had been spoken to on a number of occasions about his unco-operative and confrontational attitude, although there was no proof before the court of previous fights or threats to physically harm co-workers. While other fighting incidents or assaults may not have taken place, the court concluded that grounds for summary dismissal existed. This conclusion was reached by considering the isolated altercation together with the less serious instances of conflict. An additional fact in support of dismissal was the existence of a company rule that specifically stated that fighting was a ground for suspension or termination. It was found that the employee was fully aware of this rule and that his failure to comply with it was further justification for termination.[282]

An important factor often considered in fighting cases is the effect the altercation has on the employer's business and the workplace environment. The question the employer must ask is whether the continued employment of an individual involved in a fight or assault will be detrimental to the best interests of the employer's company. The effect on the company's business was a primary concern in a case where a service manager was fired for physically assaulting a colleague in full view of a customer.[283] The altercation was indicative of the poor relations that existed among the three employees of the small propane company. Prior to the service manager's dismissal, it had become clear that his co-workers would no longer work with him and the manager had made it clear that either he or the colleague he had assaulted would have to leave the company's employ. The court concluded that the employer had had no reasonable or economically feasible alternative but to dismiss the employee. The assault and the existing personality conflicts constituted just cause for termination because maintaining harmony among the co-workers was essential for the successful and prosperous operation of such a small organization.

Another factor that plays a role in determining whether just cause for termination exists relates to where the altercation takes place. In one case, a court concluded that an employer's business would not have been prejudiced by continuing to employ an individual who assaulted a co-worker outside the work environment.[284] However, mitigating circumstances existed in this case that helped persuade the court to side with the employee. In particular, the dismissed employee had served the company well for several years and the

---

[282] See discussion under Heading 8, "Breaching Employer Policies or Rules", of this Part.

[283] *Mellish v. Hub City Propane Ltd.* (1987), 79 N.B.R. (2d) 45 (Q.B.).

[284] *Ward v. MacDonald's Restaurants of Canada Ltd.* (1987), 39 D.L.R. (4th) 569 (B.C.S.C.). See also discussion under Heading 25, "Off-work Criminal or Improper Conduct", of this Part.

assault appeared to be an isolated incident that arose in an emotionally charged situation.

In contrast, some cases have suggested that an assault that occurs outside the workplace can still adversely affect the interests of an employer's organization and justify termination[285] if neither of the employees involved in the altercation leaves the employer's company of his or her own accord. In circumstances where one employee leaves, there is likely to be little or no disruption to the employer's business as a consequence of the altercation and it will be more difficult to justify dismissing the remaining employee. The different views in cases concerning fights outside the workplace might simply be a function of the unique ways in which a particular workplace can be influenced. This is why each employment situation must be analyzed in terms of its own distinctive set of facts and circumstances.

A final consideration in this area relates to the nature of the position held by the employee who engages in the physical altercation. Absent other relevant factors, a termination is apt to be justified where the employee is a supervisor and the fighting behaviour reveals qualities that are inconsistent with his or her duties and responsibilities.[286] As with many of the grounds that can justify summary dismissal, supervisors and other management personnel are often expected to act in an exemplary manner and may be held to higher standards of conduct because their behaviour will generally influence the employees they supervise or manage.

Overview

Courts will consider and assess a number of factors when deciding if a fighting incident, altercation or assault amounts to just cause for an employee's dismissal. In this regard, a case for cause will be stronger where the following factors and circumstances exist:

1. The fight or assault resulted in serious injuries to one or more of the employees involved.
2. The employee was the aggressor or instigator and was not provoked by another employee prior to the altercation.
3. The employee had a history of violent outbursts or conflicts with co-workers and had been spoken to by the employer about his or her behaviour in this regard.
4. The fight or assault was prejudicial or harmful to the employer's business interests.
5. The other employee involved in the altercation has not left the employer's organization.

---

[285] See *Bell v. General Motors of Canada* (1989), 27 C.C.E.L. 110 (Ont. H.C.J.).
[286] See discussion under Heading 23, "Character Revelation", in this Part.

6. The workplace is such that maintaining harmony between employees is particularly important as in the case where the employer's business is small and has very few workers.
7. The fight or assault occurred in the workplace.
8. The employee was in a managerial or supervisory position.
9. The altercation was not an isolated event and did not arise as a result of emotional circumstances.
10. The employee did not have a long service record with the employer.

23 ✧ CHARACTER REVELATION

In some circumstances, the "revelation of character" principle has been accepted and applied as a ground for just cause termination. This principle recognizes that an employer may be justified in dismissing an employee without notice not on the basis of the employee's misconduct *per se*, but rather on the basis of the fact that he or she is capable of it. The fact that an employee is capable of engaging in certain kinds of behaviour can reveal a character flaw that is sufficient to warrant dismissal.

A leading case in this area is one that dealt with an employee who falsely dated a document during his employment.[287] The employee had set out the terms of an oral agreement reached some 10 months before between himself and the president of the company employing him. When the agreement was reduced to writing, the employee asked the president to sign the document, and once it was signed, falsely dated it. As a result, the document appeared to have been created and signed when the oral agreement was reached, not 10 months later. The court concluded that in these circumstances there was just cause for termination based on the fact that the employee had the capacity to do what he did. In reaching this conclusion, the court noted that the employee had compounded his underhandedness by lying about his fraudulent conduct under oath and acting deliberately to further his own interests. Ultimately, it was held that revelation of the employee's character was a sufficient ground for his termination.

Subsequent cases have made it clear that a dismissal can be justified where an employee acts in a manner that reveals a character trait, judgment and/or immaturity that is inconsistent with the employee's continued employment or is at odds with the faithful discharge of his or her duties.[288] This will be particularly true where the employee occupies a senior, supervisory or

---

[287] *Lake Ontario Portland Cement Co. v. Groner* (1961), 28 D.L.R. (2d) 589 (S.C.C.). See also discussion under Heading 5, "Fraud", of this Part.

[288] See *McEwan v. Irving Pulp & Paper Ltd.* (1995), 10 C.C.E.L. (2d) 227 (N.B.Q.B.); *Toronto (City) Board of Education v. OSSTF, District 15* (1997), 144 D.L.R. (4th) 385 (S.C.C.).

management position, and where the nature of an employer's business requires confidence and trust from its employees. In one case, for instance, the employee was vice-president of internal audit for a company that dealt with securities and, as such, was expected to be a model of integrity.[289] The court concluded that just cause for the employee's dismissal existed on the basis of his unauthorized use of company credit cards and his failure to follow the company's policy regarding expense accounts. This conduct revealed a flaw in the employee's character that made him unfit to continue in his position. Because the company lost trust and confidence in the employee, his employment was justifiably terminated. The termination was also deemed necessary to prevent damage to the company's reputation and ensure that the company maintained its integrity in the financial and securities industry.

Notwithstanding acceptance of the revelation of character principle, a termination without notice will not be justified for every mistake or error of judgment made by an employee. A case for cause is especially difficult to support where the employee has not acted fraudulently or dishonestly. In addition, authority exists for the proposition that the defence of "revelation of character" is not applicable where the alleged dishonest conduct is entirely separate from the employee's employment performance.[290] The test for determining whether just cause exists is two-fold. A company must first show that it truly believes the employee has disabling character flaws. Secondly, the company must be able to demonstrate that a reasonable and informed person would likewise conclude that the employee has character flaws that justified his or her dismissal. Unless this two-fold test is met, a summary dismissal based on the revelation of an employee's character cannot easily be supported.[291]

Overview

The concept of revelation of character permits an employer to terminate an employee without notice in certain circumstances. If the employee has engaged in conduct that reveals a character trait inconsistent with his or her duties or with continued employment, just cause for termination may exist. This will generally be the case where the employee's conduct is dishonest or fraudulent in nature and where the employer's business is one that demands the utmost confidence and trust in its employees. An employer should be able to meet the two-fold test, which requires (1) proof of the employer's belief that the employee's character is flawed and (2) proof that a reasonable person

---

[289] *Lane v. Canadian Depository for Securities Ltd.* (1993), 49 C.C.E.L. 225 (Ont. Ct. (Gen. Div.)), affd 29 C.C.E.L. (2d) 322 (C.A.).

[290] *Whitecross v. Heiltsuk Nation*, [2001] B.C.J. No. 2409 (QL), supplementary reasons [2002] B.C.J. No. 843 (QL) (S.C.).

[291] See *Paulin v. Computer-Tech Consultants Ltd.* (1994), 4 C.C.E.L. (2d) 298 (B.C.C.A.).

would come to the same conclusion. Finally, a case for cause on this basis will be strengthened where the following circumstances and factors exist:

1. It was a senior or managerial employee's character being questioned.
2. The revelations of character exposed by the employee's conduct caused damage or had the potential to cause damage to the employer's reputation or business.
3. The employee intended to be dishonest or to act fraudulently.
4. The employee received a personal gain or benefit from his or her conduct.

24 ✧ CRIMINAL CONDUCT WHILE WORKING

Engaging in conduct of a criminal nature during normal working hours is just cause for termination because such behaviour will inevitably cause prejudice to the employer and is inconsistent with the proper discharge of an employee's duties.[292] Theft and fraud are the criminal activities most often cited as justifying summary dismissal when they take place during the course of employment. However, just cause for termination can be established by any kind of illegal conduct that transpires in the workplace.

In one case, a teacher assaulted a grade three student in the classroom and the recommendation that he be fired was seen as reasonable on this basis.[293] The assault occurred after the student had taken the top off a pencil sharpener. As a disciplinary measure, the teacher rubbed pencil shavings into the student's face while holding him by the hair and also used his shoe to push or touch the student on his behind. On learning of the incident, the student's parents threatened to take legal action. The deputy superintendent of schools concluded that three options were available to resolve the matter since a peaceful settlement with the parents could not be reached: the teacher could resign without having the incident recorded in his employment file; he could be transferred to another school; or the school board could recommend that he be dismissed. The teacher chose to resign but later tried unsuccessfully to withdraw the resignation and challenge the termination of his employment. Subsequently, criminal charges were laid against the teacher and he was found guilty of assaulting the student. When he continued to challenge the loss of his employment, the board of reference hearing the matter concluded that the teacher's resignation was valid and therefore his employment had not

---

[292] Some specific types of illegal behaviour are considered under other headings of this Part, and are therefore not dealt with here. However, the comments made in each specific example apply here as well: see, *e.g.*, Heading 5, "Fraud", Heading 6, "Theft", and Heading 19, "Substance Abuse".

[293] *Gilson v. Fort Vermilion School Division No. 52* (1985), 12 C.C.E.L. 72 (Alta. Bd. of Ref.).

been wrongfully terminated. Also implicit in the board's reasons was the view that the alternatives outlined by the deputy superintendent were justified, including the option of recommending that the teacher be dismissed. The alternatives were all warranted because the teacher's conduct was excessive and criminal, and the parents expected the assault to be dealt with by the school's administration.

An employer is sometimes justified in dismissing an employee without notice following the laying of a criminal charge, even though the matter has not yet been determined by a trial. This is particularly true where the employee occupies a position of trust and has refused to comply with an employer's request to respond to the charges. In one case, for instance, a correctional centre was found to have just cause for dismissing its superintendent after criminal charges relating to breach of trust were laid against him.[294] The superintendent was the trustee of an inmate welfare fund and a public officer entrusted with the care and custody of incarcerated inmates, together with the overall administration of the correctional centre. The court concluded that the superintendent's dismissal was warranted because the nature of his position was totally inconsistent with his conduct in misusing trust funds and entering into contracts with inmates for the making of various carvings. Furthermore, the court concluded that the employer did not have to await the outcome of the criminal proceedings since an investigating committee had been established to look into the activities of the superintendent and other employees. The superintendent was invited to appear before the committee in order to respond to the charges laid against him but he expressly refused to do so. The findings of the committee substantiated ample grounds for just cause termination and, accordingly, the superintendent's dismissal was justified.

A thorough investigation is recommended before employers dismiss an employee summarily based on the commission of a criminal act in the workplace. In this regard, the employer must not act too hastily or under an unjustified cloud of suspicion in deciding to terminate the individual's employment on this basis.[295] Employers must establish just cause on a balance of probabilities;[296] however, there are varying degrees of probability within this standard and where commission of a crime is being claimed as the reason for termination a somewhat higher standard of proof may be required.[297] The employer must be able to lead strong and compelling evidence that implicates the employee with the alleged criminal act. Circumstantial or inferred evi-

---

[294] *Dennis v. Northwest Territories (Commissioner)* (1989), 28 C.C.E.L. 54, supplementary reasons [1990] N.W.T.R. 97 (S.C.).

[295] See *Conrad v. Household Financial Corp.* (1992), 115 N.S.R. (2d) 153 (S.C.T.D.), affd 45 C.C.E.L. 81 (A.D.).

[296] See discussion under Heading 11, "Onus of Proof", and Heading 12, "Standard of Proof", of Part I, "General Concepts".

[297] See *Billingsley v. Saint John Shipbuilding Ltd.* (1989), 23 C.C.E.L. 300 (N.B.Q.B.).

dence will be insufficient. Furthermore, where an employer fires an employee and asserts without reasonable foundation that he or she committed a criminal act, the courts have in some cases awarded the employee punitive damages. Punitive damages do not compensate the employee for financial losses that have been sustained as a result of wrongful dismissal but, rather, are intended to punish the employer. They are awarded in exceptional cases where the employer has acted in a harsh, vindictive, reprehensible and malicious manner.[298]

Even when the illegal conduct does not occur during an individual's regular work hours, a summary dismissal can still be justified if the behaviour takes place while the employee is involved in a matter connected to the employer's business or is using the employer's resources. However, just cause for termination does not exist unless there is evidence that the employee has in fact engaged in criminal activity. In one case, a service technician employed by a cable systems company was dismissed for reasons that included apprehension about his alleged illegal conduct.[299] The technician's girlfriend was in charge of a local community channel that had a profit-sharing arrangement with the cable company. After his regular work hours, the technician often used the company's van and equipment to assist his girlfriend in operating the channel. The company seemed to permit this practice on account of its arrangement with the channel. While assisting his girlfriend and driving the company van one evening, the technician was stopped by R.C.M.P. officers who searched the van looking for drugs. Although none were found, the company later learned that the R.C.M.P. was investigating the technician for drug-related activities and the officers intended to "catch him in the act". Shortly thereafter, the employment of the technician was terminated. The company alleged that there were several problems with his work performance and behaviour and that the R.C.M.P. search was the "culminating incident" justifying dismissal. The company felt that termination was warranted by the incident because of the technician's already blemished employment record. Furthermore, because of the continuing investigation of his activities, there was concern about the company's interests and reputation should the technician be "caught" while driving the company van. After considering the facts, however, the court took the view that most of the company's claims about the technician's misconduct were either unfounded or not sufficiently serious to warrant just cause for termination. In respect of the search incident, the court concluded that there was no evidence of the technician having done anything that was illegal or detrimental to the company's image. While the incident may have occurred in the course of the technician's employment (he was using the company van to assist an organization that

---

[298] *Conrad v. Household Financial Corp.*, *supra*, footnote 295.
[299] *Parsons v. NI Cablesystems Inc.* (1994), 5 C.C.E.L. (2d) 282 (Nfld. S.C.).

shared profits with the company), it did not warrant discipline nor did it amount to a culminating incident justifying dismissal.

Overview

Just cause for termination can be established where an employee engages in workplace criminal conduct or illegal activities in the course of employment. A case for cause on this basis will be strengthened by the following factors, together with those recognized under the headings of grounds for termination that consider specific examples of illegal conduct:

1. The employer has strong evidence implicating the employee with the criminal act being alleged.
2. A thorough investigation of the alleged criminal activities was undertaken by the employer.
3. The employee occupied a position of trust.
4. The criminal behaviour was wholly incompatible with the employee's duties and responsibilities.
5. The employer's interests were prejudiced by the employee's conduct.
6. While the criminal activity did not take place during the employee's regular work hours, it occurred while the employee was involved in a matter connected to the employer's business or was using the employer's resources.

25 ✧ OFF-WORK CRIMINAL OR IMPROPER CONDUCT

Employed individuals are generally free to do what they wish on their own time outside of the workplace. Even so, this right is subject to exceptions and in certain circumstances an employee's conduct can amount to just cause for termination even though it does not arise during normal work hours or in the course of employment. A specific exception relates to off-work criminal behaviour that can justify an employee's dismissal where particular factors or conditions are present. A case for cause can also be established by off-work conduct that is not criminal in nature but is considered "improper" because it detrimentally affects the employment relationship.

On a number of occasions, courts have recognized that an employee's criminal activities may warrant dismissal even though they occur outside of the work environment. The courts have decided in this manner because criminal activity reveals character traits that are often incompatible with continued employment.[300] This happened in one case, for instance, where an advertising manager was dismissed after pleading guilty to charges of assault

---

[300] See also discussion under Heading 23, "Character Revelation", of this Part.

and nuisance.[301] The manager had assaulted a female employee one evening at his residence after having consumed a large quantity of alcohol. For some time prior to the incident, the manager and the employee had been intimately involved, although the employer was unaware of this when the decision was made to dismiss the manager. Rather, the manager was dismissed because his assault of a subordinate female employee was seen as unacceptable conduct for a member of management, given that he and the victim worked in a relatively small department. The court concluded that the manager's conduct and the nature of his character revealed by the conduct amounted to just cause for termination. Moreover, the court noted that his behaviour was inconsistent with both his duties as a supervisor and the respect that employees owe one another.

Criminal conduct outside of the work environment is likely to amount to cause for termination where the employee's position requires that he or she follow or impart ethical standards. In one case, a part-time lecturer at a university's school of business administration was convicted of filing false insurance claims.[302] His employment contract was ultimately terminated when the conviction came to the attention of the school's dean. After the court had considered all the facts, it concluded that the termination of the lecturer's employment contract was warranted because he had engaged in conduct that was immoral, dishonest and deceitful and the school's reputation would likely have been prejudiced had the lecturer remained on staff. This was especially true because the subject matter he taught included the topic of business ethics. It was difficult to see how the lecturer could instruct students on ethical practices in business were he himself guilty of criminal and unethical conduct in his dealings with the business community. Accordingly, just cause for dismissal will exist where an employee's off-work criminal conduct conflicts with the proper discharge and performance of his or her employment duties.

A case for cause is not likely to succeed if the employee has been accused of criminal conduct outside of the work context but is still awaiting trial. In one case, just cause for termination was not established where an employee was dismissed because criminal charges had been laid against him.[303] The charges related to an incident that occurred between the employee and a transvestite prostitute while the employee was on holidays. As a result of the incident, the employee was charged with assault causing bodily harm, administering a noxious drug and possession of a weapon for a purpose dangerous to the public peace. The event was published in a local newspaper and

---

[301] *Bell v. General Motors of Canada* (1989), 27 C.C.E.L. 110 (Ont. H.C.J.). See also discussion under Heading 22, "Physical Fights or Altercations", of this Part.

[302] *Pliniussen v. University of Western Ontario* (1983), 2 C.C.E.L. 1 (Ont. Co. Ct.). See also discussion of this case under Heading 4, "Dishonesty", of this Part.

[303] *Ryan v. University of British Columbia* (1987), 44 D.L.R. (4th) 550 (B.C.S.C.).

when his employer learned about it the employee was forced to take a leave of absence. He was told that he could return to his job if acquitted of the charges, but before the trial took place the employee was dismissed, despite the fact that one of the charges against him had already been dropped. Ultimately, the court concluded that the employer had acted inappropriately in discharging the employee on the basis of a grossly exaggerated newspaper report and by not applying the maxim that states that an individual is "innocent until proven guilty". Moreover, it was said that before his employment was terminated, the employee should have been given a chance to explain his version of the incident and the employer should have verified the status of the criminal proceedings. For all these reasons, the employee was wrongfully dismissed and entitled to damages.

Even though an employee may ultimately be convicted for his or her off-work criminal behaviour, the conviction does not automatically constitute just cause for termination. The type of offence, the nature of the employee's job and the circumstances of the conviction must always be considered. In one case, for example, the misconduct took place before the employee was hired and did not relate to the duties and responsibilities the employee was required to perform.[304]

Where an employee is required to be absent to serve a prison sentence, this will not automatically amount to just cause for termination. For instance, a driver-salesman employed by the same employer for 23 years went on a medical leave of absence that was scheduled to last fewer than two months. However, while on leave, he was sentenced to four months in jail and 18 months' probation for two criminal convictions that were unrelated to his work. The employer temporarily extended the employee's leave, then terminated him one month before he was scheduled to be released from jail. The Ontario Court of Appeal held that owing to the employee's "length of service, his unblemished record and the demonstrated ability of the [employer] to cover his absence there was nothing approaching just cause for this termination".[305]

Similarly, just cause for a dismissal will probably not exist where an organization is unable to show that it has been prejudiced by the employee's off-work criminal activities or by the laying of criminal charges against the employee. For instance, a grocery clerk's possession of marijuana outside of the employment environment was found not to harm the reputation of his

---

[304] See *Queensbury Enterprises Inc. v. J.R. Corporate Planning Associates Inc.* (1987), 19 C.C.E.L. 48 (Ont. H.C.J.), affd 27 C.C.E.L. 56 (C.A.).

[305] *Heynen v. Frito-Lay Canada Ltd.* (1997), 32 C.C.E.L. (2d) 183 (Ont. Ct. (Gen. Div.)), revd on other grounds 179 D.L.R. (4th) 317 at para. 31 (C.A.), leave to appeal to S.C.C. refused 188 D.L.R. (4th) vi.

employer.[306] A court requires objective evidence to substantiate a company's fear that its business will be damaged as a result of criminal charges being laid against one of its employees. This is especially true where the employee is ultimately acquitted of the charges. A dismissal cannot be justified in such a situation unless a clear nexus is established between the likelihood of damage to an employer's operations and the publicity surrounding an employee's charges and trial. In other words, the employee's conduct or the criminal proceedings related to the employee's conduct must cause actual or real potential prejudice to a company's interests before just cause for termination will exist. The mere possibility of bad publicity alone is insufficient to justify summary dismissal.[307]

It has been recognized that certain convictions will affect a company's confidence in its employees more adversely than others. For example, those that are directly related to an employee's duties and involve dishonesty or a breach of trust are more likely to constitute just cause for termination. The very fact that an employee is capable of certain types of misconduct may be sufficient to justify dismissal.[308] In addition to the character of the offence, the nature of an employee's position must be considered because some occupations demand a higher standard of conduct than others. In this respect, it has been held that police officers or bank tellers convicted of theft are no longer able to meet the standard of integrity required by their jobs.[309]

Even where it is not criminal in nature, misconduct that takes place outside of normal working hours and not in the course of employment can still give rise to just cause for termination if the employment relationship is detrimentally affected. Dismissal is often justified in these situations on account of the employee engaging in "improper" behaviour that is inconsistent with his or her continued employment. In one case for example, the assistant supervisor in a bank's branch was dismissed for cause on the basis of her choice of roommates.[310] The supervisor lived with her boyfriend who in the past had been convicted of three bank robberies and who had recently been charged for his involvement in another. While this robbery did not occur at the supervisor's place of employment, it did take place in a branch of the same bank for which she worked. Moreover, the boyfriend was found counting the stolen money in the apartment that he shared with the supervisor. Shortly after he was charged, the supervisor was fired from her job and the court subsequently held that dismissal was justified. In reaching this conclusion, the court noted that co-habitation with a particular person can in some

---

[306] *Rhodes v. Zehrmart Ltd.* (1984), 5 C.C.E.L. 236 (Ont. Sm. Cl. Ct.), revd 15 C.C.E.L. 137 (Div. Ct.).

[307] See *Backman v. Hyundai Auto Canada Inc.* (1990), 33 C.C.E.L. 300 (N.S.S.C.T.D.).

[308] See discussion under Heading 23, "Character Revelation", of this Part.

[309] See *Canada (Attorney General) v. Brissette*, [1994] 1 F.C. 684 (C.A.).

[310] *Canadian Imperial Bank of Commerce v. Boisvert*, [1986] 2 F.C. 431 (C.A.).

situations create just cause for dismissal and whether it does will depend in large part on the nature and requirements of the employment in question. The circumstances of this case were such that the supervisor's conduct in co-habitating with the boyfriend was incompatible with her managerial duties and her position as a key bank employee. In particular, the activities of the supervisor's boyfriend constituted a security threat to all financial institutions, including those belonging to the supervisor's employer. Furthermore, the supervisor's association with the boyfriend was seen as having caused her to lose a characteristic that might reasonably be regarded as necessary for properly discharging the duties of her position. As a consequence, there was a corresponding loss to the employer's confidence in the supervisor and the employment relationship could therefore not have continued.

While off-work behaviour can amount to just cause for termination in certain circumstances, a case for cause will rarely succeed on the basis of an employee's sexual conduct unless it has negative work-related consequences. Absent these consequences, firing an employee for having an affair with a co-worker will not be warranted where the employer's interests and reputation have not been prejudiced.[311] It would appear that in today's society, if the employer suffers no harm, moral standards pertaining to off-work sexual conduct cannot be imposed in the workplace.

Finally, employers should note that they cannot rely on all instances of off-work misconduct to justify termination, even where the conduct in question is inappropriate and wrong. In one case, for instance, while the conduct of an employee in charge of a university's security department was considered inappropriate by the court, it did not amount to just cause for termination.[312] The employee's questionable conduct occurred while dealing with his wife's intoxication at a staff Christmas party. Because she was engaging in humiliating and embarrassing behaviour, the employee sought to take her home. On the way to the parking lot, the wife fell down three steps. The employee tried to pick her up but she resisted and he ended up pulling her to the car by the back of the collar of her coat. A witness to this incident was extremely bothered by it and filed a complaint in respect of the employee's behaviour. However, the court found that the witness's perceptions of the incident were flawed and exaggerated and the university had not properly investigated the matter before terminating the employee. The court concluded that the employee had overreacted in the circumstances and his conduct was both inappropriate and wrong. However, his behaviour was not extreme enough to irrevocably damage the employment relationship between himself and the university. Rather, the incident could have been dealt with by

---

[311] See *Dooley v. C.N. Weber Ltd.* (1994), 3 C.C.E.L. (2d) 95 (Ont. Ct. (Gen. Div.)), affd 80 O.A.C. 234 (C.A.), leave to appeal to S.C.C. refused 89 O.A.C. 318*n*.
[312] *Yeomans v. Simon Fraser University* (1996), 20 C.C.E.L. (2d) 224 (B.C.S.C.).

having the employee meet with those concerned about his behaviour. Furthermore, just cause for termination was not established for the following reasons:

1. There was no evidence that the employee had engaged in similar misconduct before.
2. His wife testified that the incident was not characteristic of their marriage.
3. There was no indication that such conduct would be repeated in the future.
4. The incident did not seriously damage the university's interests nor go to the root of the employee's contract of employment.

In general, it appears that in cases dealing with an employee's off-work behaviour employers are required to establish one of the following:

1. The behaviour has detrimentally affected their interests.
2. The behaviour has inhibited their ability to manage and direct the operations of the workplace efficiently.
3. The behaviour has rendered the employee unable to discharge his or her duties and obligations of employment.
4. The behaviour has led to other employees refusing to work with the employee.

Overview

Criminal or improper conduct on the part of an employee can amount to just cause for dismissal even though it occurs outside of normal working hours and the work environment, or not in the course of employment. While not every instance of off-work misconduct will justify a summary dismissal, the case for cause is strengthened where the following factors and circumstances exist:

1. The misconduct exposed character traits incompatible with the employment relationship.
2. The employee's misconduct and/or any publicity surrounding any criminal proceedings detrimentally affected the employer's reputation, operations or interests.
3. The misconduct impaired the employee's ability to discharge and perform his or her duties of employment properly.
4. The employee's continued employment would have had a harmful effect on the workplace.
5. The employee's continued employment would have put other employees at risk.
6. The misconduct conflicted with the position held by the employee or was directly related to the employee's responsibilities.
7. The employee was convicted for the misconduct.

8. The employee was in a position or occupation that requires a high standard of ethics and integrity.
9. The misconduct took place after the employee had begun working for the employer.
10. The misconduct caused the employer to lose confidence in the employee.

26 ✧ SABOTAGE

An act of sabotage on the part of an employee is deliberate misconduct aimed at damaging an employer's productive capacity and typically entails destroying or damaging an employer's products or property used in the employer's business. In most circumstances, such behaviour will amount to just cause for termination because employers are entitled to manage their operations without fear of an employee engaging in acts intended to undermine the employer's business. Furthermore, acts of sabotage, sometimes referred to as "industrial sabotage", are inconsistent with the proper discharge of an individual's employment duties or responsibilities. Whether the actions of an employee amount to sabotage and justify dismissal is an issue that has been dealt with primarily by arbitrators in the arbitral jurisprudence. This is partly due to the fact that acts of sabotage against an employer often occur in the context of hostile strike situations that only arise in unionized settings. However, many of the principles identified in the arbitration awards that consider dismissals based on sabotage apply with necessary modification to cases of non-unionized employees. Accordingly, they are used in this discussion for the purpose of explaining when it is that an employee's misconduct will constitute sabotage and justify a termination without notice.[313]

Sabotage is considered serious misconduct because an employer may find it virtually impossible to guard against acts of sabotage. Depending on the nature of their property and business, certain employers are more vulnerable to industrial sabotage than other employers. When an employer is particularly vulnerable, acts of sabotage are very likely to warrant termination. For instance, a technician in one case was summarily dismissed because he had damaged property belonging to his employer, Bell Canada.[314] During the course of a lawful strike, the technician jammed the locks of a Bell Canada

---

[313] In a unionized workplace, an employee can "grieve" his or her discharge (*i.e.*, dismissal) through the arbitration process. A panel of one or more arbitrators ultimately decides whether or not the employee was improperly discharged. While a wrongful dismissal in the non-unionized setting gives rise to court awarded damages, the improper discharge of a unionized employee often results in the employee being reinstated.

[314] *Bell Canada and Communication Workers of Canada (Re)* (1989), 5 L.A.C. (4th) 40 (Can.).

vehicle and pried open a Bell Canada interchange box, ripping out the wires inside. As a result of the latter incident, at least eight businesses were without telephone service for several hours. The technician was found to have engaged in acts of sabotage by wilfully and intentionally putting the company's equipment out of order. The sabotage was particularly serious for two reasons: members of the public depend heavily on the company's services; and much of the company's property is exposed and unsupervised making it vulnerable to attack. The arbitration panel concluded that the technician's termination was warranted on account of the seriousness of the sabotage. Factors that provided further support for this conclusion included the technician's position, his visibility and his appreciation of the consequences that would flow from his actions. Since the technician was the local union vice-president and occupied a position of leadership and influence, he was liable to receive a more severe penalty for his misconduct than employees who did not have similar status. Furthermore, in his capacity as a union official, the technician had warned other employees not to commit acts of sabotage during the strike and he knew that the company's policy was to dismiss anyone caught engaging in such misdeeds.

In order to establish a case for cause on the basis of sabotage, an employer will have to show that the employee engaged in a deliberate act intentionally designed to damage the property or product of the employer's business. Without such a motive, a case for sabotage cannot be proved. This principle was confirmed in a case where an employee was dismissed by a meat-processing company because of misconduct the company perceived to be analogous to sabotage.[315] In the case, a food inspector saw the employee wet his hair under a water tap over a bin of meat. As a result, the meat was condemned and had to be destroyed. The arbitrator who heard this matter concluded that the employee had not engaged in an act of sabotage because he was not motivated by a desire to damage the company's products. Instead, the employee's conduct was characterized as very careless considering the importance of sanitation in a food-processing operation. Since the employee's conduct was not an act of sabotage, his dismissal was found to be a form of discipline that was too severe in the circumstances.

A dismissal may likewise be unwarranted where an act of sabotage results from "horseplay" among employees and not from malice against the employer. In one case, a company fired an employee for allegedly engaging in acts of sabotage against company property.[316] On one occasion, the employee broke the lights on a company tractor and on another disconnected the tractor's lights and rendered a co-worker's drill inoperative by cutting a

---

[315] *Burns Meats and UFCW, Loc. 832 (Morissette) (Re)* (1993), 38 L.A.C. (4th) 172 (Man.).

[316] *Inco Ltd. and USWA, Loc. 6500 (Gignac) (Re)* (1991), 20 L.A.C. (4th) 386 (Ont.).

water hose. At the time the incidents occurred, the employee and his co-worker were involved in a series of childish pranks that eventually got out of hand. While damage was caused to the company's property, this result was not intended by the employee. His actions could not be characterized as sabotage since they were not deliberately or wilfully aimed at destroying property belonging to the company. Accordingly, the employee's dismissal was not warranted as there was no evidence of malice against the company and others were also involved in the "horseplay".

On the other hand, where an employee wilfully sets out to damage an employer's property or product, dismissal can be justified even where the misconduct is discovered before the employer actually suffers any harm. The employment relationship may lawfully be brought to an end because the act of deliberately trying to sabotage an employer's operations is totally incompatible with what an employer is entitled to expect from an employee.[317]

A case for cause is likely to be established in situations where an employer has specific rules that prohibit acts of sabotage and the rules are regularly enforced.[318] Furthermore, a termination is more likely to be upheld where there is a credible witness who can attest to the employee's involvement in an incident of sabotage. These were the circumstances in a case where an employee was seen tearing apart the wires of an alarm system that restricted access from some of the exits in his employer's plant.[319] A supervisor who proved to be a credible witness saw the employee engage in this act. Such behaviour was specifically prohibited by the workplace's rules and regulations. Non-compliance with any of the rules and regulations was grounds for discipline, up to and including termination of employment. In light of the seriousness of the sabotage and the employee's awareness of its consequences, the arbitrator who heard this matter upheld the dismissal and concluded that the employment relationship had been irrevocably breached. Additional support for this conclusion existed because the employee continued to deny his involvement in the incident even when repeatedly faced with the fact that the supervisor had witnessed the event.

While an act of sabotage can amount to just cause and support a termination, certain factors may indicate that the employee's conduct was out of character and that dismissal was not appropriate. Examples of such factors include:

(a) a discipline-free work record;

---

[317] See *Oil, Chemical & Atomic Workers, Loc. 9-341 and Inmont Canada Ltd. (Re)* (1970), 21 L.A.C. 411 (Ont.), as quoted in *Bell Canada and Communication Workers of Canada (Re)*, *supra*, footnote 314.

[318] See also discussion under Heading 8, "Breaching Employer Policies or Rules", of this Part.

[319] *Redirack Ltd. and USW, Local 9088 (Re)* (1988), 33 L.A.C. (3d) 226 (Ont.).

(b) a long period of service;

(c) evidence the individual was a valuable and reliable employee;

(d) a physical or psychological impairment such as alcoholism or depression that might explain the employee's failure to appreciate the nature of his or her conduct;

(e) other emotional or family problems;

(f) apparent lack of motive for the act of sabotage; and

(g) dismissal of the employee shortly before he or she was entitled to full pension rights from the employer.[320]

Finally, an employee's conduct in destroying company property will not amount to just cause for termination where the conduct is trivial in nature or can be characterized as a lapse of good judgment. In one case for instance, a clerk employed by an insurance company destroyed an entry made in her personnel file.[321] The general content of this entry indicated that on one occasion the clerk had left the office without permission to drive her daughter to work and on another occasion she was late by ten minutes. After telling a co-worker that she found this notation to be trifling and childish, the clerk destroyed the entry by tearing it up. While the court confirmed that destruction of the document was wrong, it concluded that the clerk's conduct was not serious enough to constitute just cause for dismissal. Instead, the court indicated that the clerk's actions were better characterized as a lapse of good judgment. This conclusion was reached because the clerk had not acted in a sinister manner nor did she attempt to hide the incident.

Overview

Intentionally destroying or damaging the property or product of an employer may give rise to cause for dismissal, thereby removing the need to provide the employee with reasonable notice of termination of employment. A case for cause on the basis of sabotage will be strengthened where the following factors or circumstances exist:

1. The employer's property or product is particularly vulnerable to attack.
2. The act of sabotage in question had the potential of affecting a large number of people in an adverse manner.
3. The incident was serious in nature.
4. The employee responsible for the sabotage occupied a position of some importance and influence.

---

[320] See *Boise Cascade Canada Ltd. and CPU, Loc. 306 (Del Zotto) (Re)* (1991), 20 L.A.C. (4th) 355 (Ont.).

[321] *Connor v. Canada Life Assurance Co.* (1991), 108 N.S.R. (2d) 361, supplementary reasons 108 N.S.R. (2d) at p. 369 (S.C.T.D.).

5. The employee was aware that the consequences of engaging in an act of sabotage included termination.
6. The employee deliberately set out to damage or destroy the employer's property or product, even if no damage was ultimately caused.
7. The employee was motivated by a desire to undermine the employer's operations.
8. The employee's conduct was wilful and deliberate rather than a mere lapse of good judgment.
9. The employer regularly enforces a policy or rules that prohibit acts of sabotage and provide that the penalty for such conduct is termination.
10. There were witnesses to the employee's misconduct.
11. The employee continues to deny his or her involvement in an incident of sabotage despite the existence of one or more credible witnesses.
12. The employee is not a long-serving or exemplary employee.
13. The employee's judgment or behaviour was not affected by illness or other mitigating circumstances.
14. The employee attempted to conceal the misconduct.

27 ✧ PERSONAL APPEARANCE AND HYGIENE

There may be situations where an employer is unsatisfied with an employee for reasons related to the employee's consistent neglect of personal hygiene and/or appearance. While the employee's behaviour in this regard is not unlawful or improper *per se*, it can be incompatible with maintaining the employment relationship. A dismissal based on personal hygiene or appearance concerns can be justified if the concerns are not insignificant and if the interests of the employer's business are likely to be adversely affected. This will be especially true where an employee's responsibilities include dealing with the public and where appearance and hygiene are primary considerations because of the nature of the employer's business. Furthermore, an employer must normally provide sufficient warning that an employee's job is in jeopardy on account of hygiene or appearance problems before a case for cause on this basis can be established.

A common complaint in this area relates to an employee's untidy appearance. It was for this reason that a snack foods merchandiser fired its district manager after only five weeks in the position.[322] On one occasion in the course of a delivery, the manager's shirt was partially out of his pants and the buckles of his overshoes were flopping open. While the court recognized that this incident may have fallen short of an ideal state of dress, it was found to be trivial in nature and unlikely to offend any of the merchandiser's cus-

---

[322] *Kozak v. Aliments Krispy Kernels Inc.* (1988), 22 C.C.E.L. 1 (Ont. Dist. Ct.).

tomers. Moreover, the court said the employee had not been advised of any specific dress code and apart from that one occasion, his standard of dress never fell to a level that could be considered unreasonable. For these reasons, the incident relating to the employee's untidy appearance was not a major transgression and did not constitute just cause for his dismissal.

In another case, the operator of a hair-cutting business gave reasons relating to personal appearance for firing one of his hairstylists.[323] In particular, the operator complained that the hairstylist's clothing was untidy, his face was unshaven and his hair was greasy. The court stated that conduct inconsistent with the express or implied conditions of an employee's service will justify dismissal, although the degree of misconduct required to justify dismissal may be greater for long-term or senior level employees. In the particular circumstances, the court ultimately accepted that the employee's appearance and untidiness were factors that made him ill-suited to the employer's business. Since he had been warned about these things but refused to change, the court concluded that just cause for the employee's termination existed.

As already noted, where problems exist that relate to an employee's personal hygiene or appearance, sufficient warnings are usually required in order for the employer to establish that a dismissal was for cause. In one case, the court found that the employment of a fragrance demonstrator was terminated on account of a serious personal hygiene problem.[324] In particular, the employer and a number of witnesses testified that the employee persistently had bad body odour. In addition, the employer complained that the employee had dressed inappropriately on at least one occasion and that she often engaged in disruptive behaviour that included constant requests for higher wages, frequently calling the territory manager, monopolizing staff meetings and generally exaggerating minor work problems out of proportion. The court concluded that the employee's body odour problem together with the incidents of disruptive behaviour gave the employer sufficient cause to dismiss her. However, because the employee had only been "spoken to" twice prior to her dismissal, she had not received sufficient warning that her job was in jeopardy. Also, there was some inconsistency relating to evaluations of the employee's performance. This was demonstrated by the fact that her personnel file contained notes from senior management praising her work and sales record. In these circumstances, particularly because of the apparent satisfaction with her work, the employer was required to give the employee a warning in the clearest of terms that her job was at risk if she did not correct the body odour problem and stop engaging in disruptive behaviour. Having

---

[323] *Essery v. John Lecky & Co.* (1986), 60 Nfld. & P.E.I.R. 219 (P.E.I.S.C.).
[324] *Bagnall v. Calvin Klein Cosmetics (Canada) Ltd.* (1994), 5 C.C.E.L. (2d) 261 (Ont. Ct. (Gen. Div.)).

received no such warning, the employee was entitled to damages as she had not received reasonable notice of termination.

Overview

There may be situations where an employee's neglect of personal hygiene and appearance warrant termination of employment without notice, especially where other instances of misconduct exist. A case for cause on this basis is easier to prove where the following factors and circumstances are present:

1. The employee's responsibilities included dealing with the public.
2. Appearance and hygiene are primary considerations on account of the nature of the employer's business (*e.g.*, businesses that deal with food).
3. The hygiene or appearance problems are inconsistent with or ill-suited to the employer's business.
4. The hygiene or appearance problems are not trivial in nature.
5. Clear warnings in respect of the employee's appearance and personal hygiene were provided by the employer.
6. The employee was made aware of the fact that dismissal was imminent should the appearance and hygiene problems not be ameliorated.
7. There had been customer and employee complaints in respect of the employee's personal appearance and hygiene.
8. The employer's interests were harmed or were likely to be harmed as a result of the appearance and hygiene problems.
9. The employee's state of dress or appearance fell below a standard of reasonableness.
10. The employer has a policy in place that relates to appearance or hygiene (such as a dress code) that is consistently enforced but was not met by the employee.

28 ✧ UNSUITABILITY

An employer might consider an individual unsuitable in the employment context for a number of reasons and by reference to an assortment of criteria. When employers decide that an employee is not properly suited to the position he or she holds, they may do so on the basis of one or many factors. Some of the factors will stand alone as grounds amounting to just cause for termination and in these circumstances an employer is entitled to dismiss the employee without notice. On other occasions, however, the conclusion regarding an employee's lack of fit or suitability may not be based on recognized or sufficient grounds of misconduct that would ordinarily justify a summary dismissal. In these circumstances, the general rule is that reasonable notice must be provided if an employer wants to fire the unsuitable employee.

Having said this, there is some authority to suggest that, in and of itself, extreme unsuitability can amount to just cause for termination where the operations of an employer are prejudiced.[325] For the most part, however, a case for cause will not succeed where a regular employee is dismissed simply because he or she is not a proper fit in the employer's organization. While a company is entitled to fire an employee who it believes is unsuitable, that employee will have a right to receive damages for wrongful dismissal if proper notice of termination was not provided. This point is illustrated by a somewhat unusual case where a marketing and sales manager was fired before his actual start date with a computer software company.[326] The company's president dismissed the manager after concluding that he was not the right person for the job. The president based this conclusion on observations made of the employee at three meetings prior to the day on which he was formally required to report to work. From those observations, the president decided that the employee was unsuited for the position of marketing and sales manager because he lacked the proper degree of professionalism and credibility. The court accepted that the employee may have been unsuitable and agreed that the president was entitled to cancel the employment contract on this basis. However, the court also took the view that the president was primarily to blame for the employee's erroneous hiring because he had failed to exercise due care and caution when choosing the prospective employee. Accordingly, while the employee may not have suited the position of marketing and sales manager, the court interpreted the evidence as supporting his wrongful dismissal claim and concluded that he was entitled to damages.

While unsuitability alone will rarely support just cause for a regular employee's dismissal, different considerations apply where the employee has probationary status. The courts have indicated that, standing on its own, unsuitability can amount to just cause for dismissing a probationary employee.[327]

Overview

The dismissal of a non-probationary employee without notice is not justified on the basis of unsuitability alone unless the unsuitability is extreme in nature and prejudices an employer's operations. Even so, a case for cause can succeed where an employer concludes that the employee is unsuitable based

---

[325] See *Perham v. Canada Trust Co.* (1988), 23 C.C.E.L. 277 (B.C.S.C.).
[326] *Levi v. Chartersoft Canada Inc.* (1994), 8 C.C.E.L. (2d) 10 (Man. Q.B.).
[327] See the discussion under Heading 1, "Probationary Status", of this Part.

on recognized grounds of misconduct that on their own may amount to just cause for termination.

29 ✧ AGE/RETIREMENT

Age does not constitute just cause for termination and, therefore, employees cannot be summarily dismissed on this basis alone. Having said this, an individual's employment may in some instances be ended by way of retirement without providing reasonable notice or pay in lieu of notice. This will only be the case where a mandatory retirement policy has been established or where an employee has otherwise agreed to retire on or by a certain date.[328] In other situations, age may play a role in establishing a case for cause or in the frustration of an employment contract. Regardless of the circumstances, when the decision to dismiss an employee involves considerations of age, employers must assess the human rights legislation in their jurisdiction and, where relevant, the *Canadian Charter of Rights and Freedoms.*

Whether an employee can be dismissed without notice by way of mandatory retirement depends on a couple of factors. First, every termination based on retirement must comply with the relevant human rights legislation and possibly the Charter. Secondly, the employee who is dismissed must have accepted mandatory retirement as a condition or term of employment. In most instances, this requires the employer to establish a mandatory retirement policy that is clearly defined and communicated to all employees affected by it. The employer must also ensure that employees accept the policy at the time of hiring. If a mandatory retirement policy is established after such time, the employer should have current employees agree to the policy before it is actually enforced. Otherwise, the employer must provide employees with reasonable notice of the policy's implementation. This gives an employee the opportunity to look for other work in the event that he or she refuses to accept mandatory retirement as a condition of employment. In other words, where an employment contract does not originally contemplate mandatory retirement, a policy created at a later date does not allow an employer to impose retirement until existing employees have either accepted the policy or have received reasonable notice as to when the policy will be in effect.[329]

In certain situations, an employer may be able to dismiss an employee summarily by way of retirement even if a formal retirement policy has not been instituted. This will only be permitted where an employment contract specifies a retirement date or where such a date can be implied from other

---

[328] In this context, retirement refers to an employment contract ending because the employee has reached a certain age or has worked the number of years originally set as the required period of employment.

[329] See *Brown v. Coles* (1986), 5 B.C.L.R. (2d) 143 (C.A.).

sources, such as a company's retirement practices or the provisions of a company's benefits, compensation or pension plans. If these circumstances do not exist, an employee's dismissal cannot be justified without acceptance of a mandatory retirement policy as a term of employment. As a consequence, reasonable notice of termination must be provided in the absence of a retirement policy or other evidence from which to imply a mandatory retirement date. This will be true even though a company may believe that the industry in which it operates has a "standard" retirement age. These were the facts of one case where a company in the business of crane rentals and related services dismissed a salesman because he had attained the age of 65.[330] In the company's opinion, this was the generally accepted age of retirement and it was also appropriate for its operations. However, the court confirmed that compulsory retirement is not recognized in the common law as legal justification for an employee's termination. Instead, summary dismissal based on age is only warranted where an employer has established a clear policy or practice of mandatory retirement. In this case, there was no evidence that the company had established such a practice or policy either before or during the salesman's employment. There was also no evidence that any other company employee had been required to retire at the age of 65. Accordingly, the court concluded that the salesman was entitled to reasonable notice of his dismissal because termination by way of retirement is not justified in the absence of a company policy or practice relating to mandatory retirement.

If an employee acquiesces and consents to retirement or retires voluntarily, the employer may be released from the obligation to provide reasonable notice of termination. Be that as it may, a court will usually require that there be strong evidence of an agreement to retire before concluding that mandatory retirement was accepted. An employee's silence after being told of his or her impending retirement is insufficient proof of agreement to retire.[331] Similarly, retirement may be found to be involuntary if an employee retires because he or she believes that no other choice exists. This is likely to be the case where the employee wants to continue working and is able to do so.[332] Finally, courts will not infer that an employee knew or accepted that mandatory retirement would be imposed because of recent changes made to the employer's operations and personnel department.[333]

Where a mandatory retirement age has been properly imposed as a term of employment, an employer should take note of when an employee will reach retiring age. Employees cannot be dismissed without receiving proper

---

[330] *Heslop v. Cooper's Crane Rental Ltd.* (1994), 6 C.C.E.L. (2d) 252 (Ont. Ct. (Gen. Div.)), vard 30 C.C.E.L. (2d) 279 (C.A.).

[331] *Supra.*

[332] See *Mallet v. New Brunswick* (1982), 142 D.L.R. (3d) 161 (N.B.Q.B.), affd 2 D.L.R. (4th) 766 (C.A.).

[333] See *Stock v. Best Form Brassiere Canada Inc.* (1986), 15 C.C.E.L. 298 (Que. S.C.).

notice if they continue to work past the age of retirement. However, an agreement with an employee who continues to work can be negotiated to limit the amount of reasonable notice to be provided in the future. This agreement should be negotiated before the employee attains retirement age to ensure that it will be legally binding if and when the employee is eventually dismissed. If a timely agreement is not reached, the employer will have to provide the employee with the full amount of notice or pay in lieu of notice to which he or she is entitled. The amount of notice can prove to be significant on account of the employee's advanced age and because the employee is likely to have served the employer for a long period of time.

As already mentioned, every dismissal that involves consideration of an employee's age must be examined in light of human rights legislation and in some cases the Charter. Discrimination in employment based on age is prohibited by the human rights legislation of all Canadian jurisdictions, thereby making termination on this basis unlawful. The statutes of some provinces, however, qualify the definition of age and employers can establish a policy that requires employees to retire at 65 years of age or older.[334] Accordingly, subject to any other statutory conditions that may exist, mandatory retirement at the age of 65 or older can be a valid term of an individual's employment contract. In provinces where age is not similarly qualified, mandatory retirement at any age can only be imposed as a term of employment if the employer demonstrates that it is a "*bona fide* occupational requirement or qualification" ("BFOR"). To establish a BFOR, the employer must show that mandatory retirement has been imposed in good faith and with the sincerely held belief of being in the interests of adequate, safe and economical work performance. Furthermore, the employer must show that mandatory retirement is related in an objective sense to the performance of the employment concerned.[335] Proof of a BFOR may also be advanced in jurisdictions where compulsory retirement at 65 is permitted but employers want to retire employees before they reach that age. In contrast, federal jurisdiction employers and employees are entitled to agree on any age of mandatory retirement without employers having to prove the existence of a BFOR. In any event, the retirement age chosen by the parties must be one that is generally appropriate for the industry in question.

A term of employment that imposes mandatory retirement cannot be used to justify termination without notice if the term is contrary to the relevant human rights legislation. Reasonable notice of the retirement must be

---

[334] In Ontario, British Columbia, Newfoundland and Saskatchewan, employment age is defined with an upper limit of 65 years and therefore employees are not protected from dismissal pursuant to a mandatory retirement policy that sets the age of retirement at 65 years or older.

[335] Establishing a BFOR is also discussed under Heading 14, "Illness and Disability", of this Part.

provided in these circumstances. In one case, the court found that an understanding relating to retirement existed between a branch manager and his employer.[336] The manager understood that he was expected to retire at the age of 65 unless some other arrangement was made. The understanding was primarily based on the fact that the employer's company had a long-standing policy requiring all employees to retire at the age of 65. Furthermore, the policy was incorporated into the company's compensation and benefits plans. In any event, while the manager understood that his employment would end at the age of 65, the court concluded that he was still entitled to receive reasonable notice of termination. This conclusion was reached because provisions of the company's retirement policy were contrary to the relevant human rights legislation.

A further consideration of employers when implementing mandatory retirement policies is the potential application and effect of the Charter. The Charter applies to all legislation and other "governmental actions".[337] Section 15 of the Charter guarantees that all individuals have the right to equal protection and benefit of the law without discrimination based on age. If provincial or federal human rights laws allow employers to establish a mandatory retirement policy, this may constitute discrimination based on age and an infringement of the Charter. Similarly, a retirement policy imposed by the government or a body acting under statutory authority may amount to discrimination that violates the Charter. However, the violation may be permitted pursuant to s. 1 of the Charter, often referred to as the "the saving clause". Mandatory retirement policies and the laws that allow them are "saved" if they are seen as reasonable limits to the Charter's guarantee of freedom from age discrimination and if they can be justified in a free and democratic society. The Supreme Court of Canada has indicated that, while a mandatory policy of retirement may violate s. 15 of the Charter, this infringement can be justified if a proportionality test is satisfied. The test requires the court to make the following findings of fact:[338]

1. The retirement policy has objectives that are pressing and substantial.
2. The policy is rationally connected to the objectives.
3. In achieving these objectives, the policy minimally impairs the rights of individuals.

---

[336] *Keshen v. Carrier Canada Ltd.* (1989), 30 C.C.E.L. 107 (B.C.S.C.).

[337] In this regard, the Charter applies to government employers and is likely to apply to statutory governmental bodies, even when they are acting as employers. However, the Charter does not apply to private sector employers and may not apply to quasi-government bodies unless they are acting in a governmental capacity.

[338] See *McKinney v. University of Guelph* (1987), 46 D.L.R. (4th) 193 (Ont. C.A.), affd 76 D.L.R. (4th) 545 (S.C.C.).

4. The adverse effects of the policy do not outweigh its pressing and substantial objectives.

As a consequence, employers may be able to impose a policy of mandatory retirement that infringes the Charter where any impairment to an individual's rights is proportional to the achievement of the policy's legitimate objectives.

While age alone does not amount to just cause for termination, it can help to establish a case for cause. For example, there may be circumstances where an employee is no longer capable of performing the required duties of employment as a result of his or her advancing age, thereby giving rise to just cause for dismissal. Even so, serious performance problems must exist before just cause for termination can be established. Since the employee is likely to have a lengthy and satisfactory service record, an employer may have to exercise a substantial amount of tolerance when concerns arise relating to the employee's competence and ability to perform. In the absence of significant performance problems, advanced age alone will not constitute proof that an employee is incompetent to discharge his or her employment responsibilities.[339]

In other circumstances, an employee might retire on account of illness and disability. The frustration of contract doctrine will apply if the illness or disability is permanent in nature and has made it impossible for the employee to perform the required duties of employment. However, an employer must be able to demonstrate that the illness or disability cannot be accommodated without undue hardship.[340] In cases of retirement based on the frustration of contract, employers are not obliged to provide the disabled or ill employee with reasonable notice or pay in lieu of notice, but the terms of an employer's benefits or pension plan may require that some payment to the employee be made.

Overview

The common law does not recognize age or mandatory retirement as justification for termination. Still, age may assist in establishing just cause for termination or in frustrating an employment contract. Similarly, employers may be able to end an individual's employment without notice where mandatory retirement had been imposed as an accepted term of employment. Mandatory retirement will likely be an accepted term of employment where the following factors and circumstances exist:

---

[339] *Supra*, footnote 334. See also discussion under Heading 3, "Performance Problems", of this Part.

[340] See discussion under Heading 14, "Illness and Disability", of this Part.

1. A clearly defined policy of mandatory retirement has been established by the employer and communicated to all affected employees.
2. The policy was implemented prior to the employee's hiring.
3. If the policy was created after an employee's hiring, the employee either accepted the policy or received reasonable notice of its implementation.
4. The policy is not contrary to human rights legislation.
5. The employment contract specified a mandatory retirement age or a mandatory age of retirement can be implied from an employer's retirement practices or by the terms of an employer's benefits, compensation or pension plans.
6. There is strong evidence to demonstrate that the employee accepted mandatory retirement or retired voluntarily.
7. The employee had not continued to work past the age of mandatory retirement as defined by the employer's retirement policy or practices.

30 ✧ SEEKING LEGAL ADVICE OR INITIATING CLAIM AGAINST EMPLOYER

Seeking legal advice in respect of a matter related to one's employment or initiating a claim against an employer does not *per se* amount to just cause for termination. Once a solicitor has been consulted, however, an employee may act in a manner that serves to breach the employment contract, thereby giving the employer grounds to dismiss the employee without notice. Similarly, commencing legal proceedings against the employer prematurely or unlawfully can give rise to just cause for termination. Absent such circumstances, a case for cause will fail where it is based solely on the act of seeking legal advice, communicating through a solicitor or making a legitimate claim.

Many employees will consult a lawyer to determine whether or not they have been constructively dismissed as a result of changes made by an employer to the terms and conditions of their employment. Once a legal opinion is obtained, an employee might then allege constructive dismissal through a solicitor. If the allegation is ultimately found to be untrue, the fact that it was made does not in and of itself justify dismissing the employee retroactively. On the other hand, just cause for termination may exist if the employee's contract of employment is breached when the allegation of constructive dismissal is made. In one case, for example, a manager employed by Canada Post allowed his solicitor to send the corporation a highly confrontational letter that left little room for negotiation.[341] The letter asserted that the manager had legal claims against the corporation based on its misrepresenta-

---

[341] *Skidd v. Canada Post Corp.* (1993), 47 C.C.E.L. 169 (Ont. Ct. (Gen. Div.)), vard on other grounds 69 A.C.W.S. (3d) 684 (C.A.).

tion of the job and his constructive dismissal. Furthermore, the letter and subsequent conversations with the solicitor made it clear that the manager was not interested in preserving his employment. Rather, he wanted to leave the corporation and receive compensation for conduct that he perceived as constituting misrepresentation and constructive dismissal. The corporation ultimately terminated the manager's employment as a result of his actions and the manager commenced legal proceedings for wrongful dismissal. The court found that the corporation had not misrepresented the manager's job nor fundamentally changed the terms and conditions of his employment. Rather, the manager had made unsubstantiated claims. However, this fact alone did not amount to just cause for termination. The court recognized that the manager had a right to seek and follow legal advice in light of his perception of the situation. Notwithstanding this right, the court held the manager's conduct had breached the employment contract because it showed he was not interested in preserving his employment and the only issue he was willing to negotiate was the amount of compensation he was owed. Consequently, the court concluded that just cause for dismissal was established and that the company was justified in terminating the manager's employment.

Requesting a solicitor to review an employment agreement that is different from the one agreed to does not amount to cause for termination. In one case, an employee who had taken the three weeks' vacation he was entitled to requested an additional three and one-half weeks of leave to travel.[342] When the general manager refused his request, the employee had his solicitor write a request for the additional leave. This request was forwarded to the owner. At a meeting with the owner, the employee negotiated an agreement whereby the employee would quit his position to be hired back upon his return, provided the employee accepted a reduction in his vacation period and vacation pay. Upon returning to work the employee was presented with an employment agreement to sign. The agreement, however, was different from that originally agreed to by the owner and employee. The employee therefore requested time to have his solicitor review the new agreement. Instead, the employee was dismissed. The court concluded there was no justification for denying the employee the right to seek legal advice about the altered agreement.

Communicating with one's employer through a solicitor does not itself amount to just cause for termination. But, if the solicitor communicates an employee's intention to no longer be bound by the terms of his or her employment contract, the employer is entitled to dismiss the employee. This was the situation in a case where the employee was the manager of a bank's branch

---

[342] *Palmer v. Gallery 1 Enterprises Inc.*, [2002] N.S.J. No. 557 (QL) (S.C.), affd [2003] N.S.J. No. 114 (QL) (C.A.).

in Vancouver.[343] The bank decided to transfer the employee to another position in its New York office. The employee considered such a transfer to be a demotion and the employee had his solicitor send the bank a letter advising that he would not accept the change to his employment as the change amounted to constructive dismissal. A "proposal of settlement" prepared by the solicitor followed and demanded a certain amount of compensation for the perceived dismissal. The bank treated the letter and proposal as rejection by the employee of his employment contract and he was dismissed. Considering all the facts, the court noted that, while the bank could not require the employee to accept a demotion, an express term of his employment contract required that he be available for duty throughout the world. Since the court viewed the transfer as a lateral move rather than a demotion, it was not found to constitute constructive dismissal and the employee's initial claim was therefore unfounded. With respect to the termination of his employment, the court concluded that it was warranted by the employee's repudiation of his employment contract. That the contract had been repudiated was demonstrated by the solicitor's letter expressing the employee's intention to no longer be bound by its terms.

In some circumstances, consulting a solicitor and threatening to commence legal proceedings will support a case for cause if there is unreasonable and harmful interference to a company's management as a result. In one case, for example, legal action was threatened against an officer of a rigging company who was investigating a work-related incident.[344] The threat was made by one of the employees whose involvement in the incident was being examined. When the employee learned that the officer had acquired written statements alleging that he had been under the influence of alcohol at the material time, the employee instructed his solicitor to threaten a lawsuit unless the statements were suppressed and destroyed. The employee was summarily dismissed when he subsequently refused to withdraw his solicitor's letter, along with the threat of legal action. In the employee's action for wrongful dismissal, the court recognized that an employer has an inherent right to investigate a work-related incident and produce a report that describes the conduct of any employees involved. In this case, the company was conducting its investigation in a reasonable manner and had properly given the employee an opportunity to provide his account of the incident. The employee's demand that the officer suppress and destroy evidence properly available to the employee's superiors was extremely inappropriate. By having his lawyer threaten legal action against the investigating officer and by subsequently refusing to retract the threat, the employee had made internal resolution of the work-related incident highly improbable. The court concluded that the

---

[343] *Reber v. Lloyds Bank International Canada* (1985), 18 D.L.R. (4th) 122 (B.C.C.A.).
[344] *Cunningham v. Kwikasair Ltd.* (1980), 111 D.L.R. (3d) 618 (B.C.S.C.).

employee's termination was justified because his conduct was unreasonable and it amounted to harmful interference with the company's internal management.

Generally speaking, a case for cause is established if an employment contract is breached while an employee exercises his or her right to seek legal advice. The type of conduct that can breach the employment contract will necessarily depend on the facts and circumstances of each particular situation. However, it is almost always true that, where an employee is a senior executive and in a fiduciary position, the duty owed to the employer will be much greater than that of an hourly paid or very junior employee. Where a senior executive persists in promoting his or her own interests and through a lawyer advances a position that fundamentally conflicts with that of management, just cause for termination will exist.[345] This is especially true where the solicitor writes a letter to the employer in a demanding and forceful manner. These were the circumstances in a case where an organization's senior executive was persistent in his view that he owned the patent to a product he had designed during the course of his employment.[346] Management was of the view that ownership belonged to the organization. The court concluded that the executive's dismissal was warranted because the position he was taking was entirely incompatible with that taken by the organization. In particular, the executive's fiduciary duty was breached by his continued persistence in the matter which consisted mainly of having his solicitor advance the incompatible position he had taken.

An employment contract is also breached where an employee commences a lawsuit for wrongful dismissal while still employed. In such situations, just cause will be found to exist because suing an employer for wrongful dismissal is inconsistent with a continuing employment relationship. In one case, for example, a real estate development officer commenced an action for wrongful dismissal against the company for which he worked.[347] The terms of his employment had consisted of equity participation in certain projects engaged in by the company. The officer was removed from the last project he was involved in when the company received client complaints about his performance. He was told he would be kept on salary until another project became available. The officer came to feel that his removal from the project in return for some undefined position constituted constructive dismissal. As a result, when no new project was found after 48 days, the officer commenced a lawsuit against the company in which he alleged that his

---

[345] See also discussion under Heading 17, "Breaching Fiduciary Duties", of this Part.

[346] *Helbig v. Oxford Warehousing Ltd.* (1985), 20 D.L.R. (4th) 112 (Ont. C.A.), leave to appeal to S.C.C. refused [1985] 2 S.C.R. vii.

[347] *Hulme v. Cadillac Fairview Corp.* (1993), 1 C.C.E.L. (2d) 94 (Ont. Ct. (Gen. Div.)), affd 81 A.C.W.S. (3d) 815 (C.A.), leave to appeal to S.C.C. refused 236 N.R. 188*n*.

employment contract had been breached. Effective that day, the company severed its relationship with the officer. The court concluded that the officer had not been constructively dismissed when taken off the project and that it was unrealistic to expect a new position in 48 days or less given the nature of the development business. His lawsuit had therefore been brought prematurely. Furthermore, the court found that it was inconsistent with a continuing employment relationship for the officer to be suing his employer for wrongful dismissal. As such, the company was entitled to dismiss the officer on the day the lawsuit was commenced.

In contrast, a request to have legal counsel present when being questioned by an employer will not warrant an employee's termination so long as the request is reasonable given the circumstances. A request is reasonable where the employer suspects that the employee has engaged in serious misconduct such as theft. In this situation, the employee should not be dismissed summarily for his refusal to answer questions without a lawyer.[348] Termination of employment on this basis will likely amount to wrongful dismissal and the employer will be held liable for damages.

Similarly, unless the employee's conduct serves to repudiate an existing employment contract, making a complaint or bringing a legitimate claim against the employer does not warrant termination or justify an employer's failure to call the employee back to work. In one case, for instance, the employee complained to management about what she considered a health and safety risk to herself, to other workers and to the employer's operations generally.[349] As a result of this complaint and the employee's refusal to work a shift where her health and safety were threatened, she was laid off and never recalled to work. The employee subsequently filed a complaint with the appropriate provincial authority alleging that she had not been provided with the statutory notice of termination or severance pay to which she was entitled. In addition, the employee commenced legal proceedings against her employer for wrongful dismissal damages. The court concluded that the employer had acted unlawfully in terminating the employee's employment because she had a legal right to refuse work that was likely to endanger her health and safety and the employee's decision to bring claims against the employer for statutory and common law benefits did not justify the employer's failure to recall her to work.

In addition to issues of health and safety, employees are statutorily entitled to make complaints in respect of other matters as well. For example, all jurisdictions have laws that give individuals the right to file a human rights complaint in the appropriate circumstances and their employment cannot be

---

[348]   See *Wilson v. T. Eaton Co.* (1980), 6 A.C.W.S. (2d) 503 (Ont. H.C.J.).

[349]   *McLean v. Humpty Dumpty Foods Ltd.* (1994), 144 N.B.R. (2d) 63 (Q.B.). See also discussion under Heading 11, "Refusing to Perform Unsafe Work", of this Part.

terminated for doing so. Termination by an employer on this basis amounts to wrongful dismissal and is also contrary to human rights legislation. Any employer who fires an employee for filing a human rights complaint may be required to reinstate the employee and/or pay the employee a substantial amount of damages.[350]

A termination is similarly not justified if it is based on the fact that the employee sought legal advice with respect to an unreasonable deduction in his or her pay. An example of this principle can be found in a fairly old case where an employee's solicitor wrote to the employer and courteously asked that he pay the employee the amount that had wrongfully been deducted from his wages.[351] Although the employee was eventually paid, he was subsequently dismissed for complaining about the deduction through his solicitor and refusing to withdraw the solicitor's letter before receiving what he was owed. The court concluded that the dismissal was unwarranted as the employee had acted within his legal rights and had done nothing that could be construed as offensive.

Just cause for termination will likewise not be established where a lawyer writes to an employee's company for clarification of its position in respect of the employee's employment. In such a case, a dismissal without notice based on the employee's conduct in consulting a lawyer and communicating through counsel is unjustified. This is especially true where the terms and conditions of employment have been fundamentally changed by the employer and therefore amount to the employee's constructive dismissal. In these circumstances, the employee is entitled to determine his or her legal position by consulting a solicitor.[352]

Overview

Seeking legal advice, communicating through a solicitor or making a claim against the employer are not in and of themselves grounds for just cause termination. However, where an employee's conduct serves to repudiate the employment contract, the employer may be entitled to dismiss the employee summarily. In this regard, a case for cause is strengthened where the following factors or circumstances are present:

1. As a consequence of seeking legal advice, the employee made an unfounded claim of constructive dismissal and showed no interest in preserving the employment relationship.

---

[350] See also discussion under Heading 20, "Participation in Harassment", of this Part.
[351] *Clark v. Capp* (1905), 9 O.L.R. 192 (Div. Ct.).
[352] See *Zarantonello v. Forest Industries Flying Tankers Ltd.* (1994), 5 C.C.E.L. (2d) 96 (B.C.S.C.).

2. A solicitor was used to communicate the employee's intention not to be bound to the terms of his or her employment contract.
3. The employee was a senior executive and he or she used a lawyer to advance a position entirely incompatible with the fiduciary duty owed to the employer.
4. As a result of the employee obtaining legal advice and communicating through a solicitor, there was harmful and unwarranted interference to an employer's management and operations.
5. Legal proceedings for wrongful dismissal were commenced while the employee was still employed.

Just cause for termination will likely not be established where the following circumstances exist:

1. The employee's lawyer wrote to the employer for clarification of its position in respect of the employee's employment.
2. With or without the assistance of counsel, the claims asserted and communicated were valid and legitimate.
3. The employee was acting within his or her legal rights.
4. The employee's request to have legal counsel present when being questioned by the employer was a reasonable one given the facts of the situation.

31 ✧ LOOKING FOR OTHER EMPLOYMENT

In the course of running their operations employers may learn that one of their employees is seeking alternate employment. While the initial reaction in these circumstances may be a desire to dismiss the employee immediately, a case for just cause solely on this basis cannot be maintained. Looking for another job does not in and of itself amount to just cause for dismissal.

It has generally been accepted that an employee can do certain acts in preparation for leaving his or her employment so long as the current employer is not prejudiced as a result. An employee will especially be justified in seeking alternate work while still employed where it is felt that his or her current job is no longer secure. These circumstances arose in one case where an advertising and merchandise show manager began looking for other employment while still employed by a company in the hardware business.[353] The manager sought alternate work when a number of managerial employees were dismissed and he learned that the company was having financial and management difficulties. However, the manager did not accept the first job offer he received because he felt compelled to complete the preparations for the company's upcoming merchandising show. In spite of his commitment to

---

[353] *Mack v. Link Hardware Co.* (1978), 92 D.L.R. (3d) 757 (Alta. Dist. Ct.).

the show, the manager's employment was terminated after the company became aware of his search for another job. The company said the manager was dismissed on account of its concerns about how the merchandising show was shaping up. The court was satisfied that the manager was carrying out his duties in a satisfactory manner and that the company's alleged concerns about his performance in respect of the show were unfounded. The court ultimately concluded that the manager's dismissal was primarily based on his seeking other employment and that such conduct did not amount to just cause for termination.

During a search for another job, an employee could potentially engage in behaviour that is prejudicial to the interests of his or her employer. Summary dismissal may be warranted in these circumstances. Whether the conduct is in fact prejudicial and constitutes just cause will depend on the particular fact situation. In the case of the advertising and show manager just noted, the company had also maintained that termination was justified on the basis of letters the manager had written to potential employers. These letters contained unfavourable comments about the company's current and future status. The court found that such statements were made by the manager in an effort to explain his reasons for seeking another job rather than with an intent to harm the company. While unflattering, the statements had caused no damage to the company's business nor was the company able to prove that potential harm to its interests or reputation existed. Consequently, the court concluded that the statements, though perhaps ill-advised, did not amount to a breach of the manager's duty to serve his employer with loyalty. As such, they did not give rise to just cause for termination.

Although an employee is permitted to do certain things in contemplation of leaving a company, the employee cannot solicit the company's current customers in order to obtain their future business on a personal basis. This is contrary to the employee's duty to be faithful to his or her employer and can justify dismissal without notice.[354]

The issue of just cause for termination does not arise if an employee resigns to seek alternate employment. The employment contract will come to an end because notice is given of the employee's intention to stop working for the employer on a particular date. Before acting on what appears to be a resignation, a company must ensure that the employee in question has in fact resigned. A resignation cannot be implied where the employer has simply been told that the employee is looking for another job. In one case, for example, a vice-president of finance sought alternate employment after his employer undertook a reorganization of its operations.[355] As a result of

---

[354] See *Wessex Dairies Ltd. v. Smith*, [1935] 2 K.B. 80. See also discussion under Heading 16, "Conflicts of Interest", of this Part.
[355] *Mosher v. Twin Cities Co-Operative Dairy Ltd.* (1984), 5 C.C.E.L. 72 (N.S.T.D.).

changes to his title and responsibilities, the employee felt that his prestige and status had been substantially eroded. He advised senior management of his intention to seek other employment and said that, if successful, he would provide adequate notice of his intention to resign. A few months later, a financial officer was hired to replace the employee and carry out his duties. The employer took the position that the employee had tendered an open-ended resignation that was to take effect when a replacement was found. The court rejected the employer's position and concluded that the employee's conduct did not constitute a resignation. The court said the employee had merely expressed dissatisfaction with recent changes to his position and had indicated that he would look for other employment while continuing to work for the employer. Since the employee did not resign, he was found to have been dismissed from his job when his replacement was hired. The court concluded that the dismissal was not justified because looking for other work is not itself a ground for termination. The court went on to say that this was true regardless of whether an employee sought alternate employment openly or did so in a secretive manner.

In a later case, another court concluded just cause for termination does not exist where an employee says he is not resigning but is seeking alternate employment while continuing to work under protest.[356] The employee in this case was the director of relations and information for an Ontario university. Believing that a fundamental change had unilaterally been made to his job, the director advised his employer in a letter that he would have to look for another job. His employment was subsequently terminated because the employer treated the letter as a resignation, despite declarations by the director to the contrary. The court concluded that no resignation had in fact been tendered and that the employee's expressed intention to seek alternate employment did not amount to just cause for dismissal. Therefore, termination of the director's employment was wrongful and he was entitled to damages.

Overview

Looking for alternate employment will not itself constitute just cause for an employee's dismissal. However, it may be possible to support a case for cause on this basis if the following circumstances exist:

1. During a search for alternate employment, the employee engaged in conduct that is harmful to the employer's business or interests.
2. The employee failed to carry out his or her duties and responsibilities in a satisfactory manner while seeking alternate work.

---

[356] *Moore v. University of Western Ontario* (1985), 8 C.C.E.L. 157 (Ont. H.C.J.).

3. While still working for an organization, the employee attempted to solicit its customers to obtain their future business on a personal basis.

In the absence of these circumstances, an employment relationship cannot be severed without notice where the employer has only been told that the employee is looking for another job. The employment relationship cannot be considered at an end until the employee clearly tenders a resignation. If the employee has in fact resigned, the employment relationship ceases and the issue of just cause for termination does not arise.

32 ✧ GARNISHMENT

Garnishment generally refers to the situation where a creditor seeks satisfaction of a debt from property or money owed to the debtor by a third party. Where the debtor is employed, the creditor may succeed in obtaining a garnishment order for a fixed amount that attaches to his or her wages. Where such an order is obtained, the employer is legally required to garnish the employee's wages and to make available to the creditor the sum of money provided for in the order.

Employers who are compelled to garnish an employee's wages cannot dismiss the employee without notice on this basis. This is specifically prohibited by the employment standards legislation of most jurisdictions. As a result, the fact that a garnishment order has been or will be made against the employee's wages does not constitute just cause for termination.

An employee's failure to disclose to the employer the existence of any prior or future garnishment orders is also unlikely to amount to just cause for termination. In one case, for example, a serviceman was summarily dismissed because he did not tell his employer about two garnishment orders that were being effected against him.[357] The employee's wages were already being garnished by two other creditors and the employer became concerned about his potential liability to satisfy these garnishees. When the employer confronted the employee and admonished him about his financial situation, the employee did not advise the employer that two other garnishment orders were being effected against him. The employee was ultimately fired when the employer learned of the additional orders. An employment standards officer concluded that dismissal was not warranted because an employee does not have a legal duty to disclose to an employer the existence of other garnishment orders. Accordingly, the employee was entitled to notice of his termination.

---

[357] *484093 Ontario Ltd. (Re)*, E.S.C. 1142 (December 18, 1981 — Hunter).

Overview

An employer cannot dismiss an employee summarily on the grounds that garnishment proceedings are or may be taken against the employee. Just cause will similarly not be established on the basis that an employer is or may be required to pay to a third party money that is owed by the employer to the employee. The prohibition against termination also applies to any attachment orders made against the employee under a specific statute or regulation, such as laws relating to child or spousal support. Finally, a case for cause is unlikely to be established because of an employee's failure to disclose the existence of garnishment orders.

33 ✧ REDUNDANCY

There are many reasons why an employee's job or position may become superfluous or unnecessary. An employer's motivation for eliminating a job or position frequently stems from economic considerations. On other occasions, a job or position will no longer be required because an organization decides to change its focus. In either case, the jobs and positions that are being removed have become redundant. While employers are entitled to dismiss workers for reasons of redundancy, a dismissal cannot take place without appropriate notice or pay in lieu of notice being given. Redundancy is not a ground for just cause termination.

If a company decides to eliminate a position in order to decrease its costs and expenses, the employee who occupies that job is often dismissed as a result. The employer in such circumstances continues to have the obligation to provide the employee with reasonable notice of termination and failure to do so may entitle the employee to damages for wrongful dismissal.[358]

Similarly, a dismissal without notice cannot be justified where an employee's job becomes redundant after an organization changes its focus. In one case, for instance, a production co-ordinator's job was made redundant after the controlling interest of the organization employing him changed hands. The controlling interest was acquired by a group of companies who quickly varied the emphasis of the organization's business. As a result, the work performed by the production co-ordinator was no longer required and he was dismissed. The court concluded that redundancy did not justify dismissal without reasonable notice. As a consequence, the employee was entitled to damages for wrongful dismissal.[359]

---

[358] See *Baker v. United Grain Growers Ltd.*, [1978] 5 W.W.R. 370 (Alta. S.C.).
[359] *Gillespie v. Bulkley Valley Forest Industries Ltd.* (1973), 39 D.L.R. (3d) 586 (B.C.S.C.), affd 50 D.L.R. (3d) 316 (C.A.).

There are many examples in the case law confirming that redundancy does not constitute just cause for a termination nor does it remove the employer's obligation to provide reasonable notice. This principle continues to hold true despite the current economic climate in which downsizing and reorganizations are the norm. An employer can attempt to argue that the amount of notice owed to an employee should be reduced where the individual is dismissed due to prevailing economic circumstances or lack of work. This argument will usually fail, however, particularly where an organization is in an industry that has been suffering as a whole. In these circumstances, it is the employee who might successfully advance an argument for greater notice because similar or related employment will take longer to find. In one case, for instance, a hospital had to reorganize and eliminate a specialized position on account of the depressed health care industry.[360] Despite this fact, the hospital still had a duty to provide the displaced employee with reasonable notice. The court concluded that the employee was entitled to a significant amount of notice on the basis of several factors. One of the factors included recognition that similar employment might never be available to the employee because of the nature of her previous job and the prevailing economic climate.

While a company is obliged to provide reasonable notice in cases of redundancy, dismissed employees have a reciprocal duty to mitigate their losses. This may require an individual to accept alternate employment that is offered by the employer and failure to do so can reduce an employee's award of damages for wrongful dismissal. Generally speaking, however, the employee will not have to accept an offer of employment if the new position is substantially different from the one previously held. This is especially true where the position involves a demotion or the circumstances are such that acceptance of the new position will result in the employee having to endure unreasonable working conditions, a loss of prestige, or humiliation and embarrassment.[361] If a particular industry is suffering or declining, an employee may be required to accept a position with another employer that is unrelated or different in nature from the job previously held. Generally though, courts will not reduce an award of damages simply because the employee has limited his or her job search to a specific industry or type of position. This will particularly be the case where certain jobs are not suited to the employee on account of limitations that can include the employee's age, health, abilities, licensing requirements and location needs.[362]

---

[360] *Trudeau-Linley v. Plummer Memorial Public Hospital* (1993), 1 C.C.E.L. (2d) 114 (Ont. Ct. (Gen. Div.)).

[361] *O'Grady v. Insurance Company of British Columbia* (1975), 63 D.L.R. (3d) 370 (B.C.S.C.). See also discussion under Heading 16, "Mitigation", of Part I, "General Concepts".

[362] *Trudeau-Linley v. Plummer Memorial Public Hospital, supra*, footnote 360.

Overview

It is clear that a case for cause cannot be established based solely on reasons of redundancy. Even though a job or position may become redundant for a number of reasons, the employee who is dismissed as a result is entitled to receive reasonable notice of termination or pay in lieu of notice. However, this entitlement is subject to the employee's duty to mitigate his or her losses. Issues of mitigation aside, where the required notice or pay is not provided in cases of termination due to redundancy, employers are apt to find themselves fighting and losing claims of wrongful dismissal.

34 ✧ SALE OF BUSINESS

The sale of a business will never amount to just cause for termination. In this context, a sale refers to the selling of an organization's assets as a going concern. Because an employment contract cannot typically be assigned without the consent of both the employee and employer, the sale of a business acts to terminate all employees where it results in the change of an employer's legal identity. This will consequently give the employees a right to sue their former employer (the vendor of the business) for wrongful dismissal and to be awarded damages for not receiving reasonable notice of termination.[363]

Having said this, it should be noted that the employee in such a situation still has a duty to mitigate losses arising from the termination of employment. In most cases, this means the employee must accept a position with the new employer (the purchaser of the business) if one is offered on the same or substantially the same terms as the position previously held. Even where the offer of employment constitutes a change in an employee's responsibilities, the employee will likely be required to accept it unless doing so would amount to a demotion.

This was demonstrated in a case where a company's president had both manufacturing and distribution responsibilities before the assets of the business were sold to another corporation.[364] Prior to actually taking the assets, the purchasing company offered the employee a future position as head of its distribution division. Even though the financial terms associated with the new position were more favourable than those of the employee's former job as president, he rejected the offer because the new position lacked manufacturing responsibilities. When the sale of the business effectively took place, the employee was fired without notice or compensation and he subsequently sued his former employer for wrongful dismissal. After examining the facts, the court said the position offered by the purchasing corporation carried respon-

---

[363] *Addison v. M. Loeb Ltd.* (1986), 25 D.L.R. (4th) 151 (Ont. C.A.).
[364] *Buchanan v. Canada Valve Inc.* (1987), 39 D.L.R. (4th) 268 (Ont. H.C.J.).

sibilities substantially similar to the employee's former job. Moreover, while the employee's preferences and career objectives were relevant considerations, the court said they did not outweigh his overarching duty to act reasonably. Although there was no issue of just cause and it was clear that the employee had been wrongfully dismissed, the court awarded him no damages. Instead, it concluded that the employee's losses were attributable to his unreasonable failure to mitigate his damages by accepting the purchaser's offer and as a result the losses were not recoverable.

A more difficult issue arising in connection with the sale of a business is whether an employee who accepts an employment offer from the purchaser is entitled to receive credit for his or her past service with the vendor (the former employer). This is an important consideration for the purposes of salary, bonuses and reasonable notice upon termination of employment in the future. In one Ontario case, an employee had worked in a grocery store for 25 years prior to the business being sold by a creditor-appointed receiver.[365] The employee accepted employment with the purchaser but was dismissed without cause some 18 months later when the business was sold to another company. At trial, the court concluded that the employee had only been employed for 18 months for the purpose of assessing the notice period to which he was entitled. Based upon that length of service, reasonable notice was found to be six months. On appeal, the court increased the notice period to 12 months. It noted that an employee's length of service was only one of the factors to consider when determining a proper award for wrongful dismissal damages and in most cases courts give employees some credit for past employment with a predecessor employer.

A different approach was taken by the British Columbia Court of Appeal in respect of an employee who had been employed by a company for 26 years prior to the sale of its business.[366] The employee continued his employment with the purchaser for another 10 years before being dismissed. The court took the view that, when a business is acquired as a going concern, an implied term of the employment contracts between the purchaser and employees who continue to work for the business is that credit will be given for past years' service with the vendor. The implied term can be negated by an express term to the contrary and employees then have the option to sue the vendor for wrongful dismissal. In the British Columbia case, there was no "express term to the contrary" because the purchaser had not advised the employee that his past service would not be taken into account. Consequently, the implied term was not negated and the employee was credited with his full 36 years of service when the award of damages for wrongful dismissal was calculated.

---

[365] *Addison v. M. Loeb Ltd.*, *supra*, footnote 363.
[366] *Sorel v. Tomenson Saunders Whitehead Ltd.* (1987), 39 D.L.R. (4th) 460 (B.C.C.A.).

In at least one New Brunswick case, another method was used for assessing reasonable notice in a sale of business situation. There, an employee had been employed by the vendor of a business for 15 months and by the purchaser of the business for seven months thereafter, at which time the employee was terminated for allegedly using a company vehicle without authorization.[367] After assessing the allegation, the court concluded that the new employer (the purchaser) had not satisfied the burden of proof required to establish just cause for termination and the employee was found to have been wrongfully dismissed. However, the court held that the notice period to which he was entitled was properly based only on his seven months of employment with the purchaser. In its reasons for using the seven-month period, the court explained that where an employee is offered a job with a purchasing company on substantially the same terms as his former position, he must accept it in order to satisfy the duty to mitigate losses associated with the termination of employment. Since there was no evidence in this case to suggest the parties intended otherwise, the court was prepared to apply the common law principle which states that employment terminates when a business is sold. The employee would therefore have an action against the vendor only if his new employment did not last beyond the notice period to which he would have been entitled based on his former years of service. Otherwise, in an action against the purchasing company, the company would only be liable for damages based on the actual length of time it employed the employee.

Overview

The sale of a business as a going concern does not on its own amount to just cause for dismissing its employees. When such a sale happens, the employment of all the business's employees is terminated. The vendor may be held liable for wrongful dismissal damages unless the employees refused to accept job offers from the purchaser on substantially the same terms (or better) as their former employment.

Depending on the jurisdiction, courts have used different approaches when calculating the appropriate reasonable notice for an employee who is subsequently dismissed by the purchaser. Employers must therefore look to the recent case law in their provinces or jurisdictions to determine what approach will be applied. In Ontario, for instance, employees who accept employment with purchasers and who are subsequently terminated without cause can expect to receive some credit for their past service with the vendor. This will particularly be so where a purchaser fails to advise employees that credit for their past service will not be given. Employers should refer to the applicable employment standards legislation of their provinces or jurisdic-

---

[367] *MacLean v. Saunders Home Comfort Ltd.* (1992), 152 N.B.R. (2d) 241 (C.A.).

tions since service with a former employer (the vendor) may be included in an employee's statutory entitlement upon termination by the new employer (the purchaser).

PART III

✧ THE TERMINATION ✧

Few employees are going to be pleased about being fired, but a poorly handled termination can make matters worse by leaving an employee emotionally upset, bitter, perhaps even violent. A poorly handled termination can also disrupt an employer's operations and adversely affect the morale among other employees. Furthermore, if the disgruntled employee subsequently launches a lawsuit, an employer could wind up having to pay a large wrongful dismissal award. The award can include damages for bad faith discharge by an extension of the reasonable notice period (typically referred to as *Wallace* damages),[1] damages for failing to provide reasonable notice, damages for an employee's mental distress, aggravated or punitive damages for treating an employee in a reprehensible manner and perhaps even damages for harm or loss to an employee's reputation. To avoid these consequences, the employer must properly plan, prepare for and conduct a termination. In doing so, the employer must recognize that the most important aspect of all firings is the termination interview and the letter that accompanies or follows the interview. Employers need to know how to prepare for a termination, how to conduct the termination interview and what to do afterwards so that possible pitfalls can be avoided. Court decisions reached after the *McKinley* Supreme Court case[2] have focused on the contextual approach to just cause termination,[3] thereby rebalancing the rights of employees and the managerial concerns of business efficacy. This new emphasis highlights the need for proper preparation for and execution of a termination, and includes careful drafting of the termination letter, allowing employers to protect their own interests while at the same time maintaining the dignity and self-respect of the employee being dismissed.

---

[1] See the discussion under Heading 8(a), "Wallace Damages", of Part I, "General Concepts".

[2] *McKinley v. B.C. Tel* (2001), 200 D.L.R. (4th) 385 (S.C.C.).

[3] See the discussion under Heading 4, "Dishonesty", of Part II, "Grounds for Termination".

1 ✧ PRE-TERMINATION

(a) Planning for Termination

The first step in any termination is to map out a plan. The threat of damages being awarded for bad faith discharge of an employee makes it critical for employers to properly plan the termination of an employee. In addition to the manner in which the employee is dismissed, the court will also consider the following factors when determining the appropriate length of the reasonable notice period as damages for bad faith discharge: the employee's length of service, age, the nature of his or her employment, the history of the employment relationship, the employee's qualifications and the availability of similar employment. As key elements in forming the plan and in order to avoid *"Wallace"* damages, the employer needs to address the following 10 key questions:

1. Why exactly is the employee being terminated?
2. Who should undertake to fire the employee (spokesperson and witness)?
3. Who will take over the responsibilities of the employee being dismissed (one person, several persons, elimination of some duties)?
4. Who should be contacted after the termination in terms of customers, clients, suppliers, etc.?
5. When should the termination take place?
6. Where will it occur?
7. Should there be an outplacement counsellor available at the termination interview?
8. How will the employee be removed from the building after the termination interview?
9. What paperwork should be ready at the termination interview (letter, offer of settlement, release, reference)?
10. How much damage can the employee cause "on the way out" and how can that be minimized?

In preparing a response to the question of why an employee is being fired, a company should carefully review the individual's employment record and any performance reviews. The expectation is that this exercise will provide sufficient reasons to support termination. It is important to stress at this point that having good "reasons" for dismissal is not the same as having "cause" for dismissal. Reasons are very important for communication purposes and corporate integrity, and useful in response to any human rights complaints; however, many cases that involve good reasons will not amount to just cause for dismissal without notice. It is very important for an employer to be satisfied with its reasons and to be comfortable with the decision to fire an employee. The employer must believe that the decision is the correct one to make and must project its confidence in that belief to other employees, shareholders (if any), customers, suppliers and the general public. In this respect, the reasons for dismissing an employee should be objective and unemotional. It is only after assembling all of the reasons for dismissal that an employer should turn to the stricter test of determining whether there is a solid basis to allege just cause for termination.

The next item to think about is who to choose for the termination task. The choice should be someone in management and in most cases the individual's direct supervisor or manager. A representative from the human resources or personnel department also should be in attendance during the termination interview to answer any questions the employee might have and to serve as a witness to the termination itself.

Another "who" question that needs to be answered concerns the replacement for a fired employee. Who is going to perform the duties and responsibilities originally assigned to the departing employee? A company must decide whether an individual from within the organization should be considered or if it would be better to recruit externally for a candidate to fill the newly vacant position. Alternatively, an employer may choose to eliminate the duties and responsibilities of the position entirely or combine its functions with one or more existing positions. The decision as to the dismissed employee's replacement will often depend on the company's financial position, its organizational structure and the nature of its workplace. In any event, an employer should plan ahead so that the duties and responsibilities of the employee are transitioned with little or no interruption.

A final "who" inquiry is aimed at determining which individuals or contacts outside the organization must be told about an employee's termination and how quickly. Certain customers, clients and suppliers will need to know right away that the employee is no longer with the company, particularly if they have been dealing exclusively with the employee for business-related matters. The employer must ensure that these individuals are promptly contacted so that they experience no delay or difficulties in service.

The question of when to fire an employee and carry out the termination interview is an important one. Timing can be critical because a termination might affect the workplace, other employees and the customers, clients or suppliers of an organization. Another factor to consider is whether the employee's contract of employment refers to any specific notice requirements or related provisions in respect of termination. The prudent employer will take the time to obtain this information from an employee's file before deciding when to conduct a termination. Additional details the employer may wish to note while examining the file are the dates of birthdays or anniversaries. It is also useful to make some inquiries about an employee's schedule to determine the dates of any special events the employee has planned in the near future. As a courtesy and in light of *Wallace*,[4] firing an employee on one of these important days should be avoided. Similarly, in most workplaces with regular business hours, employers should avoid dismissing the employee on a Monday or Friday. People tend to be emotionally weaker on Monday mornings and when a termination occurs on a Friday, independent legal advice is difficult to obtain. In this respect, employers must not discourage an employee from seeking such advice. The best "terminating" days are therefore Tuesdays, Wednesdays or Thursdays. As for the time, employers should endeavour not to fire an individual too early in the day. It is probably best to advise employees that they are being dismissed closer to the day's end when fewer co-workers, customers and clients are likely to be around. It is generally not a good idea to give the employee much advance notice of the meeting in which he or she is to be fired. Uncertainty about the meeting's purpose may cause the employee to become distressed and agitated long before the termination actually occurs.

The last but equally important question that must be addressed relates to the setting for a termination. The location should be one that is private and discreet. The office of a manager tends to be a good choice or, alternatively, arrange to meet in the employee's office if he or she has one. Avoid using offices that others can see into or that are in a different location or building. When deciding where the termination will be conducted, employers should consider whether they want the employee to leave the premises immediately. If they do, the termination should occur in a place from which the employee can exit easily. It is usually best to have employees leave as soon as possible, unless they are given working notice of the termination. Whether an employee is asked to leave immediately will depend in part on the level of trust an employer has in the individual and on the position that he or she occupied within the company. In most cases, it will not be necessary to have a security person escort dismissed employees back to their desks or to watch them retrieve their belongings. Having said this, an employee's exit should be monitored so that privacy is balanced with security. As well, steps should be taken to ensure that employees cannot re-enter the company's premises after hours. In this regard, employers should immediately collect an employee's keys and/or security passes and, where applicable, any passwords used to access the company's offices or computers must be changed. It is particularly important to ensure that employees who have been able to access the company's computer systems from outside the office are completely cut off.

---

[4] *Wallace v. United Grain Growers Ltd.* (1997), 152 D.L.R. (4th) 1 (S.C.C.).

(b) Preparing Termination Letter and Final Release Form

After an employer has planned the details of the termination, the next step is to prepare a termination letter that will be ready when the termination interview occurs. In some cases, it is acceptable to conduct the meeting and to follow up shortly afterwards with a letter; however, it is generally preferable to have the necessary paperwork ready for the meeting. It is never acceptable to dismiss an employee without paperwork. The letter serves as formal notice of the company's decision to end the individual's employment. Careful thought should be put into drafting the letter so that it provides the employee with all essential and required information while still protecting the company's interests. Moreover, the letter should be clear and concise although its particular wording, especially in terms of the articulation of reasons, will necessarily depend on whether just cause for termination is being alleged and whether there is any realistic concern about a human rights complaint. There is no room in the letter for unnecessary criticism or harshness. Diplomacy and tact are always recommended.

(i) *Termination for Cause*

In a case where cause is being alleged, termination is normally effective immediately. The termination letter should be brief but still provide a general description of the reason or reasons why the employee is being fired. At the same time, the employer must exercise caution and refrain from being too specific about the grounds amounting to just cause for dismissal. Otherwise, a company's ability to structure a defence against a wrongful dismissal claim can be unduly restricted.

A letter of termination for cause does not usually contain provisions for financial compensation or continuation of benefits. In some cases, the employer may make a "without prejudice" offer of settlement or at least suggest that such an offer could be forthcoming. In all cases, the employer is required to pay any outstanding sums owed to the dismissed employee such as vacation pay and earnings for the hours worked up to the date of termination. An employer will also have to provide the employee with the minimum statutory termination or severance pay, unless an exemption in the applicable legislation says otherwise.[5]

Where termination is for cause, it is not necessary to ask the employee to execute a final release in which the employee promises not to sue the employer on the basis of the termination unless a "without prejudice" offer has been made.

---

[5] See the discussion under Heading 4, "Statutory Notice, Termination Payments and Severance Payments", of Part I, "General Concepts".

There may be cases where cause is believed to exist but the employer does not wish to justify dismissal on this basis. For example, an employer may wish to offer a gratuitous payment for compassionate reasons and/or to avoid future litigation. In such circumstances, the termination letter should set out terms for financial compensation on a "without prejudice" basis and "without admission of liability". If the employee declines to accept the offer and chooses instead to commence a wrongful dismissal lawsuit, the employer can still rely on the existence of cause to justify the termination.

(ii) *Termination Without Cause*

Where just cause for termination does not exist, the termination letter will set out terms for the period of notice to which the employee is entitled. A company either could allow the employee to continue working for the entire reasonable notice period or provide the employee with pay in lieu of notice in the form of a "severance package". A combination of working notice and pay in lieu of notice could be offered as well. Regardless of the way an employer chooses to satisfy the requirement for reasonable notice, the actual date of termination must be stated; that is, whether the termination is effective immediately or is to take effect on a specified future day. If the employer decides to provide a severance package rather than permitting the employee to work the notice period, the details for financial compensation must be precisely set out in the termination letter or in an accompanying offer.

In the case of a dismissal without cause, a company should endeavour to have the employee execute a final release. This document is normally attached to the termination letter and, if executed, frees the employer from any future demands the employee might make. The release also acts as the employee's promise not to commence legal action on the basis of the termi-nation. While it may not be legally enforceable, the release should include an undertaking by the employee not to file a human rights complaint in respect of the termination.

2 ✧ TERMINATION INTERVIEW

After planning the termination and preparing the letter of termination, the employer reaches the point where it is time to meet with the employee and conduct the termination interview. The nature of the termination interview and the steps to follow depend largely on whether the employee is being offered a severance package or financial compensation. Dismissals based on cause usually involve a brief termination letter that very generally explains why the employee is being fired. What the letter does not typically have are any terms for compensation or an appended final release. The employer will have nothing to say in respect of the terms of a severance package because none is being offered. Nor must an employer explain the significance of a final release because the employee is not being asked to execute one.

A termination interview should be of short duration, no more than 10 to 15 minutes, and a representative from human resources should be in attendance. The employer should avoid the practice of permitting an employee to have a family member, friend or lawyer present at the termination interview. Employees have been known to ask that this be allowed where they suspect or anticipate being fired.

When it comes to advising the individual that he or she is being terminated, an employer should get right to the point. The best approach is to tell the employee at the outset and within the first few sentences of the interview. There is no advantage in soft-selling a termination. Also, avoid getting into any protracted debate about the employee's abilities or the merits of the termination and stay away from a renegotiation of dismissal terms. Once the employee has been advised of the termination, the employer should quickly move on to discuss the contents of the termination letter. Where the employer intends to provide financial compensation despite the potential existence of just cause for termination or where a severance package is offered because the dismissal is not for cause, the terms of compensation and any other proposed benefits should be highlighted. If the employer has chosen to offer relocation or job-placement counselling, it should be made available immediately and the employee should be so advised.[6] In many cases, it is common practice to have a counsellor available to meet with the employee immediately following the termination meeting.

Both the original and a copy of the termination letter should be given to the employee. In addition, the employee should be given a final release to sign if financial compensation is being proposed. By signing it, the employee acknowledges receipt of the termination letter and purports to release the employer from all further claims or demands arising from the termination. Although it is advantageous to have an executed final release for all terminations not justified by cause, the employer must be careful not to force or pressure an employee into signing one. Courts have been known to disregard the existence of a release if there is any suspicion that it was executed under duress. As a consequence, there is no guarantee that a final release will prevent an employee from initiating litigation over the termination at a later date or that such litigation will necessarily fail because the employee appeared to release the employer from further claims or demands. To show that an employee acted willingly, a prudent employer will allow the employee a rea-

---

[6] Even in cases where just cause is asserted, there may be reasons why the employer may want to offer the employee outplacement counselling.

sonable period of time to consider both the final release document and the terms of the financial compensation or severance package offered. Seven to 10 days is usually deemed to be a sufficient amount of time for this purpose. Some employees are anxious to sign right away and employers are equally keen to put the matter to rest. Even so, "keen" employees should be encouraged to contemplate the offer and take it with them for overnight review and reflection. At the very least, they should be provided with a private office and telephone and careful notes should be taken of what was said and done.

Some employers prefer to use the "soft release" approach which refers to the use of general release language in the termination letter. This approach typically uses broad release language in non-legalistic terms and is often "triggered" when the employee cashes the severance cheque. Employers like to use this approach because it is less threatening to the employee. However, brevity has its limitations and employers who use this informal approach cannot expect to receive the court's assistance if the employee decides to commence litigation after the severance cheque is cashed. Generally, a court wants to be satisfied that in accepting payment the employee knew that he or she was promising not to sue the company and that the employee was given sufficient time to obtain independent legal advice.

Where a company complies completely with its legal obligation to provide an employee with reasonable notice including continuation of health care and other employment benefits during the notice period, there is little risk to the employer. However, where existing privileges such as short-term and long-term disability benefits are not continued and where a final release from the employee is not obtained, the employer may be exposed to significant damages for loss of the discontinued benefits. This is sure to be the case if the employee suffers some form of disability during the notice period for which coverage would have been in place but for the termination.

In the opinion of the authors, prudence would dictate that a formal release document be used in every case unless the employee was not entitled to health care benefits. Understandably, some employers may be prepared to take the risk and not use a formal release where the employee's entitlement to common law reasonable notice is minimal.

An alternative, which still falls short of the security of a formal release but is rarely challenged, is to use a sign-back method. An employee is provided with two original copies of the termination letter that include the offer of settlement. A sign-back clause in short form (two or three sentences) using standard release language appears after the signature block. Sign-backs are often very effective and easy for employees to accept, especially if the settlement is reached at an early stage or the monetary amount involved is insignificant. However, sign-backs should be abandoned and the employer should return to a formal release policy as soon as the employee engages counsel.

At the point in the termination interview where the paperwork is handed over, things are likely to have become tense and stressful. It is a good idea to hold all phone calls and allow no other interruptions during the interview. They will only prolong the discomfort. It is important to avoid any kind of argument with the employee. The decision is made. The time for discussion and reconsideration is over. If it is appropriate to do so, a company might consider thanking the employee for past contributions to the organization, especially where the termination is based on downsizing or redundancy factors and not on the employee's conduct or work performance. However, before concluding the interview, whatever the reasons for dismissal, an employer should ask the dismissed employee to return any company keys, access cards, company property or credit cards. The individual should then be allowed to return to his or her office or work station and to leave the premises unescorted, assuming there are no security issues or concerns of potential violence. The ideal approach to an employee's departure is low-key supervision. For instance, employees should be permitted to remove their personal belongings from the company's office at an arranged time and supervision or monitoring of the employee's departure should be discreetly exercised. At the same time, caution must be taken to ensure that an employee does not wrongly remove items that belong to the employer such as company reports, customer lists or personnel data, and that an employee cannot create havoc with the employer's computer systems on the way out the door.

3 ✧ POST-TERMINATION

Once the termination interview is over and the employee has left, the following steps must be taken to properly complete the termination process.

(a) Documenting Interview

It is a good idea to record immediately all details of the termination interview in the employee's personnel file. The length of the meeting, the employee's reactions, specific matters that were discussed and any anticipated concerns should be documented. Employers often fail to adequately record the termination meeting, especially as it was likely unpleasant and time-consuming; however, these details could prove helpful at a later date. For instance, dismissed employees might subsequently allege that they were fired in a harsh manner and as a result suffered mental distress or a psychological illness. By having a set of notes which document the termination interview completely, a company is able to rebut the accusations of a dismissed employee and prove that the termination was in fact conducted fairly and inoffensively.

(b) Informing Staff About Termination

The employee's co-workers and colleagues must be told about the termination. It is better that they hear it from the employer or management than through workplace rumours and gossip. A brief memo announcing the employee's departure with little or no detail will suffice in most cases. If details are provided, employers must avoid using disparaging and negative remarks that would make reaching a settlement more difficult and create the risk, for the individuals involved as well as the company, of being sued for defaming the employee's character. If appropriate, the employer may want to speak to some of the staff members on an individual basis. For instance, this approach might be appropriate where the employee worked very closely with a few individuals or where the decision to terminate the employee was made on the basis of several complaints made by a few colleagues.

(c) Notifying "External" Individuals

Some of the company's customers, clients and suppliers may need to be notified of the employee's departure. These individuals should be assured that the organization's operations will not be interrupted or upset by the termination. An explanation as to why the employee was dismissed is not normally required. If one is provided, however, every effort must be made to avoid any damage to the employee's reputation. Otherwise, the employer might be liable for defamation of the employee's character.

(d) Completing Administrative Tasks

First, the employee's "Record of Employment" should be filled out promptly with the reason for termination clearly and accurately described. Next, the employer must deal with the employee's benefits to ensure that they are either maintained or discontinued, as set out in the termination letter. This is a good time to review the letter in its entirety so that the employer can be reminded of any outstanding obligations that must be fulfilled.

The cancellation of any company credit cards, calling cards or access cards in the employee's possession is another detail that must be looked after. Depending on the size and character of an organization, there also may be matters of a technological nature to consider, such as modifications to the company's phone, mail and computer systems. All of these concerns should be dealt with as soon as possible as a precautionary measure against possible retaliation by the terminated employee.

(e) Considering Provision of References

Where just cause is being alleged, most employers choose not to provide the employee with any kind of reference or reference letter. An employer who decides to provide a reference despite the employee's termination for cause must exercise caution in so doing. While it is generally in the employer's interest to see the employee re-employed as soon as possible, providing a reference in these circumstances should be done conditionally or on a without prejudice basis. If a reference is provided in this manner, it is less likely to be inconsistent with the employer's position that cause existed in the event that litigation follows. Many organizations have policies on the giving of references. If a reference or reference letter is appropriate, an employer must be truthful and not mislead another employer into hiring a troublesome employee. There have been cases where companies have been sued for misrepresenting a former employee's credentials and work record.

Threatening to withhold a reference or reference letter unless the employee accepts the compensation or severance package being offered is a grave mistake. This bargaining technique will invariably back-fire because it is evidence of duress that the employee can rely on in any future court action. Furthermore, it may lead to a larger award of damages if litigation does result and the employee can prove that the failure to receive a reference or reference letter made it more difficult to secure alternative employment. In most circumstances and where the termination is on a without cause basis, the best course for an employer to follow is to provide a candid reference or reference letter regardless of whether or not the employee agrees to accept the terms of severance or compensation proposed.

Certainly, in cases where cause is not a factor, the authors strongly support the issuance of accurate and generally positive reference letters and consistent oral references. This should be a centralized task so that the employer can control the message. Even when there is not much good to say or the employer wants to be cautious, every employer should at the very least be able to describe its business, the duties and responsibilities of the departed employee and the duration of employment.

4 ◆ PRACTICAL CONSIDERATIONS

The task of terminating an employee is never a pleasant experience and the person responsible for the actual termination will often feel extremely uncomfortable. On the other hand, some individuals can make the decision to dismiss too easily and without due consideration of the effects a termination can have on the employee, his or her family, co-workers and the workplace.

The proper "firing" approach falls somewhere between agonizing over the event and dismissing an employee without a second thought. Hesitation to the point of anguish about whether or not to terminate an employee is not recommended, but neither is the "trigger happy" impulsive termination that lacks thought, understanding and compassion.

Because a termination could have serious consequences for both the organization and the individual employee, it is hoped that this book will assist employers with making the right decision when considering if just cause for termination exists. Whether a termination is with reasonable notice, with pay in lieu of notice or on the basis of just cause, employees will almost always feel bitter and disappointed after it is over. Employers only make things worse by acting aggressively or with insensitivity, or by alleging just cause for termination when, in fact, none exists.

Whenever possible and where the circumstances require it, employers and their respresentatives should treat the departing employee with respect even when you may have cause for dismissal. Every individual, regardless of shortcomings as an employee, deserves to be treated with dignity when their employment is being terminated. Showing compassion, understanding and respect will help dismissed employees accept their fate and will foster greater loyalty and respect in the remaining employees towards the employer.

The authors believe that even termination for cause can be a "win-win" situation. An organized approach and a commitment to treat the employee with respect will greatly increase the chances of a satisfactory conclusion for both employer and employee.

The following is a list of questions and practical considerations that, if addressed by the employer with care, will help bring every kind of termination to the desired conclusion for both parties.

1. Has a proper investigation been conducted? Always make an informed decision based on all the facts that exist at the time. An investigation of the alleged incident prior to termination will reduce the risk that you have acted on incorrect information.

2. Has the employee been confronted with the allegations and been provided with an opportunity to respond? If appropriate, hearing the employee's side of the story prior to termination will help you in assessing all the facts in the case.

3. Is there a written employment contract that outlines specific causes for termination? If a written contract exists, carefully check the termination provision. It may contain grounds for termination that will be difficult to prove or it may provide that the severance payment obligation is minimal. In either case, termination without cause may be the better approach.

4. Has the employee's file been thoroughly reviewed to consider previous performance and any disciplinary record? Unrelated performance problems and/or a strong discipline record will assist you in building a case

for just cause termination. In any event, being able to show that the employee has either a performance problem or discipline record will create a favourable picture for the employer and may encourage settlement.

5. Has a progressive discipline policy been enforced, along with documented warnings for each incident of misconduct? Have progressively stricter sanctions been imposed? A properly structured and applied discipline policy will help you, as an employer, to avoid potential *Wallace* damages for bad faith discharge.

6. Have you as an employer directly or indirectly condoned the employee's behaviour? Look at your response to the misconduct by this particular employee and any responses to similar conduct by other employees.

7. Is there a lesser sanction that is more appropriate in the circumstances? In view of the contextual approach taken by the courts, establishing just cause requires proportionality between the misconduct, the circumstances and the punishment. For example, a longer service employee must engage in a more serious act of misconduct before termination for cause will be warranted.

8. Is there any reason why the termination should not proceed on a specific date? Is there an operations or security concern or is the date a "sensitive" date for the employee such as a wedding anniversary or birthday? You should choose the termination date carefully. In most cases, the termination can easily be postponed to a date that avoids such "special days".

9. Is there just cause at law to terminate? You may be convinced that you have cause but have you checked to see that the law agrees with you? Never allege cause, when none exists especially in light of the potential for a court to award *Wallace* bad faith discharge damages to the employee. Be careful about alleging cause where your case is uncertain or key facts may be in dispute. It is always a sound practice to consult with an independent human resources professional or employment lawyer before carrying out the termination.

10. Choose the right person to conduct the termination interview and the right lawyer to defend you should litigation ensue. Choosing the right person to conduct the termination will ensure that it is handled in a professional and courteous manner. The lawyer you choose, should the case proceed to litigation, is equally important in order to avoid delay and disruption to your organization and to minimize legal costs.

11. Tell the employee the truth about why he or she is being terminated. It is not entirely clear whether there is a legal obligation to advise the employee of the reason for dismissal. However, by misleading the employee or relying on a specific reason that cannot be proven, the employer is apt to lose any wrongful dismissal action that follows. The best approach is to keep the reason accurate but general enough to encompass several different legal causes for termination. For example, the particular act of stealing $100 could be described as "theft", "dishonesty", "breach of trust",

"breach of company policy", or "revelation of character". The authors suggest that you always provide a reason where a clear reason exists.

12. Always consider whether any recent information, acquired following the termination, may be helpful in establishing just cause. In certain cases, termination will be appropriate before a full investigation is possible. This should not prevent the employer from completing a thorough investigation after the termination.

13. While supporting documentation is not required for all situations, some cases for cause depend heavily on a properly documented file. If your case is litigated, it will be stronger where such a file exists. In this respect, notes in a file will likely be given little weight. Any incident on which you intend to rely should have been brought to the employee's attention, preferably in writing.

14. If litigation ensues, consider mediation or arbitration as a less expensive alternative.

15. There is always the possibility that compassionate statements or inadvertently aggressive comments made by an employer during a termination interview could, if recorded, be misinterpreted by a court. It is wise therefore not to allow a termination interview to be recorded. While it is not recommended that an employee be physically searched, be certain that any meetings with the employee are not surreptitiously recorded. Often employees follow advice (from various sources including U.S. television shows and lawyers) to tape any conversations with their employers. These recordings may be admissible during a trial so do not dismiss the possibility that it could happen to you. If there is any suspicion on your part, one way to minimize this risk is to confirm with the employee before a meeting begins that he or she is not carrying any kind of recording device.

16. Surveillance of the employee after a termination is another issue that has arisen frequently. While this form of observation during employment has been accepted by courts and arbitrators, reasonable grounds should exist for it and the employer should have exhausted other less intrusive ways of getting the necessary information. Surveillance must always respect the dignity and privacy rights of the individual employee. Observation that follows a termination can attract court sanctions if it is seen as being unjustified, unreasonable or a violation of privacy rights. Unless extremely strong reasons exist, employers should not engage in surveillance following the termination of an employee as an aid or tactic for use in wrongful dismissal litigation. While there may be exceptional circumstances, surveillance after termination should generally be avoided.

17. If you are unsure about any issues, consult a lawyer who specializes in employment law and understands the philosophy of your company with respect to human resources. Sound legal advice will always help minimize your risks in a termination case.

APPENDIX A

✧ SUMMARY OF SIGNIFICANT SUPREME COURT OF CANADA AND COURT OF APPEAL CASES ✧

✧ SUPREME COURT OF CANADA DECISIONS

- *Fraser v. Canada (Public Service Staff Relations Board)* (1985), 23 D.L.R. (4th) 122 (S.C.C.)

Conflicts of Interest – Insubordination – Criticizing Operations

See discussion under Heading 7(b)(iii), "Criticizing Operations", of Part II, "Grounds for Termination"

Fraser, an employee of Revenue Canada, publicly criticized the federal government's policies on metric conversion and the entrenchment of the *Canadian Charter of Rights and Freedoms.* He received two suspensions and was eventually terminated when he persisted in his criticisms. The Supreme Court of Canada held that Fraser's effectiveness as a public servant was damaged because of his public statements. The court agreed with the Public Service Staff Relations Board that there was a balance to be struck between a public servant's right to free speech and the competing interest of loyalty to the government, and that Fraser's statements were so critical that they were "unlikely to instil confidence in a clientele [persons subject to tax audits] that has a right to expect impartial and judicious treatment" (p. 132). There was, therefore, just cause for the dismissal.

- *Sobeys Stores Ltd. v. Yeomans* (1989), 64 D.L.R. (4th) 234 (N.S.C.A.), leave to appeal to S.C.C. refused 68 D.L.R. (4th) vii

Performance Problems – Incompetence

Yeomans had worked for Sobeys Stores for 10 years when he was dismissed on the ground of incompetence. The Nova Scotia Supreme Court, Appeal Division, upheld the Labour Standards Tribunal's ruling that the employer did not have just cause. The tribunal had determined that Yeomans' actions were examples of incompetence, but did not amount to misconduct. As a result, Yeomans was entitled to notice. The court ruled that, since s. 67A of the Nova Scotia *Labour Standards Code* provided that employees of more than 10 years could only be dismissed for just cause, and since "adequate notice had [not] been given and progressive discipline had [not] been utilized before Mr. Yeomans was dismissed", the tribunal was correct in finding that there was no just cause (p. 240).

- *Toronto (City) Board of Education v. OSSTF, District 15* (1997), 144 D.L.R. (4th) 385 (S.C.C.)

Unprofessional Conduct

See discussion under Heading 23, "Character Revelation", of Part II, "Grounds for Termination"

B had been employed as a teacher for almost 20 years and was discharged following two threatening letters that he wrote to the board of education. B was discharged "for reasons of unprofessional conduct, poor judgment, and attitudes which indicate he is no longer capable of fulfilling his duties as a Teacher under the Education Act". Following his discharge, B wrote a third abusive letter to the board. The Supreme Court of Canada ruled that the board had just cause to dismiss B as B was clearly guilty of significant, possibly extreme, misconduct. In so ruling, the Supreme Court overturned an arbitration board's decision that B could return to teaching, finding it patently unreasonable. In a concurring judgment, L'Heureux-Dubé J. stated that, in this case, "the two offensive letters are of such gravity as to seriously prejudice the grievor's status as a role model [and] [t]herefore . . . in themselves, constitute just cause for discharge" (para. 92).

- *Wallace v. United Grain Growers Ltd.* (1997), 152 D.L.R. (4th) 1 (S.C.C.)

Bad Faith Discharge

See discussion under Heading 8, "Bad Faith Discharge", of Part I, "General Concepts"

Wallace was hired by the competitor of his former employer of 25 years. In the course of being hired, the employee sought and received assurances from his new employer concerning tenure, fair treatment and remuneration. Until his summary dismissal 14 years later, the employee was the employer's top salesperson. The employer originally alleged cause for dismissal, only to withdraw the allegation on the eve of the trial. As a result of the manner in which he was dismissed, the employee had difficulty finding replacement work. He also required psychiatric treatment for the psychological and emotional distress caused by the dismissal and false allegations made against him. The Supreme Court of Canada ruled that employers have an obligation of "good faith and fair dealing" in the manner in which dismissals are carried out because employees are most vulnerable and in need of protection at the time of dismissal. Accordingly, the court stated that employers should treat employees fairly, reasonably and decently at the time of dismissal. Where this does not occur, the notice period may be dramatically increased by the courts.

- *Dowling v. Halifax (City)* (1998), 158 D.L.R. (4th) 163 (S.C.C.), revg 136 D.L.R. (4th) 352 (N.S.C.A.), affg 15 C.C.E.L. (2d) 299 (S.C.)

Fraud – Near Cause

See discussion under Heading 9, "Near Cause", of Part I, "General Concepts"

Dowling was dismissed for a series of allegations that, had they been true, would have constituted just cause. However, the trial judge found no factual basis for the allegations. The employer contended that additional facts that had come to light after Dowling's dismissal did constitute just cause. Even so, the trial judge determined that at one point in time "the City would have had clear grounds to seriously reprimand Mr. Dowling, but not to summarily terminate his employment as an employee with 25 years service and a decent record" (para. 34 (S.C.)). In assessing the amount of notice to be awarded, the trial judge adopted the principle of "moderated damages" to reduce the amount of notice. On appeal, the Nova Scotia Court of Appeal ruled that there was authority for the application of the "near cause" or "moderated damages" principle. The Supreme Court of Canada rejected all arguments relating to near cause and remitted the case to the Trial Division to determine the appropriate amount of notice.

- *McKinley v. B.C. Tel* (2001), 200 D.L.R. (4th) 385 (S.C.C.)

Just Cause – Contextual Approach – Dishonesty

See discussion under Heading 7, "Just Cause – The Contextual Approach", of Part I, "General Concepts", as well as the discussion under Heading 4, "Dishonesty", of Part II, "Grounds for Termination"

Mr. McKinley took a leave of absence from work due to health problems after 16 years of service. He expressed an interest in returning to work in a less stressful position, but B.C. Tel did not offer him alternative employment. When, eventually, B.C. Tel terminated Mr. McKinley, he rejected the accompanying offer of severance and commenced a wrongful dismissal action. At first, B.C. Tel argued it had offered Mr. McKinley a reasonable compensation package and had used its best efforts to locate an alternative position for him. Then, three days into trial, B.C. Tel discovered a letter from Mr. McKinley's physician and changed its defence to allege that he had lied about his medical condition and the available treatments. Based on this letter, B.C. Tel claimed that McKinley had deliberately withheld the fact that he could have safely returned to work if he took certain medication. The Supreme Court of Canada rejected the approach that "any" dishonesty is grounds for dismissal. Instead, the court adopted a contextual approach that looks at the nature and seriousness of the misconduct. Each case must be examined in light of its own particular facts and circumstances. The test adopted by the Supreme Court was to ask whether the employee's dishonesty gave rise to a breakdown in the employment relationship.

- *Machtinger v. HOJ Industries Ltd.* (1992), 91 D.L.R. (4th) 491 (S.C.C.)

Reasonable Notice – Statutory Notice

Machtinger and Lefebvre were both employed for seven years at HOJ, a new and used car dealership. Their employment contracts stated that no cause was needed for the employer to dismiss them without notice. Both were dismissed without cause, with the employer providing each with four weeks' pay in lieu of notice. The *Employment Standards Act* ("*ESA*") of Ontario dictates a minimum notice period of four weeks for employees with seven years of service. The Supreme Court of Canada ruled that it is not possible to contract out of the minimum notice periods found in the *ESA*. If an employment contract dictates a notice period that is shorter than the statutory provision, it is deemed null and void and cannot be considered to determine the intentions of the parties. Should the employment contract be found null and void, the common law presumption of reasonable notice is applicable and the courts will determine the appropriate notice period taking account of the length of service, the nature of employment, the age of the employee and the availability of comparable employment based on the employee's training, experience and qualifications. Policy considerations dictate the use of common law reasonable notice when an employment contract is deemed void to prevent employers intentionally attempting to contract a lower notice period with the only possible consequence being a court-ordered enforcement of the *ESA* minimum standards.

- *Heynen v. Frito Lay Canada Ltd.* (1997), 32 C.C.E.L. (2d) 183 (Ont. Ct. (Gen. Div.)), revd on other grounds 179 D.L.R. (4th) 317 (C.A.), leave to appeal to S.C.C. refused 188 D.L.R. (4th) vi

Absenteeism and Lateness – Off-Work Criminal or Improper Conduct

See discussion under Heading 4, "Dishonesty", of Part II, "Grounds for Termination"

Heynen was employed as a driver-salesman for 23 years. He went on a medical leave of absence that was scheduled to last less than two months. However, while still on leave, he was sentenced to four months in jail and 18 months' probation for two criminal convictions that were unrelated to his work. The employer temporarily extended Heynen's leave, then one month before he was scheduled to be released from jail it terminated him. Frito Lay claimed that Heynen's absence presented difficulty as it had to arrange for coverage of his route. Furthermore, it was restructuring its sales force and employees had to bid on new routes, which Heynen could not do because he was incarcerated. The trial judge dismissed both assertions stating that "in the context of 23 years of loyal and effective service, and bearing in mind that Hostess serviced his route with a replacement driver-salesman for the nine weeks immediately before [his termination date]", his absence was only a "minor inconvenience" (para. 41 (Gen. Div.)). Furthermore, the employer was in touch with Heynen while he was in jail and could have arranged for an alternate method of bidding on the new routes. The Court of Appeal upheld this ruling.

*   *Simpson v. Consumers' Assn. of Canada* (1999), 41 C.C.E.L. (2d) 179 (Ont. Ct. (Gen. Div.)), revd 209 D.L.R. (4th) 214 (C.A.), leave to appeal to S.C.C. refused 214 D.L.R. (4th) vi

Participation in Harassment

See discussion under Heading 20, "Participation in Harassment", of Part II, "Grounds for Termination"

Simpson was dismissed by his employer following six incidents of sexual harassment. The trial judge found for Simpson, ruling that there was no just cause. The trial judge confirmed that the six incidents occurred, but discounted them for various reasons, including that the events happened outside the workplace, that the events occurred with the consent of the female employees, and that there was no sexual harassment policy in the workplace. The Court of Appeal overturned the trial decision. It ruled that the trial judge "failed to consider the totality of the conduct, and to view it objectively". In the Court of Appeal's view, termination was justified as "[Simpson's] conduct consisted of several incidents and ongoing situations, which although not repeated conduct with one person, amounted to a pattern of sexually harassing conduct". In addition, "because [Simpson] was the executive director of the Association and the supervisor to whom the employees reported, his obligation to the Association was to ensure that sexual harassment did not occur, and to set the standard of a workplace which protected both the employees and his employer from complaints of offensive conduct" (paras. 83-4 (C.A.)).

✧ COURT OF APPEAL DECISIONS

• *Komperda v. Hongkong Bank of Canada*, [2000] O.T.C. 619 (S.C.J.), affd 141 O.A.C. 373 (C.A.)

Breaching Employer Policies or Rules

See discussion under Heading 8, "Breaching Employer Policies or Rules", of Part II, "Grounds for Termination"

The employee worked at a bank and was employed in a position of trust. She engaged in three instances of cheque kiting. Following the second instance, the employee signed a memorandum agreeing to certain conditions, including that any future action by the employee representing a breach of trust could result in her immediate suspension or termination. After the third instance of cheque kiting, the employee was dismissed. The plaintiff's claim of wrongful dismissal was dismissed at trial; the Court of Appeal dismissed the appeal. The bank had just cause to terminate the employee because she had been in a position of trust and had been warned twice.

• *Thompson v. Lex Tec Inc.*, [2000] O.T.C. 130 (S.C.J.), affd 149 O.A.C. 106 (C.A.)

Physical Fights or Altercations

See discussion under Heading 22, "Physical Fights or Altercations", of Part II, "Grounds for Termination"

The plaintiff arrived one hour late to work, following which a confrontation took place with his supervisor. The supervisor demanded an explanation, but the plaintiff did not reply as he had been at a medical clinic and was embarrassed to disclose the reason for his lateness. Following repeated inquiries by his supervisor, the plaintiff responded with profanity, pushed his supervisor and left the work site. The next day he was terminated. The trial judge found that there was no just cause, and the Court of Appeal agreed. The court cited *McKinley v. B.C. Tel* (2001), 200 D.L.R. (4th) 385 (S.C.C.), in support of the proposition that an employee's misconduct should be judged in the context of his overall employment relationship. The trial judge was correct to consider that such context "included the respondent's employment history with his employer, his relationship with . . . his immediate supervisor, [his immediate supervisor's] role in the relevant events, the actual nature of the misconduct, and the effect, if any, of the misconduct on the employer's business". The trial judge noted that the altercation "did not demonstrate that [the plaintiff] constituted a danger or threat of violence to other employees in the workplace" (para. 1 (C.A.)). Consequently, the decision to terminate for cause was unjustified.

* *Hoffman v. VRP Web Technology Inc.* (2001), 12 C.C.E.L. (3d) 255 (Ont. C.A.)

Disloyalty

See discussion under Heading 16(d), "Miscellaneous Conflicts", of Part II, "Grounds for Termination"

The Ontario Court of Appeal upheld a trial court ruling that there was no just cause for dismissal where an employee had merely requested "a negotiation for corporate restructuring and a more central role for himself in [the company] . . . As a shareholder, he had every right to ask for a negotiation on a proposal to purchase more shares" (para. 8).

* *O'Donnell v. Bourgault Industries Ltd.* (1999), 182 Sask. R. 117 (Q.B.), affd 277 W.A.C. 132 (C.A.)

Misrepresentation Prior to Hiring – Dishonesty

See discussion under Heading 10, "After Acquired Cause", of Part I, "General Concepts"

The Court of Appeal upheld a judgment of the Court of Queen's Bench that there had been just cause for dismissal. The existence of just cause was based on two findings of fact. First, "the appellant misrepresented his qualifications when he applied for employment and . . . did not measure up to the qualifications of his own resume". Second, "the appellant was dishonest in attempting to claim for moving expenses which had been paid by his former employer" (paras. 1-2 (C.A.)). Applying the doctrine of after acquired cause, the employee's dishonesty with respect to the moving expenses, which was discovered after his dismissal, constituted just cause.

* *Battams v. S.L.H. Transport Inc.* (2002), 277 W.A.C. 222 (Sask. C.A.), revg 211 Sask. R. 319 (Q.B.)

Performance Problems – Neglect of Duty

See discussion under Heading 7(a), "Disobedience", of Part II, "Grounds for Termination"

A transport truck driver was dismissed. He claimed that his employer forced him to do peddle runs in breach of the terms and conditions of his employment. The Court of Appeal found there was just cause, overturning the trial judgment and stating that, "the evidence . . . does not support the respondent's position that his terms and conditions of employment excluded any requirement that he do peddle runs. Rather, they support the appellant's position that all highway drivers were required to do peddle runs if necessary, and that the only reason the respondent was able to avoid them as he did, was the availability to him of better runs to bid on by reason of his seniority. Accordingly, when the respondent refused to bid on the peddle runs available to him, or to consider the other alternatives offered by the company, the company had cause to terminate his employment as it did" (para. 2).

•   *Chambers v. Omni Insurance Brokers* (2002), 17 C.C.E.L. (3d) 179 (Ont. C.A.), revg 145 O.A.C. 162 (Div. Ct.)

Performance Problems – Incompetence

See discussion under Heading 13, "Condonation", of Part I, "General Concepts"

Chambers' employer claimed that there was just cause by reason of incompetence. It based this assertion on a series of events that took place between 1996 and 1998. Most of the events cited in support of the allegation of incompetence occurred before the employer offered to renew Chambers' employment contract. The trial judge found that, although the events prior to the renewal of the employment contract should not be overlooked entirely, the legal principle of condonation dictated that they be considered of little significance: "I place very little significance on those complaints, or on those problems, considering that Mr. Chambers was offered a continuation of his position by the letter of September 1998". The Divisional Court overruled the trial judge, stating that since further examples of incompetence occurred after the employment contract was renewed, the events occurring prior to the renewal could be considered "whenever any new misconduct occurs, the old offences may be invoked and may be put in the scale against the employee as cause for dismissal". The Court of Appeal disagreed, stating that "unless the trial judge has completely ignored the previous conduct, the appellate court must accord deference to the trial judge's decision about the weight to be given to it" (all quotes at paras. 43-6 (C.A.)). Accordingly, the Divisional Court's ruling was overturned, and the trial judgment was restored.

•   *Mitchell v. Paxton Forest Products Inc.* (2002), 286 W.A.C. 205 (C.A.), affg 2001 BCSC 1802

Performance Problems – Neglect of Duty – Breaching Fiduciary Duties

The Court of Appeal dismissed an appeal from a trial court's finding that there was no just cause. The trial judge found that the employer "had not proven dishonesty or breach of duty . . . nor any abuse of privileges such as the use of a car or credit card". The trial court stated that failing to prove that the employee had been disloyal, or that he had breached any of his obligations to the company, meant that there was no just cause for dismissal. Moreover, "poor management is not grounds for summary dismissal" (paras. 70 and 68 (Q.B.), para. 5 (C.A.)).

- *Nickson v. Industrial Security Ltd.*, [2001] N.B.R. (2d) (Supp.) No. 86 (Q.B.), affd 253 N.B.R. (2d) 297 (C.A.)

Performance Problems – Neglect of Duty

See discussion under Heading 3(c), "Neglect of Duty", of Part II, "Grounds for Termination"

The plaintiff was employed as a "monitor" with a company that provided night patrols. He had a tendency to continually question his supervisors and was given a letter warning him that this behaviour would no longer be tolerated. More than a year later, during an incident that took place while he was on duty, the plaintiff failed to notify headquarters when he was aware he should have done so. The trial judge found that the employer had established just cause, and the Court of Appeal agreed. The trial judge stated that the plaintiff's misconduct "destroyed the trust that his employer was entitled to have in him. In my view, a watchman's failure to immediately report such an emergency situation is comparable to a cashier's failure to ring in a sale or an employee's dishonest dealing with employer's property" (para. 54 (Q.B.)).

- *Belzberg v. Pollock* (2003), 23 C.C.E.L. (3d) 22 (B.C.C.A.), affg 2002 BCSC 1766

Performance Problems – Neglect of Duty

See discussion under Heading 3(c), "Neglect of Duty", of Part II, "Grounds for Termination"

The case involved a partnership of three individuals concerned with the management of a bar. One of the partners was terminated by the other two for his alleged "failure to carry out the duties that were assigned to him, and his lack of initiative". The trial judge found, and the Court of Appeal agreed, that the allegations "must be examined in light of the relationship between the three partners". The partners lacked experience in the management of this type of business. Moreover, the trial judge noted that it was the very action of the defendants, namely removing the plaintiff from the management of the enterprise, that contributed to the plaintiff's lack of involvement. As such, they were in no position to complain, and there was no just cause to terminate the plaintiff.

- *Hyland v. Royal Alexandra Hospital* (2000), 5 C.C.E.L. (3d) 63 (Alta. Q.B.), affd 26 C.C.E.L. (3d) 186 (C.A.)

Breach of Trust

See discussion under Heading 4, "Dishonesty", of Part II, "Grounds for Termination"

The plaintiff was an auditor at the hospital. In a transaction unrelated to his employment, he attempted to avoid paying the GST on the purchase of a new vehicle. The hospital maintained that the plaintiff's dishonesty constituted just cause for dismissal since it showed a lack of exercise of good judgment. Sound judgment was essential to the plaintiff's position and the credibility of the audit department. The trial judge found, and the Court of Appeal agreed, that there was just cause to terminate the plaintiff's employment. The trial judge noted that, had the plaintiff's evasion become public knowledge, the effectiveness of the hospital's audit department might be called into question: "From the public's perspective it would seem somewhat bizarre; the Hospital's auditor, who ensures compliance with matters such as inventory controls and taxation law, has engaged in questionable efforts to avoid payment of GST on his personal vehicle . . . The maintenance of public confidence in financial accountability and regularity were important to the operation of the Hospital . . . [therefore] the Hospital had proper cause to summarily dismiss the Plaintiff" (para. 28 (Q.B.)).

✧ BIBLIOGRAPHY ✧

Ball, S.R., *Canadian Employment Law* (Aurora: Canada Law Book Inc., 1996)

Christie, I.M., G. England and W.B. Cotter, *Employment Law in Canada*, 2nd ed. (Toronto: Butterworths, 1993)

D'Andrea, J.A., D.J. Corry and H.I. Forester, *Illness and Disability in the Workplace: How to Navigate Through the Legal Minefield* (Aurora: Canada Law Book Inc., 1995)

Echlin, R.S., "Taking a Strong Position: The Rightful Dismissal", in *Recent Trends in Just Cause* (Toronto: Insight, 1991)

Echlin, R.S., "The Law and Sexual Harassment in the Workplace: Where We've Been and Where We're Heading", in *HR Law Symposium* (Toronto: Human Resources Professional Association of Ontario, 1995)

Echlin, R.S., and C.M. Thomlinson, *For Better or For Worse*, 2nd ed. (Aurora: Canada Law Book Inc., 2003)

Echlin, R.S., and M.L.O. Certosimo, *Just Cause: The Law of Summary Dismissal in Canada* (Aurora: Canada Law Book Inc., 1998)

Echlin, R.S., and J.M. Fantini, *Quitting for Good Reason: The Law of Constructive Dismissal in Canada* (Aurora: Canada Law Book Inc., 2001)

Echlin, R.S., and M. MacKillop, *Creative Solutions: Perspectives on Canadian Employment Law*, 2nd ed. (Aurora: Aurora Professional Press, 2001)

Elliott, C.J., *Employment Equity Handbook* (Aurora: Canada Law Book Inc., 1994)

Ellis, M.V., "An Overview of Fiduciary Duties in the Employment Law Sphere", in *Employment Law: Views From the Bench and Bar* (Toronto: Canadian Bar Association, Ontario Branch, and Law Society of Upper Canada, Continuing Legal Education, 1993)

Gilbert, D.G., J. Mastoras and L.A. Liversidge, *A Guide to Workers' Compensation in Ontario*, 2nd ed. (Aurora: Canada Law Book Inc., 1995)

Grosman, B.A., and J.R. Martin, *Employment Law in Canada: A Guide for Employers and Employees* (Aurora: Canada Law Book Inc., 1991)

Halsbury's Laws of England, 4th ed., Vol. 16, p. 437, para. 644

Harris, D., *Wrongful Dismissal*, 3rd ed. (Toronto: De Boo, 1984)

Knight, J.G., L.S. Goodfellow and C.J. Overholt, *Employment Litigation Manual* (Markham: Lexis Nexis Butterworths, 2004)

Knight J.G., P. Leiper and K. Williams, *Canada Labour Code Quick Reference Guide*, 2004 ed. (Toronto: Thomson Carswell, 2004)

Levitt, H.A., *The Law of Dismissal in Canada*, 3rd ed. (Aurora: Canada Law Book Inc., 2003)

Mole, E.E., ed., *Wrongful Dismissal Practice Manual* (Toronto: Butterworths, 1984)

MacKillop, M., and K. Taylor, *How to Conduct a Workplace Investigation* (Toronto: Thomson Carswell, 2004)

Mosner, C., and M. Rogers, eds., "Probationary Employees Fired for Legitimate Reasons" (1985), 11:7 *Hiring & Firing* 3

Parry, K.A., and D.A. Ryan, *Employment Standards Handbook*, 3rd ed., 2 vols. (Aurora: Canada Law Book Inc., 2002)

"Racial and Sexual Harassment in the Workplace" (client seminar, Borden & Elliot, Toronto, 1995)

Sproat, J.R., *Employment Law Manual: Wrongful Dismissal, Human Rights and Employment Standards* (Toronto: Carswell, 1990)

The Duty to Accommodate: The Legal and Practical Aspects of Integrating People with Disabilities into Your Workforce (Mississauga: Insight, 1991)

Waddams, S.M., *The Law of Damages*, 4th ed. (Aurora: Canada Law Book Inc., 2004)

✧ INDEX ✧

ABSENTEEISM AND LATENESS
absenteeism, 90-91
case law, 210
generally, 89-90
grounds for termination, as, 92-3
lateness, 91-2
overview, 93-4

ABSENTING. *See* LEAVING WORK WITHOUT PERMISSION

ACCOMMODATION, DUTY OF, 103-104

AFTER ACQUIRED CAUSE
described, 23
pre-hire misrepresentation, 213
weight, as issue of, 24

AGE
agreement to retire, 172-3
BFOR, establishment of, 173
capacity to perform employment duties, 175
Charter protection, 171, 173
  equality rights issues, 174
generally, 171
human rights legislation protection, 173
illness and disability, 175
mandatory retirement policies, 171, 173-4
overview, 175
reasonable notice of retirement, 173-4
retirement policy, 171-2

ALCOHOL. *See* SUBSTANCE ABUSE

ALTERCATIONS. *See* PHYSICAL FIGHTS

NEGLECT OF DUTY — *continued*
described, 47
multiple instances requirement, 49
prejudice suffered by employer, 49
reasonableness of performance requirements, 49
seriousness requirement, 47-8
warning requirement, 48-9
wilfulness requirement, 48

NOTICE
(*See also* REASONABLE NOTICE)
cap re managerial employees, 6
common law, at, 4
redundancy and, 186-7
retirement, of, 173-4
sale of business and, 189-90
statutory. *See* Statutory notice
Wallace damages and, 17

ONUS OF PROOF, 24-5

OVERTIME. *See* SHIFT WORK OR OVERTIME, REFUSING

PERFORMANCE PROBLEMS. *See* CARELESSNESS;
  INCOMPETENCE; NEGLECT OF DUTY
overview, 50-51

PERSONAL APPEARANCE
body odour, 168
generally, 167
job requirements and, 168
overview, 169
untidy appearance, 167

PERSONALITY CONFLICTS
abuse and rudeness, 147
factors considered, 147
generally, 147
overview, 148
"proper fit" issue, 148

PHYSICAL FIGHTS
case law, 212

WALLACE DAMAGES. *See* BAD FAITH DISCHARGE

WARNINGS
carelessness, 46
discipline, 30
documentation of, 29
incompetence, 42
neglect of duty and, 48-9
unco-operative behaviour, 131

WORKERS' COMPENSATION, 102

WRONGFUL DISMISSAL
action for while still employed, 179
Canada Labour Code remedies for, 10-11
constructive dismissal versus, 9
punitive damages for, 156
redundancy claims, 186